D1224003

PRIDE IN THE JUNGLE

CREATING THE NORTH AMERICAN LANDSCAPE

Gregory Conniff
Bonnie Loyd
Edward K. Muller
David Schuyler
Consulting Editors

Published in cooperation with
the Center for American Places,
Harrisonburg, Virginia

PRIDE IN THE JUNGLE

Community and Everyday Life in Back of the Yards Chicago

THOMAS J. JABLONSKY

THE JOHNS HOPKINS UNIVERSITY PRESS / Baltimore and London

Frontispiece: Back of the Yards Neighborhood Council's message board (in 1973) at the Forty-seventh and Damen community field built atop the one-time city dumps. For many years this was the site of the annual Back of the Yards Fair sponsored by the Council. Recently the land has been developed as a shopping mall. Courtesy of Chicago Historical Society. Photograph by Casey Prunchunas. ICHi-06998.

The Johns Hopkins University Press
2715 North Charles Street
Baltimore, Maryland 21218-4319
The Johns Hopkins Press Ltd., London

Library of Congress Cataloging-in-Publication Data

Jablonsky, Thomas J.
    Pride in the jungle : community and everyday life in Back of the Yards
Chicago / Thomas J. Jablonsky.
        p.   cm. — (Creating the North American landscape)
    Includes bibliographical references (p.   ) and index.
    ISBN 0-8018-4335-9 (hc)
    1. Chicago (Ill.)—Social life and customs.   2. Stockyards—Social aspects—
Illinois—Chicago.   3. Human geography—Illinois—Chicago.   I. Title.
II. Series.
F548.5.J32   1993
977.3'11—dc20   92-12969

For my parents, Rudolph J. and Ann T. Jablonsky,

and for their parents.

These loving people—and thousands of their neighbors—

were the Back of the Yards community during the interwar years.

Contents

Acknowledgments

Deserving recognition for making so much of the data collection enjoyable as well as rewarding are the eighty-four women and men from the Back of the Yards who shared their lives, first with me and now with each reader. Their recollections, whether explicitly included in this book or not, were helpful and are deeply appreciated.

Thanks must also go to the patient and courteous staff members at the Chicago Historical Society, especially those in the Manuscript Division and in the Prints and Photographs Division. Similar kindness was demonstrated by the hardworking librarians at the Back of the Yards Branch of the Chicago Public Library. They trusted me when they had no reason to.

A special nod of appreciation is due Robert Slayton of Chapman College. His generosity to another generation of scholars has already been demonstrated by his depositing microfilm copies of the Joseph Meegan Papers as well as of the *Journal Town of Lake* and the *Back of the Yards Journal* in the Back of the Yards Library. Moreover, although Professor Slayton and I do not agree concerning the grass-roots origins of the Neighborhood Council or the degree of ethnic segmentation present within the community by the 1930s, his genuine affection for the people of the Back of the Yards was always an energizing "fill-up," whether we had one of our enthusiastic debates over many cups of coffee or just a mild-mannered telephone conversation.

Research for this book was supported at critical moments by both the National Endowment for the Humanities and the American Historical Association, the latter through its Albert J. Breckinridge Program for Research into the Americas.

Anonymous readers at the *Journal of Geography*, as well as Michael H. Ebner and Lizabeth Cohen, who served as peer reviewers for the Johns Hopkins University Press, also deserve my appreciation for their suggestions, as do Anthony R. de Souza and Patricia Mooney Melvin as editors who included related essays on the Back of the Yards in their publications. I want to acknowledge the wonderful encouragement and timely support of Carol Jacklin, Lois Banner, Fred Shelley, and most especially Terry Seip. In addition to reading several drafts of my manuscript, Curt Roseman always insisted that this book could be a valuable bridge between the curiosity of geographers and that of historians. George F. Thompson, president of the Center for American Places and my editor at the Johns Hopkins University Press, believed in the potential of this study even when it was a long way from completion. And finally, to Pamela D. Jablonsky, who understood what this project meant to me, words can never express my regard and love.

Introduction

Saul Alinsky, the celebrated post–World War II urban activist, began his life's work in the Back of the Yards community of Chicago. Years later, while reminiscing about his apprenticeship in the streets, Alinsky characterized the Back of the Yards as a "slum across the tracks from across the tracks."[1] Two-thirds of a century earlier, Upton Sinclair had crafted an even less flattering depiction in his muckraking novel centered on Chicago's historic Union Stock Yards. First published in 1905 and noted more for touching America's stomach than its heart (as Sinclair himself ruefully remarked), *The Jungle* presented a sickening tale of the wretched conditions that greeted Eastern European immigrants whose final destination, some six miles southwest of downtown, was the Windy City's memorable "Stockyards District."

The reality of such wretchedness both horrified and fascinated an army of University of Chicago faculty and students. They left the comfortable academic confines of Hyde Park and journeyed like explorers from another age into a fragment of Chicago that was unbelievably different from their own. But these twentieth-century adventurers had only to take a voyage of two and a half miles to find their New World. In the mid-1890s the University of Chicago established a settlement house near the mammoth tangle of packinghouses, railroad lines, and stock pens. From the safety of this base camp, dozens of researchers, most of them associated with the Chicago school of sociology, scoured the area for information, much of it highlighting the most awful aspects of local life. They detailed conditions in the Back of the Yards through surveys, interviews, observational studies, and ecological mapping. Everything a socially sensitive Progressive Era American might want to know about infant mortality and outdoor privies, "retardation" and the square footage of apartments, or drunkenness and ethnic cultures was measured, weighed, labeled, and presented in published pieces and graduate theses. Most of these projects were completed by 1923, however. As the Back of the Yards evolved beyond its "immigrant" phase, the attention of university researchers wandered toward other captivating corners of that great urban laboratory called Chicago.[2]

As a result, these earnest reformer-scholars never witnessed firsthand the fascinating transformation of the Back of the Yards from an infamous immigrant slum to a rather cohesive, rehabilitated working-class neighborhood. With roots in the opening decades of the twentieth century, this metamorphosis took place in large part from 1918 to 1941. The following pages focus on these interwar years, a time when the original "Stockyards District" of Upton Sinclair and the Chicago school of sociology evolved into the "Back of the Yards" community. According to historian Robert Slayton, the transformation was highlighted by the emergence of a "local democracy" guided, for the most part, by an indigenous elite.[3] But the emergence of the Back of the Yards as a showcase for community-sponsored action required more than a handful of exceptional individuals. Rather than being considered the *cause* of communal unity, the emergence of the Back of the Yards Neighborhood Council in 1939 might instead be seen as the institutional expression of geographic and sociocultural processes that, admittedly, benefited from the leadership of a few talented people.

Generational succession took place in the Back of the Yards not only across time but also across space, across a landscape where ordinary people acted and aged. This book considers how everyday spatial behaviors influenced—and in turn were influenced by—family, ethnicity, religion, education, recreation, and politics. My intention has been to employ spatial considerations, especially from the "standpoint of user behavior,"[4] as a consistent theme (rather than as an episodic condition relegated to specific moments or chapters) and to see how these considerations reshape our understanding of residential life in a rather familiar—given its popularity in the scholarly literature—corner of Chicago. Geography is used here to augment questions typically asked by community historians. I hope that historians will be intrigued by the explanations that geography offers to those who are curious about urban ethnic history and, at the same time, that geographers will find value in the conclusions derived when some basic disciplinary themes are played out in a case study from the past.

During the period of initial settlement, everyday life in the Back of the Yards was home centered, with an emphasis on family and ethnic traditions. But for succeeding generations born in the United States, the centrality of home and family diminished as relationships with nonfamily and nonethnic agencies such as schools, city parks, and local shopping strips were incorporated into the cognitive map of everyday life. Over time, an elaborate behavioral threshold bridged private and public space. Among second- and third-generation residents, "home" as a fixed point for structuring reality grew in geographical distance and social complexity. The Americanization of the Back of the Yards involved spatial as well as social, cultural, economic, and political acculturation.[5] Residents took the community's legacy of an urban slum and turned this questionable heritage into something positive and dynamic. They found a way to be proud of coming from what had once been called a jungle, developing spatial and psychic attachments to their piece of Chicago that went beyond mere words.

For a great many residents, an authentic "sense of community" seems to have existed in the tenements and along the streets of the Back of the Yards by World War II and for some years thereafter.[6] A perception of where they belonged socially and territorially[7] combined with a new broader ethnic identification, a redefinition of religious loyalty, and generational succession to create a moment in the community's history that was epitomized but not dominated by the Back of the Yards Neighborhood Council. Most Back of the Yarders never participated actively in the Council, but they tacitly endorsed its actions because it struck the right chords, said the right things, asked for the right improvements. In this way the Back of the Yards Neighborhood Council, itself a historically noteworthy development, can be seen as the culmination of processes that were unfolding at individual, family, block, neighborhood, and community levels.

To retrieve the past at more intimate scales of analysis, we need a variety of scholarly sources and research strategies. Urban historical geographers typically conduct their research at scales broader than the family and the residential block. One unfortunate consequence is that their insights into the character of everyday life have not significantly influenced historians who are interested in the evolution of urban immigrant communities. All too often historians use the spatial dynamics of the neighborhood or city under examination merely as a two-dimensional backdrop for a series of more highly valued social or political activities. In reality, seldom is the geographical context so innocent or incidental.

For example, the built environment in the Back of the Yards played a distinctive role in the lives of residents during the interwar years. Before the widespread distribution of automobiles and television, everyday life in the Back of the Yards could be spatially self-contained, isolated from the goings-on of the rest of Chicago, let alone the nation and the world. Many residents, of course, left the community for work, school, shopping, or recreation. But traveling in and out of the area took some effort. On three sides, the Back of the Yards was surrounded by railroad tracks, manufacturing plants, packing-houses, and stockyards, formidable barriers to movement on foot and even by streetcar. On its fourth side, the boundary between the Back of the Yards and neighboring West Englewood was Fifty-fifth Street or Garfield Boulevard, a six-lane parkway with a forty-foot-wide grassy median. Back of the Yards residents viewed "the Boulevard" as the southern limit of *their* community, an "edge" that separated the greenhorn district of the Back of the Yards from the middle-class, third-generation Irish and German neighborhood of West Englewood. The Back of the Yards was isolated both physically and socially from adjacent communities within Chicago, and its residents were remarkably conscious of when they left their part of town and when they reentered it. Patterns of territoriality repeated themselves in thousands of instances over time. Back of the Yards residents came to perceive their community—and themselves in a collective sense—as distinct from the rest of Chicago. Unlike the situation in today's faceless suburbs, movement in and out of the area was a definite act, at once physical, visual, and psychological.

The research on human spatial behavior in cities is, understandably, well developed among geographers, urban planners, landscape architects, and environmental psychologists. Of particular value for urban historians are studies of the cultural landscape and of environmental perception. Insights drawn from the concepts of "place ties" and "sense of place" can be invaluable when measuring motivations and values in past societies. Of particular note is *Topophilia*, Yi-fu Tuan's classic study of environmental perception, attitudes, and values. Tuan has observed that, for working-class people, "awareness of neighborhood seems to be made up of concentric zones, highlighted in varying degrees by the type and intensity of experience they have of them. The core of awareness centers on the home and the street or a segment of the street." Beyond that point, "the home base working-class people may identify strongly with a few other spots, usually within walking distance of home. These are the favorite recreation areas, the local bars, and perhaps the settlement house."[8]

Historical and cultural geographers as a rule, however, do not study these behavioral patterns at the level of the individual, the residential block, or the local neighborhood. Perhaps, as Asa Briggs notes, it is left to historians, poets, and novelists "to restore the sense of experience through a particular place." Historians, he says, must "concern themselves with the sense of place and what has made and still makes it." Kathleen Neils Conzen has made this point in observing that the "task of local history thus becomes the analysis of the changing consequences of locality, of place itself, for those living within a place and for society at large."[9]

Fortunately, the Chicago school of sociology's riveting interest in urban ecology ensures that the data and analyses gathered and developed in the Back of the Yards during the early part of this century reflect concern for environmental factors working upon common folk. Moreover, oral history provides a way to reclaim the bits and pieces of individual and group behavior from bygone eras. But those who use this technique need to realize that some colleagues, especially from outside the profession of history, remain skeptical of its reliability. In truth, the frailty of the human memory is all too often evident. At least the dead are consistent, notes Daniel Aaron in citing Aldous Huxley. The "living relic" (an informant), Aaron notes, tends to tidy up "embarrassing disorders," reverently concealing skeletons "in a hidden closet." Moments too painful to recount or too deeply buried to remember can be overlooked and, warns Ronald Grele, are "always filtered through memory and ideology." They can also be "influenced by the language ability of the person talking." Yet, as John Bodnar argues, asking common questions of a significant number of people promotes "comparability and the emergence of systematic patterns in the recorded information."[10] Patterns do appear when the oral histories are of sufficient number and quality. In this spirit, then, processes as opposed to singular events were the focus of the eighty-five oral histories I gathered for this book.

Most of my informants agreed to meet with me and then to be interviewed as a result of personal appeals to local senior citizens' clubs. During the first century of settlement, about 90 percent of the Back of the Yards population is thought to have been at least nominally Roman Catholic. Although dramatic changes are now under way within the community, many residents from fifty years ago still live in the neighborhood or return for a monthly "Golden Agers" meeting at "their" old parish. Others attend a senior citizens' club sponsored by the Back of the Yards Neighborhood Council. A gratifying number of these women and men were willing to share their valuable hours with a bearded stranger from Los Angeles.

In the course of the research and writing, this project evolved into a form of historical ethnography. For years anthropologists have debated the benefits and disadvantages of what they characterize as "insider" research, conducted by individuals who are also members of the group under study. Proponents of insider research, says John Aguilar, maintain that "outsiders lack member knowledge—existential participation in a society's covert culture of implicit rules and ineffable sentiments and orientations." Those who uphold the opposing viewpoint emphasize the advantages gained by coming fresh to a culture, with the "ability to stand back perceptually and cognitively" and "more readily abstract from behavioral data a society's unconscious cultural grammar as well as record its conscious vocabulary." Moreover, distancing should help avoid the problem of overidentification.[11] I was born in the Back of the Yards, and though I was raised elsewhere on Chicago's South Side, I retained family ties to "the old neighborhood." I have made a conscious effort to draw upon the best of both of these ethnographic perspectives while striving to minimize their attendant disadvantages.

To underscore the scholarly curiosity that drove this project from the outset, I have organized the chapters within a sociospatial framework. The opening chapter examines the evolution of an urban industrial landscape that eventually dwarfed the surrounding residential streets. Through their domination of the local economy and, just as insidiously, through their manipulation of the local landscape, the entrepreneurs who created the great Union Stock Yards and adjoining Packingtown in the years after the Civil War profoundly influenced the quality of life within the communities of Bridgeport, Canaryville, McKinley Park, and Back of the Yards. Furthermore, the city's irresponsibility added to the evil conditions under which these people had to live. In the Back of the Yards neighborhood, industrial and municipal landscapes—by virtue of their configuration and size as well as the health hazards they presented—shaped the nature and vitality of community life during the course of the twentieth century.

With the nonresidential landscape established, I turn in chapter 2 to the tens of thousands of human beings, mostly immigrants from Eastern Europe, who flooded into the area looking for work. Within a short time they overwhelmed the existing supply of housing. By 1901 conditions were so bad that the City Homes Association refused to include the Back of the Yards in its survey of Chicago's housing stock. A few years later Upton Sinclair permanently embroidered an image of the neighborhood upon the fabric of American history. Then social scientists from the nearby University of Chicago added their comments about life in the infamous Stockyards District. By the end of World War I, the Back of the Yards was seen as the prototypical urban slum.

The remaining chapters examine the evolution of this famous immigrant ghetto between the wars, with particular attention to and respect for the sociospatial processes then unfolding. These chapters are organized in an outward-spiraling spatial sequence beginning with the family, then moving to those social agencies immediately tied to the home, and finally expanding into the larger community: stoop summits and street vendors, ethnic churches and city parks, movie theaters and municipal politics, and finally a communitywide organization known as the Back of the Yards Neighborhood Council. My aim is to stitch together, in a holistic fashion, sociospatial activities of everyday life, from the mundane and intimate to the singular and grandiose. Together, they created for many residents of the Back of the Yards a sense of community, an experience whose effects still linger.

PRIDE IN THE JUNGLE

1

THE SETTING
An Industrial Landscape

The incentives were typical of nineteenth-century entrepreneurial adventures: visions of large profits, combined with fears about potential competition, motivated a resourceful band of Chicago businessmen to envision and then the following year, 1865, to develop a central stockyard facility even as the nation struggled to survive a civil war. Chicago had dethroned Cincinnati as America's "Porkopolis" by early 1862, but far-sighted civic and business leaders, looking beyond the distraction of current hostilities, worried that its economic position would be challenged anew in spite of a well-established railroad network, a growing maze of lines linking Chicago with the East Coast as well as the upper Midwest. When the Civil War was over—presumably with a Northern victory—Cincinnati would once again be free to exploit the Ohio River as its primary conduit to the country's hog growers. Furthermore, Chicago's current advantage was compromised by the decentralization of its privately operated stockyards. Already this antiquated system was starting to impede the growth of the market as the flow of livestock into the city threatened to overwhelm the existing yards. The newest facilities were southeast of downtown near Lake Michigan. Older and smaller yards operated to the south and west of the city's business center. In the expansive prairies southwest of Chicago was another set of pens at the Brighton Stock Yard.[1]

Anticipating peace at a time when President Lincoln would assuredly have appreciated their optimism, stockyard owners, railroad executives, and a few packers made plans for a central establishment that would safeguard Chicago's position in the hog trade while ensuring accessibility to all interested parties. In early 1865 the Union Stock Yards and Transit Company was organized. With working capital of $1,000,000, its first task was to find a site

1

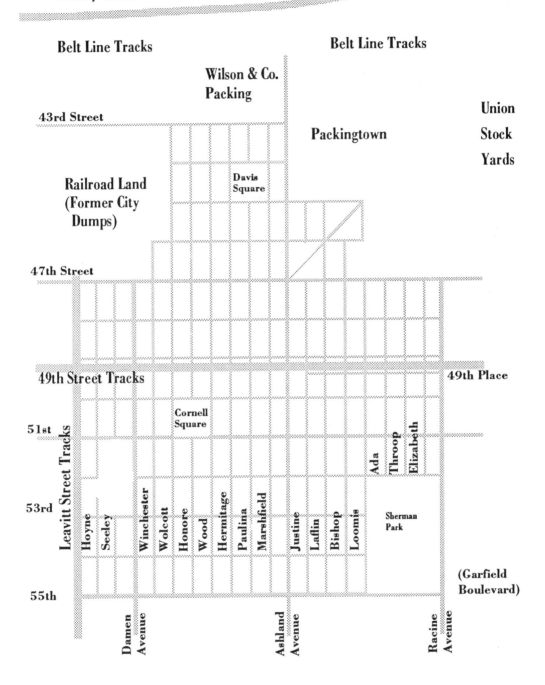

Bubbly Creek

Belt Line Tracks

Belt Line Tracks

**Wilson & Co.
Packing**

Packingtown

**Union
Stock
Yards**

43rd Street

**Railroad Land
(Former City
Dumps)**

Davis
Square

47th Street

49th Street Tracks

49th Place

Cornell
Square

51st

Leavitt Street Tracks

Ada
Throop
Elizabeth

53rd

Hoyne
Seeley
Winchester
Wolcott
Honore
Wood
Hermitage
Paulina
Marshfield
Justine
Laflin
Bishop
Loomis

Sherman
Park

(Garfield
Boulevard)

55th

Damen
Avenue

Ashland
Avenue

Racine
Avenue

Residential streets in the Back of the Yards, as well as major industrial and
transportation elements.

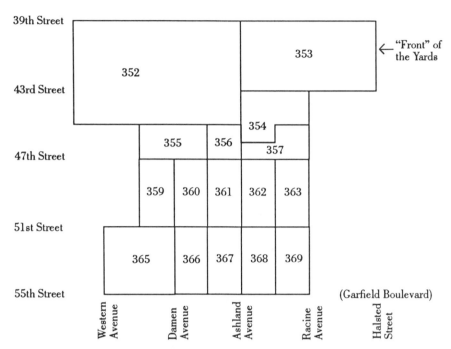

Master map for Back of the Yards census tracts in 1920.

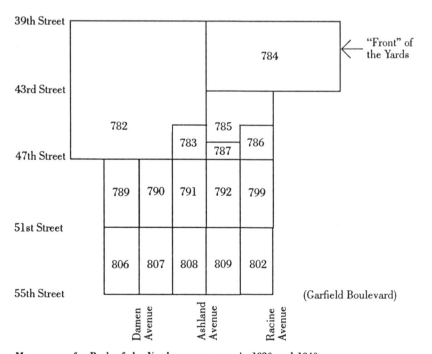

Master map for Back of the Yards census tracts in 1930 and 1940.

appropriate for an enterprise as noxious as an oversized barnyard. Most livestock entered Chicago from the south and southwest, so representatives of the stockyard company concentrated their search for available land along the city's southern edge, as close as possible to the slaughtering and packing plants alongside the south branch of the Chicago River. A suitable 320-acre stretch of low-lying prairie was located in the Town of Lake. Like most of greater Chicago, it suffered from severe drainage problems. Nonetheless, investors became convinced they had found an ideal spot: close to the river, removed from residential areas, and available at a reasonable cost from a recent mayor of Chicago, "Long John" Wentworth. The sale price was $100,000.[2]

In truth, their half-section of land was largely a swamp. Marsh birds and bullfrogs combined with hogs, cattle, and sheep in a cacophony of animal noises during the yards' first few years of operation. Assigned the task of redeeming this swamp was Octave Chanute, a railroad engineer who later worked with the Wright Brothers. Within months Chanute's work crews installed thirty miles of sewers and drains, built acres of pine-plank stock pens, and laid fifteen miles of track. The first stock train entered the yards on 26 December 1865. Through skillful direction and some good fortune, the Union Stock Yards became an immediate success. In its second full year of operation, the complex handled nearly two million hogs, an increase of 50 percent over the preceding year.

While the Great Fire of 1871 destroyed the center of Chicago, several miles to the north, at the rate of sixty-five acres an hour, consuming $125,000 in property each minute for more than a day and a night, the Union Stock Yards, though constructed almost entirely of wood, stood unaffected. The giant conflagration destroyed over 16,000 buildings, eighty business blocks, eight bridges, 15,000 water-service pipes, and $200 million worth of property. Yet the morning after the fire, trains loaded with livestock rolled into the Yards as if nothing had happened. The relocation of major manufacturing concerns including the McCormick Reaper complex into an area northwest of the stockyards brought the edge of Chicago's South Side industrial district close to the yards. Within a decade the stockyards were handling over four million hogs annually in addition to an increasing number of cattle and sheep. In 1880 the livestock received totaled almost nine million. By the end of the nineteenth century the incredible sum of 400 million animals had passed through the Yards during its brief history.[3]

At the center of this activity was the two-story Exchange Building, standing tall amid the rail lines and stock pens. The offices of the Union Stock Yards and Transit Company occupied most of the first floor, while dozens of commission firms competed for space upstairs. At one point over two hundred commission firms worked out of the Union Stock Yards. The telegraph expedited the flow of commercial information from buyer to seller and from processor to distributor, so two rooms were dedicated to this newest weapon

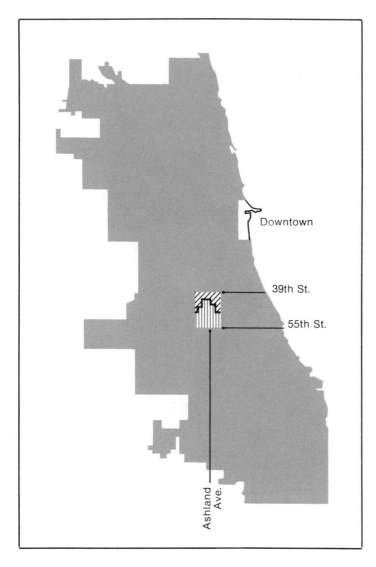

Union Stock Yards and Packingtown (diagonal shading) and the Back of the Yards community (vertical shading) in relation to the city of Chicago.

in a businessman's arsenal. Seven years after its opening, the Exchange grew to include a wing for the Union Stock Yard National Bank. Capitalized in 1868 at $100,000, this institution was unscathed by the panic of 1873. In 1888, when its first charter expired, the bank reorganized under a new name and built its own headquarters building designed by the famous Chicago firm of Burnham and Root. The three-story red-brick Live Stock National Bank of Chicago was noted for its Italian mosaic floors, Belgian marble counters, French plate-glass windows, and terra-cotta frieze at the entrance featuring a cowboy, livestock grower, and steer's head. Above the front entrance rose a four-sided clock tower with a distinctive cupola and weather vane. Over time the bank came to epitomize the success of the Union Stock Yards in general.

Stock pens. Courtesy of Chicago Historical Society. Series of 1903 by Griffith.
ICHi-04084.

In 1895, for example, it handled $500 million in aggregate deposits.[4]

In spring 1867 John Sherman, a cofounder of the Union Stock Yards and
Transit Company, became superintendent of the stockyards. Sherman set out
not only to provide the most up-to-date and efficient facilities available in the
livestock business, but also to offer his colleagues personal amenities that
would please the big-time ranchers and corporate executives who dominated
this trade. Down the street from the Exchange Building, he renovated the
Transit House, a six-story, three hundred-room hotel that, until its destruction in a 1912 fire, boasted one of Chicago's better restaurants: a fifty-cent
meal included a second steak at no extra charge. Through its corridors and
reading rooms, says W. Joseph Grand, passed "millionaires from San Francisco, Montana and Wyoming, capitalists, cattle kings, stock raisers and
well-to-do business men of the city who are lovers of good cheer, of old wine

Live Stock National Bank, 1962 *(left)*. Exchange Avenue, which leads to the "front" gate of the stockyards, begins under the iron archway. Bank entrance to the right fronts on Halsted Street. Courtesy of Chicago Historical Society. Photograph by Bob Riemer.

Union Stock Yards, looking north in 1934 *(below)*. A portion of the south branch of the Chicago River can be seen in the upper left corner. Packingtown is at the center left, the Exchange Building is in the center of the photograph, and Halsted Street is at the right. Courtesy of Chicago Historical Society. DN A-6843.

Transit House, about 1910 *(above)*. Building fronts on Halsted Street, with Exchange Avenue (leading to the main gate of the stockyards) off to the right. Courtesy of Chicago Historical Society. Photograph probably by J. W. Taylor. ICHi-04088.

Dexter Park Pavilion, about 1900 *(below)*. Halsted Street is on the right. Courtesy of Chicago Historical Society.

Root and Burnham's front gate of the Union Stock Yards, with security office to the left, about 1905. Courtesy of Chicago Historical Society. Barnes-Crosby photograph. ICHi-04049.

and juicy beef." It was, added Bertram Fowler, "Dodge City, Cheyenne and Old Tascosa mixed with the flavor of the prairies and salted by the rich brogue of Emerald Avenue. The high-heeled boots of Texas, Montana and Wyoming hooked on the brass rail of the Transit House bar with the cowhide boots of the corn belt farmers and the stockhandlers of the yards." The hotel's admirers claimed that more wealth was housed under the roof of the Transit House than anywhere in greater Chicago.[5]

A few blocks to the south, Dexter Park offered both trotting and running tracks. Later Dexter Park Pavilion was built for horse and livestock shows. With its own water and electric power plants, fire and police departments, and eventually a four-mile elevated streetcar system, the Union Stock Yards complex was for the business elite who worked there a pleasant, sometimes even elegant, male world of profit and collegiality.[6]

The main entrance to the Union Stock Yards was midway between Halsted Street (where the Transit House was situated) and the Exchange Building (which was, appropriately, on Exchange Avenue). The original wooden gate was replaced in the late 1870s by a rough-faced triple-arched limestone portal. The headquarters of the stockyards police force adjoined it. Both structures were designed by Daniel Burnham and John Root, who had built John Sherman's house in 1874. Two years later, Burnham became Sherman's son-in-law. The gate for the "front" of the Yards, with walls five feet thick and a central arch seventeen feet high, admitted presidents and laborers, bankers and butchers—and cattle on the way to slaughter.[7] For nearly a century the gate stood as a monument to the boldness that John Sherman and his colleagues exhibited in building the greatest stockyard complex in American history. (Even today, a largely forgotten historical landmark, the symbolic front gate still stands astride Exchange Avenue, so the roadway must split and curve around it.)

By 1900 the Union Stock Yards had surpassed every investor's dream. The Union Stock Yards and Transit Company employed a thousand people; commission firms employed another fifteen hundred. The stockyards provided its customers with 130 miles of belt track and 50 miles of streets and alleys connecting to pens, both covered and open, capable of handling 50,000 cattle, 200,000 hogs, and 30,000 sheep. The original site was expanded in increments until a combination of rail yards and stock pens stretched for a mile north and south and half a mile east and west. One scenario the Union Stock Yards and Transit Company had not planned for was the relocation of Chicago's slaughtering and packing companies to the cabbage fields west of the stock pens. At first the smaller packers resisted a move into the Town of Lake. They worried about the expense involved and speculated about the real intentions of their larger competitors, who generally supported the relocation. But more ambitious packers realized the advantages that awaited them south of Thirty-ninth Street. Packers looked forward to relief from city restrictions, including a particularly outrageous prohibition against driving cattle through Chicago's streets from 8:00 A.M. to 5:00 P.M.[8]

A visionary in this relocation campaign was Philip Armour. In 1872 he paid the same price ($100,000) for 21 acres next to the stockyards that John Sherman and his cohorts had paid seven years earlier for their original 320 acres. Armour's first project was the construction of a huge pork house. Soon afterward came America's first large chill room. As early as 1879, Armour and Company's net worth had climbed to $2 million, with profits of $700,000. At the time, it was recognized as the world's wealthiest packing-house. Spurred along by the development of the refrigerated rail car, by the late 1870s about half of Chicago's packers had followed Armour's move into what became known as the "Packers' Addition." Between 1870 and 1890, Chicago began to earn its reputation as "hog butcher for the world" as its meat-packing industry grew 900 percent. By 1900 meat packing was Chicago's largest industrial employer, paying 10 percent of the wages and supplying a third of the manufactured goods in an advanced and highly diversified city economy. This expansion continued into the next century. From thirty-nine plants with 25,345 workers earning $12,876,000 in 1899, by the end of World War I Chicago had forty-six plants with 45,695 workers earning $69,864,000. At the same time, the Union Stock Yards had grown to a capacity of 75,000 cattle, 50,000 sheep, 300,000 hogs, and 5,000 horses. It had expanded to 475 acres with 13,000 pens, twenty-five miles of streets, and ninety miles of water pipes fed by six artesian wells. Records were set in terms of livestock receipts throughout the first quarter of the twentieth century. In November 1908 the one-day record for cattle was set at 49,128; in October 1911 the record for sheep was set at 71,792; and in December 1924 the record for hogs was set at 122,749.[9]

Statistics alone, however, fail to capture the impact the stockyards and packinghouses made on the daily lives of South Side residents. Nearly one square mile in area, the railroads, stock pens, and packing plants dominated the local landscape; and as geographer Robert Mitchell has observed, landscape "is a receptacle for continuity and change, a palimpsest that can be 'read' for what it contains as well as for what it represents symbolically." The combined stockyards and packinghouse district contained tens of thousands of human beings and animals, millions of tons of brick and wood, and a frightening abundance of noise and smoke. This awesome medley represented economic vitality and wealth as well as basic survival through day labor. The yards, in essence, conditioned the nature of everyday life for nearby residents.[10]

The stock pens, by virtue of the acreage they covered and the tens of thousands of animals they housed, bombarded residents with noxious sights, sounds, and smells every hour of every day. For locals there were no holidays from the unrelenting reminders of the Union Stock Yards, only days when adjoining neighborhoods received their share of the assault. By itself the stockyards would have dominated any landscape and defined the nature of adjacent sections of Chicago. In combination with the massive packinghouses, the yards shaped the image of the entire South Side of Chicago: blue-collar, ethnic, and aesthetically unappealing.

Packingtown was actually a mosaic of subdistricts, each created by a major packer. In the early days, when land was cheap and easily available, packers had the luxury of using space prodigally. Empty lots, for instance, became "hair fields" where hog bristles dried before being used in paint brushes. With advances in industrial research, packing companies became more efficient until they eventually found a use for every part of the hog but the squeal. Each new product demanded space, often requiring a separate building, until one company's subdistrict might consist of two dozen structures, many five to ten stories high. Swift and Company, for example, occupied nearly eight square blocks between Forty-first and Forty-third Streets. Within this complex were approximately thirty buildings of various sizes, including a five-story general headquarters with 2,200 employees and a continuation school (for youngsters who had not completed two years of high school), a print shop for producing company stationery and can labels, and several warehouses as well as the various slaughtering and processing plants. Swift, like its major rivals, developed a long list of by-products, including margarine, gelatin, furniture glue, violin strings, surgical sutures, buttons, hairbrushes, chessmen, knife handles, perfume, soap, and cleansers.[11]

Stock pens in the early 1880s *(above)*. Courtesy of Chicago Historical Society. ICHi-04074.

"Bird's-eye view of Armour and Co.'s Chicago plant" *(opposite, top)*. From Bushnell, "Some Social Aspects of the Chicago Stock Yards," 153.

Looking northeast from near Forty-seventh and Loomis in 1924 *(opposite, bottom)*. Packingtown is in the foreground, with the Exchange Building amid the stock pens in the upper center. What remains of the stockyards slip can be seen at upper left as it curves eastward along the northern edge of the rail yards. Community at top right of photograph is Bridgeport, home of both Mayor Daleys. Gross (later McDowell) Avenue is the diagonal street at lower left. Most of the buildings on both sides of Gross Avenue exiting Packingtown were saloons "closed" by Prohibition. Courtesy of Chicago Historical Society. ICHi-04090.

"Panoramic view of Union Stockyards, Chicago," about 1909. Courtesy of Chicago Historical Society. Photograph by Max Rigot. ICHi-14408.

Odors from these operations permeated not only the clothing of the workers but the air of the surrounding neighborhoods as well. Although city boosters might characterize the fragrance as a "comforting smell" or "the aroma of a thriving trade," residents remember it very differently. Among all the companies in Packingtown, the most notorious for its olfactory sins was the rendering firm of Darling and Company. Open wagons loaded with bone bits, damaged hides, dead cats and dogs, leftover meat from local butcher shops, and "big gobs of fat" collected around the main plant at Forty-second and Ashland. The vehicles would "sit in the sun, smelling up the whole neighborhood." Streetcar customers traveling along Ashland Avenue were especially vulnerable during the summer, when the windows were open and the car would lurch to a halt near the front of Darling as the tracks dipped under the railroad viaduct. Riders gagged, covered their mouths with handkerchiefs, and occasionally became ill from the unbearable stench. One visitor from the West Side recalls moving to another seat as the streetcar drew near the Back of the Yards because she assumed that a workman who had just stepped aboard was the source of the terrible odor. When she continued to experience the aroma, she wondered how it could be emanating from a single person. Was it the entire streetcar? Her date (and eventual husband) clarified matters for her.

Relatives from the North Side of Chicago never understood why family

Looking north across cabbage fields toward Packingtown, about 1910–15; Ashland Avenue is to the left. Courtesy of Chicago Historical Society. ICHi-01869.

members chose to live amid such awful smells. Upton Sinclair described this experience with gritty texture:

> And along with the thickening smoke they began to notice another circumstance, a strange, pungent odor. They were not sure that it was unpleasant, this odor; some might have called it sickening, but their taste in odors was not developed, and they were only sure that it was curious. Now, sitting in the trolley car, they realized that they were on their way to the home of it—that they had travelled all the way from Lithuania to it. It was now no longer something far off and faint, that you caught in whiffs; you could literally taste it, as well as smell it—you could take hold of it, almost, and examine it at your leisure. They were divided in their opinions about it. It was an elemental odor, raw and crude; it was rich, almost rancid, sensual, and strong. There were some who drank it in as if it were an intoxicant.

Back of the Yards residents learned to live with these odors, but decades later they still argued over just how far the aromas of Darling and Company, the stockyards, and Packingtown carried. In his study of the Back of the Yards community, Robert Slayton cites the experience of a Catholic nun newly assigned to Guardian Angel Day Care Center, four blocks south of Darling and Company: "[I] was taking care of the children. I thought they all had their pants full, excuse the expression. I was looking around. I said, 'Oh my goodness, who made in their pants?'"[12]

The buildings of Packingtown eventually filled the one-time cabbage fields and became entwined in a tangle of rail tracks, cobblestone roadways, an elevated streetcar line, and animal runs. These long wooden ramps—a mile long sometimes—guided the animals from the ground-level stock pens to the killing floors, usually about halfway up the slaughtering houses. Rising fifty feet and occasionally enclosed on all four sides, the most remarkable runs were the double-decker ramps owned by Wilson and Company, the only packing firm west of Ashland Avenue. Running atop a forest of concrete pylons, these ramps snaked their way out of the stockyards, along the southern edge of the Belt Line tracks, then across Ashland Avenue to a building at the northern edge of the Wilson slaughtering facilities. Ironically, amid this jumble of buildings, rail lines, and runs was a lovely garden with a graceful horseshoe-shaped pathway fronting the Wilson Company headquarters off Ashland Avenue. Always well tended, the flowers and lawn provided a colorful oasis in the gray industrial landscape.[13]

Above this maze of buildings and runs, the horizon was studded with towering brick smokestacks. From the twin towers of the Union Stock Yards power plant at Thirty-ninth Street in a westerly arc through Packingtown, the giant funnels pushed skyward like mushrooms. But they bore an ominous significance, for the heavy black smoke that poured from their mouths hung over the adjoining residential neighborhoods, raining a constant shower of soot. Photographs from early in the century capture a skyline dotted with these smokestacks and shrouded in an eerie layer of smoke. Even years later, one resident recalls, there was always a haze over the district. Again, Upton Sinclair gave this landscape life: his characters were left standing upon the corner

> staring; down a side street there were two rows of brick houses, and between them a vista: half a dozen chimneys, tall as the tallest of buildings, touching the very sky—and leaping from them half a dozen columns of smoke, thick, oily, and black as night. It might have come from the center of the world, this smoke, where the fires of the ages still smoulder. It came as if self-impelled, driving all before it, a perpetual explosion. It was inexhaustible; one stared, waiting to see it stop, but still the great streams rolled out. They spread in vast clouds overhead, writhing, curling; then, uniting in one giant river, they streamed away down the sky, stretching a black pall as far as the eye could reach.

Fortunately for those who lived in the Back of the Yards—and unfortunately for their counterparts near the "front"—Chicago's prevailing south and southwesterly breezes pushed the evil haze toward the communities of Bridgeport and Canaryville.[14]

The trains that brought in livestock and carried out processed goods ringed the stockyards and packinghouses with a noose of steel. The rights-of-way they moved along carved up Chicago's neighborhoods, creating "edges." Edges, according to the late urban planner Kevin Lynch, establish boundaries between sections of a city or between activity zones (such as a residential area and a commercial district). Edges can be mountains, rivers, freeways, parking lots, grassy medians, or cinder-block walls. In the Back of the Yards, "hard" edges were established by a belt of railroad tracks wide enough to create both a physical and a visual barrier between the area and the working-class neighborhoods to the north and west. Individual residents learned to accept cattle cars and boxcars clanking past their homes at all hours of the day and night. But at the level of community life these tracks had a dramatic impact. They defined boundaries for the Back of the Yards, and as has been found with earthen dikes in northern Germany, these human-made landscape elements began to shape the nature of community life by isolating the area from adjoining neighborhoods. The tracks, like the dikes, "literally bound the region off and symbolically unite[d] the inner world" of nearby residents. [15]

The largest of these transportation corridors was a mammoth snarl of tracks that constituted the northern and western extensions of the stockyards. The Chicago Junction Railway managed these tracks for the Union Stock Yards and Transit Company as part of a belt system that wove its way around and between the pens and packinghouses. Except for an underpass at Ashland Avenue, this mile-long web of rails sealed off the Back of the Yards from the McKinley Park community to the north. Another cluster of tracks alongside Leavitt Street blocked interaction between the Back of the Yards and Gage Park to the west, also for a mile. The situation was unintentionally worsened early in the century when Chicago passed an ordinance requiring railroads to elevate their rights-of-way. The city council was responding to the growing number of rail accidents involving pedestrians. One such incident in the Back of the Yards had nearly cut a man in two. Yet the rail companies dawdled in complying. As late as 1923 residents who lived near the Leavitt Street tracks recall viewing President Harding's funeral train roll by at ground level. Not until the late 1920s, after decades of procrastination, did the railroad companies raise their tracks onto embankments ten to fifteen feet high. This safety measure completed what had already become a behavioral reality. Except for an occasional youngster "junkin'" along the tracks for glass, metal, or coal, the Leavitt Street tracks shut off residents of the Back of the Yards from the inhabitants of Gage Park. Once the tracks were raised, even visual contact between the two areas ceased; access was possible only through the Forty-seventh, Fifty-first, and Fifty-fifth Street viaducts. [16]

One should recognize, however, that a ribbon of rails slicing through the community did not automatically constitute an edge shutting one area off from another. The Forty-ninth Street tracks were a case in point. During the early 1880s the Chicago Junction Railway and the Grand Trunk Railroad

Looking east from approximately Ashland Avenue with the stockyards slip and rail yards for incoming stock at the center left and stock pens at the center and to the right, about 1923–26. Packingtown can be seen in the foreground. Courtesy of Chicago Historical Society. ICHi-04089.

built, at ground level, four sets of tracks adjacent to Forty-ninth Street. In contrast to the delay in raising the Leavitt Street tracks, the CJR and the Grand Trunk responded to the elevation ordinance with dispatch. By 1906 the job was completed.[17] A solid dirt and concrete wall about sixty feet wide and twelve to fifteen feet high rose like a surface rupture. The embankment ran the entire length of the community, presenting what appeared to be a formidable barrier to north-south movement. Yet from its earliest days, even as freight trains chugged along at ground level, sometimes within fifteen feet of homes, these tracks never interfered with the normal activities of adults or children. Street and community life were unaffected by the presence first of the tracks and later of the earthen embankment. It never mattered whether one lived north or south of the Forty-ninth Street tracks. This casual detachment was influenced by two factors. First, the embankment was only a fraction of the width of the huge switching yards south of Thirty-ninth Street or of the embankment along Leavitt Street. Second, and more important, when the tracks were raised, viaducts were constructed for every street they crossed. This meant an underpass every block from Leavitt Street east to Racine Avenue. Every house was near a street that provided easy access to the other side of the tracks, and residents unconsciously incorporated the tracks into the residential landscape. This embankment became as much a part of the local scenery as the cobblestone streets, the electric streetcars, and the corner grocery.[18]

Threatening the health of those who lived near the Belt Line tracks was what locally—and rather kindly—was known as "Bubbly Creek." The south branch of the Chicago River, as it left the Loop, oozed southward until Twenty-fifty Street, where it angled southwest. Along this stretch, in the Bridgeport community, were the city's first slaughtering and packing plants.[19] The river at this point still had a weak current, but it could not flush the stream clean of the pollutants dumped into it by the rendering and packing companies. Near Ashland Avenue the south branch split into its western and southern forks. The south fork meandered toward the Union Stock Yards. In time it split into east and west branches north of Thirty-ninth Street. The east branch ran along the northern edge of the stockyards near the rail lines. Designated the Union Stock Yards Canal Slip, the waterway expedited the movement of lumber and other heavy materials into the stockyards. The west branch, known as Bubbly Creek, ran for more than a mile to Western Avenue along what would have been Fortieth Street. This narrow sliver of slimy water earned its nickname because nineteen packing companies discharged their waste into its waters. The pollution dumped into Packingtown's open sewer is thought to have equaled the waste of one million people. In time Bubbly Creek became a stagnant cesspool only blocks from homes south of Forty-third Street. Continually rising to its surface were bubbles of gas released by the decaying matter at the bottom: thus the name. Local legend claims that the diameter of these bubbles had to be measured in feet. One eruption was said to have encircled a boat. In calmer moments residents recall bubbles five to eight inches across. They remember workmen on a small barge skimming the slime off the surface and collecting it in fifty-gallon drums. The water was so dense that Bubbly Creek never froze. Even today, where the south fork ends north of Thirty-ninth Street alongside a city pumping station, an endless multitude of greasy bubbles defines the surface of the waterway. Its consistency is still like crankcase oil.[20]

Cries of outrage against this open sewer and its thousands of attendant flies and mosquitoes went unheeded despite valiant efforts by Mary McDowell, director of the University of Chicago Settlement House (which was less than six blocks south of Bubbly Creek). Only expansion of the Central Manufacturing District, a large industrial park north of the stockyards, saved the community from continued exposure to the creek. In 1915 directors of the Central Manufacturing District, having filled their original space of 260 acres east of Ashland and north of Thirty-ninth Street, eyed an undeveloped strip of 100 acres north of the Belt Line tracks, south of Thirty-ninth Street and west of Ashland Avenue. Bubbly Creek was filled in with earth from excavations for the buildings, many of which were six stories high and several hundred feet wide. Rail tracks to service them were then laid over what had once been Bubbly Creek. After the "Pershing Road development" was completed (Thirty-ninth Street was renamed for the general in 1921), residents south of the Belt Line could not even see McKinley Park in the distance. Now the entire northern horizon of the community was an unbroken vista of rail yards and factories. As a souvenir, a stump of Bubbly Creek abutted Ashland Avenue until after World War II, continuing to produce smells that sickened passers-by and to provide breeding grounds for next summer's crop of mosquitoes.[21]

The city's contribution to the blighted landscape was four huge holes into which Chicago dumped the garbage from half a dozen South Side wards. Thomas Carey, alderman for the Back of the Yards during the early twentieth century, had originally mined this land for clay that was processed at his on-site brickyard. Over time, four pits were excavated. One hole, west of the Leavitt Street tracks, had been completely filled by 1909. The other three holes (of five, ten, and six acres) were east of the tracks from Forty-first to Forty-seventh Streets. Across Damen Avenue (the eastern edge of the dumps) and Forty-seventh Street (the southern edge) were homes. The packinghouses used one of these dump sites to burn waste; a fire smoldered continuously, surrounded by a pool of fetid water. At two of the sites professionals paid a fee to pick through the debris. After they had finished, local women and children scavenged for old mattresses, bottles, wooden boxes, worn garments, and even fragments of food. Photographs from the first decade of this century

---

Small portion of the former Quartermaster Corps buildings *(opposite, top)*. Part of the Central Manufacturing District's Pershing Road development. Some of these buildings are now used as the headquarters of the Chicago Board of Education. Photograph by P. Jablonsky.

Packingtown, looking north in 1929 *(opposite, bottom)*. Racine Avenue is at the right, separating the stockyards from the packinghouses. At the upper left is the Central Manufacturing District's Pershing Road development, built adjacent to what was once Bubbly Creek. A stump of the creek meanders along the top of the photograph. To the north of the Central Manufacturing District's buildings is the community of McKinley Park. At the lower left is Gross Avenue, with supposedly "closed" saloons lining the exit from Packingtown. Left of center, below the CMD buildings, is Wilson and Company, fronting on Ashland Avenue. Wilson was the only major packer west of Ashland. The curving roadway can be seen enclosing a beautiful flower garden in front of the headquarters buildings. To the south of this garden, along the west side of Ashland Avenue, the one-story buildings are a portion of old Whiskey Row. Courtesy of Chicago Historical Society. ICHi-04091.

"Women leaving dumps *(above)*. From Breckinridge and Abbott, "Housing Conditions in Chicago."

"One of the city dumps" *(below)*. From Breckinridge and Abbott, "Housing Conditions in Chicago."

Children "harvesting" a Christmas tree from the city dumps, about 1915. Courtesy of Chicago Historical Society. ICHi-01870.

show women in babushkas and heavy woolen peasant clothing competing with the pickers' horse-drawn wagons amid mounds of garbage. Another photograph features six youngsters probably under thirteen, with one in a wicker baby buggy, standing beside a tired-looking Christmas tree surrounded by rubble. In the background of some of these photographs one can see the two-story frame houses that lined the "dumps," and behind them are the packinghouse smokestacks with their great clouds of black smoke hovering overhead.[22]

The health hazards of these open-air dumps were fully appreciated by everyone who lived nearby. Given the political naïveté of the newly arrived immigrants, however, the only interested person with the know-how to contest this situation was Mary McDowell. But she had to contend with politicians who sought to protect one of their own, in this case Alderman Tom Carey. When he worked in the Union Stock Yards, Carey lived at Forty-third and Wood, half a mile west of Packingtown, across the street from the Belt Line tracks and near the Wilson Packing Company plant. Later he moved to Forty-second and Western. No doubt he dismissed complaints about the garbage by responding that since *he* lived near the pits, what was the problem? But that defense broke down after 1905, when he moved to a classier neighborhood close to the lakefront. The Chicago *Tribune* stepped up the attack in an article of 27 October 1909, charging that fumes from the dumps poisoned infants. The paper cited statistics showing that 127 babies under two years old had died in the Twenty-ninth Ward in the previous six months. Half of them had lived within three blocks of the dumps, and fifty children under age twelve had been observed the day before playing around the filth and refuse.[23]

The city avoided taking immediate action by shunting the issue aside to an investigative committee. Petitions were received by the city council and the health department; they too were quietly filed away. Arguments for closing the dumps were met with a smug "What can we do?" Officials claimed that closing the Back of the Yards dumps would only transfer the nuisance somewhere else. Finally, in 1913, McDowell's efforts began to realize success, but only after Illinois women were enfranchised. The "garbage lady," as the social worker was dubbed, finally coerced the city into covering the remaining pits. Only under constant and, finally, politically potent pressure had the city consented to consider the health and welfare of its residents before the preferences of its manufacturing elite.[24]

The presence of the stockyards, the packinghouses, the railroads, and their associated businesses contributed significantly to the city's reluctance to eliminate the dumps. After all, Chicago was the railroad hub of the country, and the livestock industry (from cattle cars to canned ham) was the city's largest manufacturing enterprise. In addition, the area around the stockyards and Packingtown "looked" like an industrial zone, with only a few unimpressive workers' "cottages" dotting the horizon. The bleak industrial landscape around the railroad tracks, Bubbly Creek, and the dumps undercut the urgency of cleaning up "aesthetic unpleasantries" in what seemed to be a wasteland. That the Back of the Yards residents were primarily working-class foreigners, recent arrivals from overseas, and not the professional upper middle class of Hyde Park helps explain why environmental hazards were allowed to exist, even into the twentieth century. But another important reason lay in the nature of the physical landscape in this part of Chicago. The area—especially for stockyard executives, city officials, and outsiders who would have been preoccupied with the pens and packinghouses—looked, smelled, and sounded like an industrial district. Residential streets were an afterthought—except for those who lived there. The focus for at least the first half-century after the stockyards opened in 1865 was on developing that enterprise. The stockyards and packinghouses symbolized the entrepreneurial spirit of John Sherman and his visionary colleagues. The smokestacks, standing tall atop mountains of brick, heralded Chicago as the prototypical industrial city:

Stormy, husky, brawling,
City of the Big Shoulders.[25]

As for the poor unfortunates who chose to live nearby, they simply had to take their chances.

2

THE CONTEXT
An Ethnoreligious Landscape

When cattle cars first rumbled into the Union Stock Yards on the day after Christmas 1865, the surrounding landscape was a marshy prairie with a few isolated houses and shanties but otherwise desolate. A few years later, as part of his packinghouse venture, Philip Armour allowed a handful of trusted employees to erect "cottages" on company land. Other packers followed his lead. Within a few years fifteen families, mostly Irish, had moved in. Small clusters of frame dwellings resembling the mining towns of the Far West more than the big city of Chicago (with its energetic rebuilding after the Great Fire) sprang up, with the quaint names "Armour's Patch," "New Patch," "Stone's Patch," and west of Ashland Avenue, "back o' the yards."[1]

These "patches" constituted prairie outposts a mile or so from what was then developing into Chicago's South Side "Main Street." Up and down Halsted at the "front" of the yards, saloons, meat markets, grocery stores, livery stables, furniture stores, the Transit House, and still more saloons created one of the busiest commercial developments outside the city itself. Halsted Street businesses served the stockyards, railroad companies, and packinghouses as well as the nascent working-class district of Canaryville, east of the yards. Two miles to the south around Sixty-third Street, the streetcar suburb of Englewood attracted white-collar workers and supervisors from Packingtown. All these enterprises—including the Union Stock Yards and Packingtown—were springing up within the Town of Lake. Six miles square, the town stretched from Thirty-ninth Street (the northern border of the stockyards) to Eighty-seventh Street and from State Street on the east to "No-Man's-Land" (Cicero Avenue) on the west. Section 5 of the township housed the stockyards; sections 6, 7, and 8 evolved into the Back of the Yards community. Residents elected a town board consisting of a supervisor, an

25

assessor, a collector, and two trustees. After an amendment to the charter in 1869 they also chose a clerk, a justice of the peace, and a constable. The Union Stock Yard and Transit Company donated land on Halsted Street for a town hall. The first post office was privately owned. Three men sporting badges constituted law enforcement in the Town of Lake.[2]

Throughout the 1870s, a stream of packing companies opened plants in vacant fields west of the stockyards. Industrial expansion soon swept over the original "patch" settlements. A warehouse replaced Armour's Patch. The building was christened "Castle Garden" because newcomers from Ireland were said to pass directly from New York's port of entry, Castle Garden, to Packingtown's Castle Garden. As the number of packing plants increased, better-planned housing tracts appeared south of Forty-seventh Street. Lots 25 feet by 125 feet—common to working-class districts in and around Chicago after the fire—sold for as little as $100. A miniature version of Halsted Street complete with boardinghouses, general stores, and the ubiquitous saloons sprouted along Ashland Avenue. Late in the 1870s, German-born realtor Edward Dreyer took a page from Chicago's reemergence after the fire when he developed his "New City" project on thirty-seven acres south of Forty-seventh Street, east of Ashland Avenue. Dreyer conceptualized a showcase of working-class housing complete with sidewalks and water-main hookups. Forty homes were built and eleven more were moved to the project site. Most were priced below $500, and stockyards workers rushed to purchase them. The project's name, New City, was used for a time to designate the area south of Packingtown. Eventually it became the term by which University of Chicago researchers and the United States Census Bureau identified the combined communities of Canaryville and Back of the Yards. But the name never really caught on with residents, though several businesses (the New City Iron Works and the New City Drug Company among them) did adopt it. Other names used for the rapidly growing residential community south of Packingtown included West Lake, Roseville, Arnoldsville, and back o' the yards.[3]

In 1889 Chicago annexed the Town of Lake. The area south and west of Packingtown inherited the name Town of Lake while other districts in the old township retained their original names, including Englewood, West Englewood, and Gage Park. Residents closer to Forty-seventh and Ashland

---

"O'Leary's saloon and gambling house" on Halsted Street near the main gate of the stockyards in 1906 (opposite, top). Courtesy of Chicago Historical Society. DN 3965.

Looking south down Halsted Street in the early 1900s (opposite, bottom). Archway on right (just beyond building with awning) spans entrance to Exchange Street. The "front" gate of stockyards is a block down Exchange. The tall building on the right is the Transit House. Courtesy of Chicago Historical Society.

"Just coming from the stockyards," 1900. Courtesy of Chicago Historical Society. ICHi-15113.

preferred the name "back o' the yards"; those who lived a little farther away clung to the historical Town of Lake. By whatever name, a "new city" was rising amid the cabbage fields beyond Packingtown. In 1887 developer Samuel E. Gross subdivided the two-block-square lot extending from Ashland Avenue to Loomis Street and from Forty-fifth Street to Forty-seventh Street and installed a diagonal street that angled northeastward from the corner of Forty-seventh and Ashland. By 1900 Packingtown had expanded to Gross's doorstep. Only a six-foot-high wooden fence separated the packing plants from the tenements along Forty-fifth Street. At the junction of Gross Avenue, Forty-fifth, and Loomis was one of the main entrances to Packingtown. Every morning and evening, thousands of workers tramped through this "back" gate. On occasion a steer would break loose, charge through the gate, and make life exciting for local residents. By the time Chicago annexed the Town of Lake in 1889, about 10,000 people were living in the "broad crescent" around the crossing of Ashland Avenue and Forty-seventh Street. This influx continued during the 1890s and turned into a torrent after 1900. By the First World War the community had reached its population peak: nearly 60,000 people lived in the area bounded by Thirty-ninth Street, Racine Avenue, Fifty-fifth Street, and the Leavitt Street tracks.[4]

Most "patch" residents were first- and second-generation Irish. Testimony to their role in settling the Back of the Yards was provided in 1938 when a park librarian founded the Back o' the Yards Old Timers' Club. The club's honor roll for the 1870s was replete with family names such as Cassidy, McCarthy, Driscoll, Riley, O'Toole, Patrick, Dooley, Flaherty, Shea, Egan, O'Brien, Carney, O'Farrell, and Flynn. Other nationalities were represented, but a preponderance of "first families" clearly traced their ancestry to the Emerald Isle. And their numbers grew steadily during the first ten years of settlement. By 1881, when Saint Rose of Lima parish was established (hence the short-lived name Roseville for the district), at least sixty families lived near Packingtown's back gates. Fifteen years later church membership had climbed to seven hundred families.

Over the next two decades, however, the neighborhood between Forty-seventh and Fiftieth Streets and west of Racine witnessed its first ethnic succession. Comparable to what Olivier Zunz found to be true in Detroit, ethnicity became the "primary organizing principle" for the spatial distribution of residents across the Back of the Yards. During the late 1890s, the original settlers migrated southward into the more comfortable environs of Englewood and West Englewood. Brick homes with electricity and even central heating proved attractive to families whose breadwinners were now foremen, floor managers, and division supervisors. As the packing industry expanded, the Irish moved up the occupational ladder or, as they had in other cities, into jobs with the municipal police, fire, and education departments. They were replaced by newcomers from Eastern Europe, members of the "new immigration." Although former parishioners faithfully returned for holy day services, Saint Rose's had become an "Irish church" surrounded by Poles. In 1920, for example, of the 42 percent of the population in the relevant census tract who were foreign-born, 47 percent were Polish and only 4 percent Irish. In the next tract over, between Loomis and Racine, the figures were 80 percent Polish and 3 percent Irish. By 1920 the Irish character of the streets south of Forty-seventh Street was largely a memory—and a fitting topic for an old-timers' club.[5]

Sprinkled among the "patch" Irish were a number of German families. Some working-class Germans had fled the heart of Chicago in the wake of the 1871 fire. Most moved into this semiwilderness because their butchering skills could be traded for decent wages. Many Germans were attracted to countryman Edward Dreyer's New City project. Like the Irish before them, German Catholics founded a national parish. In 1879 a small frame structure was built on Laflin near Forty-ninth Street. A parish school was opened at the same time in the rear of the church building. The church's location, so close to the Forty-ninth Street tracks, proved to be an annoyance as well as a danger, and so in 1886 the pastor purchased a block of land north of Fifty-first Street. By that time the congregation had grown to three hundred families. What had happened around Saint Rose's in the preceding decade replicated itself around Saint Augustine's during the 1890s. The ethnically identified church served as a magnet for other Germans. In turn, the presence of more and more German families attracted additional compatriots, even those of a different faith. Saint Martini's Evangelical Lutheran Church, built in 1884, provided a second anchor for the German community around Fifty-first and Ashland. As late as 1920, German and Austrian immigrants in the census tract immediately south of Saint Augustine's constituted 50 percent of the foreign-born population.[6]

Back of the Yards Germans contributed both economic and social stability to the community. Many became homeowners, frequently residing in the area for generations. Their economic achievements were directly related to the slaughtering and butchering skills that were still in heavy demand as Packingtown continued to expand during the eighties and early nineties. Others came as skilled craftsmen hired to direct the endless construction projects associated with the stockyards, packinghouses, and railroad yards. And finally, in the late 1890s, others moved in who brought with them experience in managing small businesses, just as commerce along Ashland Avenue expanded to serve the growing population. With this influx came the usual assortment of ethnic organizations. A German theater was established in Schumacher Hall on Forty-seventh Street, and Heitman Hall became the headquarters for the Teutonia Turnverein. A critical institution founded by local Germans and those in adjoining communities was Evangelical Deaconess Hospital at Fifty-fourth Place and Morgan Street, for many years the only hospital close to the Back of the Yards. Nearby on Halsted Street, Oswald Grove became a favorite recreational center among Germans. Its seven and a half acres included a beer hall, a dance hall, and a bowling alley for the adults and a merry-go-round for the youngsters.[7]

Before its annexation by Chicago in 1889, the Town of Lake possessed a rather primitive residential landscape. Ditches on each side of Ashland Avenue drained water from beach ridges to the south. Until they were filled in these canals fed into Bubbly Creek, giving the stream a periodic cleansing. The ditches were wide enough to let two boats pass and deep enough to drown the unwary. One early resident recalls paddling along Forty-seventh Street to Ashland and then southward to his favorite German saloon on Fifty-first. Like most of Chicago, the Town of Lake was just a few feet above the level of Lake Michigan. Puddles became miniature lakes after a summer squall. Local youths went crab hunting in these ponds, and bullfrogs provided entertainment on warm summer evenings. The first sewer lines were not laid until after annexation, and even then they were primarily along main thoroughfares. About the same time, a few streets in the community were finally paved. Because of Chicagoland's poor drainage, homeowners had to construct sidewalks. These were raised on stilts but with no standard height, and pedestrians received a strenuous workout climbing up and down sidewalk stairways every twenty-five feet as they crossed property lines. Residents also had to watch their step as loose or rotten boards threatened to send them tumbling into the muddy morass below. Concrete sidewalks first appeared in the 1890s when several prominent buildings were elevated. In the eighties, kerosene

Frame structure at 5205 South Ashland Avenue in a German and Polish neighborhood in 1917. Courtesy of Chicago Historical Society. Photograph by Charles E. Barker. ICHi-22787.

lamps operated by the township hung useless from lampposts; travelers had to carry their own lanterns to avoid the potholes and puddles. During the 1890s the city installed electric lights one block apart at street corners. Indians from Chicago's western suburbs came to Fifty-first and Ashland to sell herbs and medicine, while gypsies camped in cabbage fields that would later become Sherman Park.[8]

Before returning to the community's settlement history, let me add a brief digression on the role ethnic churches played in the spatial distribution and social development of the Back of the Yards. By all accounts, the area housed a population that was "almost entirely" Catholic—*Roman* Catholic primarily—between its founding and the end of World War II.[9] The establishment of parishes such as Saint Rose's and Saint Augustine's showed there were enough of the faithful to support a church and its inevitable grammar school. Although founded to serve the Irish families who lived south of Packingtown, Saint Rose's was actually a territorial rather than a national church. Its congregation comprised those Catholics who lived within specific geographical boundaries and were not members of a national church. The other territorial church among eleven local Catholic centers of worship was Saint Basil's—usually characterized by those who lived north of Fifty-first Street as the "rich people's church." The remaining Catholic churches were all established to serve particular national groups. Three were for Poles, and there was one each for Germans, Bohemians, Slovaks, Lithuanians, Russians, and Ukranians. (The last two did not celebrate the Roman or Western rite liturgy.)

The establishment of ethnically identified churches (all built between 1879 and 1910) inevitably attracted additional compatriots to the tenements nearest "their" church. In spatial terms these national churches were scattered about the community, at first separating nationalities into territorial pockets. Their placement promoted "German" or "Polish" or "Slovak" neighborhoods and, as Caroline Golab found in Philadelphia among Poles, those neighborhoods were identified with the parish names. The life of the street and the life of the soul were intimately bound within Slavic-American communities. After all, as Victor Greene has pointed out, "the words 'settlement' and 'parish' in Polish, Lithuanian, and Slovak are identical." National churches became sociospatial markers for the settlement history of the area and encouraged distribution of the different nationalities across the entire Back of the Yards community. This "group territoriality" tended to reduce interethnic conflict, since residential segregation by choice may be seen, in Robert Somer's words, as "one form of accommodation between two groups." Even the Mexicans who would arrive after 1920 found a territorial niche within the larger community, though they accomplished this without the assistance of a Spanish-language church.[10]

The single most important figure in the creation of a national parish, and thereby the local ethnic neighborhood, was the pastor. The role such men played in the United States was even greater than that of their Old World counterparts. William Galush has observed that there was "a striking difference from the homeland where parishioners worshiped in a church whose existence seemed to transcend time." A parish—with its spiritual, emotional, architectural, territorial, and historical legacies—was in Europe the *common* possession of its members and the attendant clergy. But in the United States the pastor—the first pastor in particular—and the original church members were the foundation for a parish with little history.

As one Polish priest noted in 1902: "In addition to their heavy clerical obligations, [priests in America] must function as collectors, builders, contractors, bankers, judges, teachers, accountants, organizers, etc." Without the "secular leadership provided at home by the nobility and the intelligentsia," the clergy were more than just interpreters and mediators between America and the new immigrants: they became synonymous with the parish. They came to embody the "complete parish" from its architectural form to the administration of its school to the way its members viewed Catholics from other parishes. The power these men accumulated was greatly influenced by

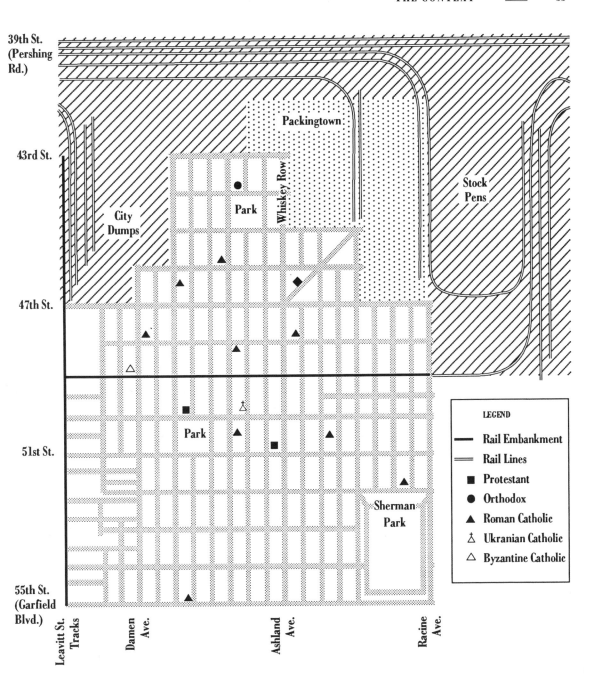

Churches and parks in the Back of the Yards community.

their length of service in Back of the Yards churches, service that lasted not just decades but generations. Rev. Stanislaus Cholewinski was pastor at Saint Joseph's (Polish) for fifty-five years, from 1910 to 1965; Rev. Louis Grudzinski was pastor at Saint John of God (Polish) for thirty-nine years, from 1909 to 1948; Rev. Francis Karabasz was pastor at Sacred Heart (Polish) from its founding in 1910 until 1966; Rev. Thomas Bobal was pastor at Saints Cyril and Methodius (Bohemian) from its founding in 1891 until 1953; Rev. Charles Florak was pastor at Saint Michael the Archangel Church (Slovak) for twenty-nine years, from 1928 to 1957; and Rev. Alexander Skrypko was pastor of Holy Cross (Lithuanian) for thirty-seven years after its founding in 1904.[11]

Although this longevity may have provided spiritual continuity for the original settlers, it tended to delay the long-term adjustment of these parishes to the changing social and cultural conditions taking place within the Back of the Yards. As local residents became more familiar with the secular, pluralistic ways of the United States and as Americanization took effect within the second and third generations, ever more tolerant, even indifferent, attitudes developed toward other nationalities. Some of the pastors, born in the old country, educated in a climate of unforgiving nationalistic feelings, and serving as caretakers of ethnic ties in their parishes, had difficulty coping with the shifting loyalties of their flocks. Marriage to a person of another nationality or in another national (although Roman Catholic) church could trigger bitter feelings that would last for years. Pastors tended to run their parishes with an iron hand in terms of finances and church policy as well as showing strong predilections for reinforcing ethnic traditions. In the first years of settlement these behaviors were valuable, since they made "the jungle" more hospitable to the greenhorns fresh from rural Eastern Europe. These strong-willed spiritual leaders helped make the Back of the Yards a home for people of a particular nationality and a particular religion. At a time when family members may still have been overseas, these ties of church and ethnicity were greatly appreciated. The real challenge came decades later, when ethnic ties no longer motivated individuals so intensely.

The transition of the Back of the Yards from a community that was 60 percent Irish and 30 percent German to one in which an overwhelming majority came from Eastern Europe started simply. Among the "first families" of the Back of the Yards were a number of Poles and Bohemians. The former, who would become the largest national group, established their first enclave near Thirty-ninth and Ashland in 1878, migrating there from other parts of Chicago's Polonia: from the Milwaukee Avenue enclave and from the city's Near West Side. In the beginning, because of the absence of "their own" church, Poles had to use Saint Augustine's. In the mid-1880s Saint Joseph's was built at the corner of Forty-eighth and Hermitage, a location noticeably removed from the more established settlements closer to Ashland Avenue. Property was certainly cheaper on Hermitage, and there was plenty of room for the two-story frame tenements that were popular and affordable.

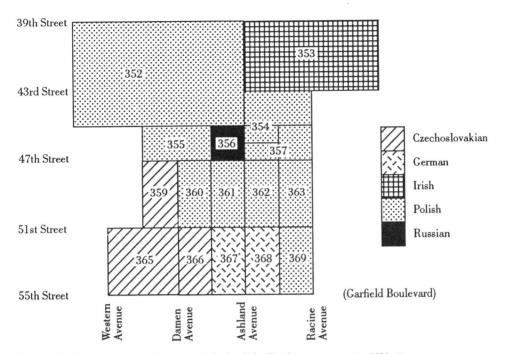

Largest foreign-born nationality in each Back of the Yards census tract in 1920. From Burgess and Newcomb, *Census Data of the City of Chicago, 1920*.

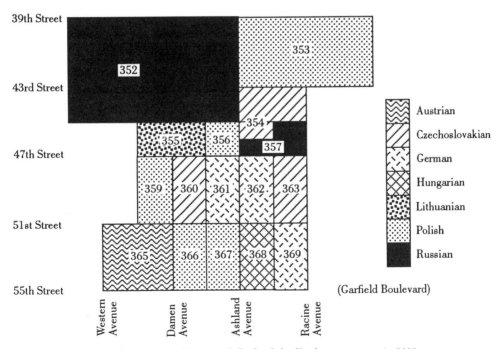

Second largest foreign-born nationality in each Back of the Yards census tract in 1920. From Burgess and Newcomb, *Census Data of the City of Chicago, 1920*.

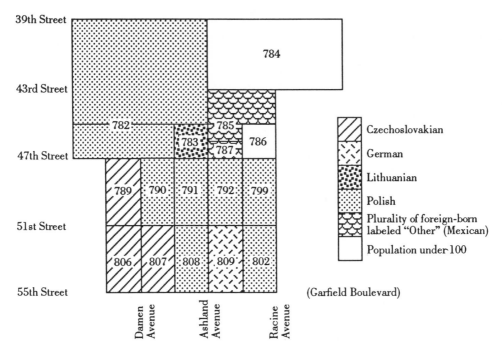

Largest foreign-born nationality in each Back of the Yards census tract in 1930. From Burgess and Newcomb, *Census Data of the City of Chicago, 1930*.

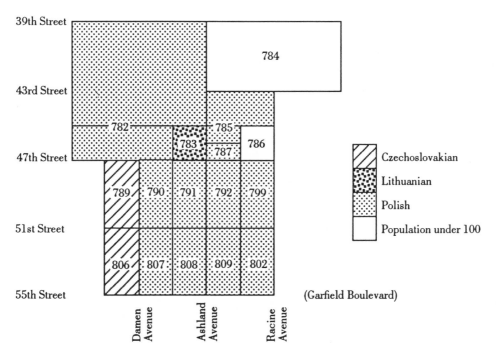

Largest foreign-born nationality in each Back of the Yards census tract in 1940. From *Sixteenth Census of the United States: Population and Housing, Chicago*.

The expandable households that were typical of Polish families in the Back of the Yards demanded all the additional space they could obtain.[12]

But the site on Hermitage was also conveniently removed from the Irish and German neighborhoods, and that may have been a factor in the choice of real estate for Saint Joseph's. Relations between the earliest settlers and the Poles started off on the wrong foot with the first large-scale introduction of Polish laborers, who served as strikebreakers during the 1884 stockyards walkout. Moreover, oral histories indicate that a considerable number of Eastern Europeans in the Back of the Yards harbored grudges against the Irish, their immigrant predecessors who subsequently became their bosses in the packinghouses or the local cops on the beat. Similarly, these first Polish families may have preferred land that was removed from the Germans near Saint Augustine's. Dominic Pacyga has successfully demonstrated that Poles bought homes in the German section of the Back of the Yards; yet other Poles bore bitter feelings toward Prussia, a nation that had helped carve Poland out of existence.

A hint of these long memories manifested itself at Saint Joseph's when its third pastor, Father Michael Pyplacz, though born in Brzeczkowice, Poland, was accused of being "more German than Polish." Several times his administration of the parish, including its funds, was questioned. Mass meetings in 1895 examined his performance. Victor Greene has shown how arguments over ethnic loyalties and control of church resources could, in certain cases, lead to congregations affiliated with the separatist Polish National Catholic church. The presence of these intensely nationalist sentiments within the Back of the Yards was reflected in the establishment of Holy Family Polish National Catholic Church at Fifty-second and Justine in a section of the community that was, ironically, heavily German. The pastor from Holy Family actively recruited parishioners from the area by going door to door.[13]

What started out as a group of Polish "scouts," as Louise Wade has nicely characterized them, became, in the late 1890s and after 1900, a rush of migrants, mostly newcomers arriving fresh from the old country. This attraction to the Back of the Yards continued until the First World War interrupted the migration plans of many families. Generally poor and reliant on the day labor system of the packinghouses, Poles chose to live where rents were cheapest. These tended to be sections of the community with aesthetically undesirable elements, including packinghouses, stockyards, railroad tracks, and the city dumps. For instance, in 1920, in the two census tracts immediately adjacent to Packingtown (Forty-fifth Street to Forty-seventh Street, Ashland Avenue to Racine Avenue) where the foreign-born were a majority, nearly two-thirds of those immigrants came from Poland. Among the foreign-born in the two census tracts south of Forty-seventh Street (including the area around Saint Rose's), as noted above, 47 percent and 80 percent were Polish. A third concentration of Poles consisted of *gorale*, or mountaineers, from the High Tatras in southern Poland who moved into a dreadful section of the community that was wedged between the Belt Line tracks on the north and the city dumps to the west. They established their own parish of the Sacred Heart at Forty-sixth and Wolcott in 1910. And finally, a fourth cluster centered around Saint John of God Church on Fifty-second Street, across from Sherman Park. This parish was established in 1906 and was appropriately—considering its proximity to the German concentration along Fifty-first Street—popular with German Poles. Among the host of religious and fraternal organizations the Poles brought with them, one of the most distinctive was the Julius Slowacki Library across the street from Saint Joseph's. Sixteen Polish organizations established the library in 1902; by 1939 it housed over three thousand volumes.[14]

Interspersed among the original settlers were a few Bohemian families. Like the Germans, they often had butchering skills that were quickly seized on by the packing companies. In the beginning, Bohemians huddled together close to the stockyards along Elizabeth, Ada, Loomis, and Throop Streets, south of Forty-seventh. Like the Germans, they translated their early economic successes into commercial establishments that over the years provided greater financial stability. They became owners of dairies, saloons, ice and coal companies, and clothing stores, as well as mom-and-pop grocery stores and bakeries. They became housing contractors and ran building and loan associations. By 1920 many of them had moved into undeveloped areas south of Fifty-first and west of Wood Street, even though their national Catholic church, Saints Cyril and Methodius, was three blocks south of Saint Joseph's at Fiftieth and Hermitage. What typified Bohemians in the Back of the Yards as well as in their other colonies throughout Chicago was their penchant for clubs, lodges, and *sokols* (athletic clubs). In addition, there was a freethinker element among Bohemians in the Town of Lake, a fact that was more important to the first generation and to Father Bobal, pastor at Saints Cyril and Methodius, than it would be to later generations.[15]

The Slovaks, who would become mistrustful cocitizens with the Bohemians in the new state of Czechoslovakia after World War I, appeared in the Back of the Yards as early as the 1880s, though they came in significant numbers only after the turn of the century. Like the Poles, with whom they got along nicely, many Slovaks found day-labor jobs in the packinghouses. Others became metalworkers who mended pots and pans or made wire products. A few possessed carpentry and woodworking skills. Generally as poor as the Polish before them and the Lithuanians who would shortly join them, Back of the Yards Slovaks lived in low-rent areas, including the residential pocket east of Ashland and north of Forty-seventh Street. A few settled south of Forty-third Street near the Belt Line tracks. The main concentration, however, was south of the city dumps between Winchester Avenue and the Leavitt Street tracks.[16]

Most Slovaks in the Back of the Yards were Roman Catholic, and in 1898 they erected a small frame church in the Polish neighborhood near Saint

Joseph's. In 1900 they moved their religious anchor closer to the center of their colony when they built Saint Michael the Archangel Church at Forty-eighth and Damen. Saint Michael's Church, a sturdy if rather plain building, served what for many years was the largest Slovak parish in the United States. Founded by the Slovak Catholic Society with the assistance of the First Catholic Slovak Union, the parish grew rapidly in the early years of the twentieth century. In 1899 the first three weddings were held at the original church. Seven years later at the new site, a record 114 marriage ceremonies were performed. Similarly, in 1898 one child received the sacrament of baptism; nine years later, 333 children were received into the church. The number of baptisms remained above 300 annually through 1920, with a record 436 in 1913.[17]

Lithuanians were the last European group to move into the Back of the Yards in substantial numbers. Only 99 newcomers from Lithuania migrated to Illinois in the last year of the nineteenth century. That number rose to 2,318 four years later and to 3,400 by 1905, a year after Holy Cross parish was founded at Forty-sixth and Hermitage. Over the next fifteen years, Chicago developed the largest Lithuanian colony in the United States and became a national cultural center with major concentrations in Bridgeport and Brighton Park as well as the Back of the Yards. For many new arrivals, "Chicago wasn't in America, but America was in Chicago." In the Back of the Yards, Lithuanians settled into the neighborhood of aging multistory apartments south of the Belt Line tracks and behind the stores fronting on Ashland Avenue. They lived along streets populated by families from Slovakia, Poland, and Russia and on more than one occasion clashed with members of the last two groups. Like their neighbors, Lithuanians found work in the packing industry. Yet by 1910 there were 112 businesses in the Back of the Yards owned by Lithuanians. Most of these establishments were grocery, meat, and candy stores that served the residents of a single block, but they also included the Knights of Lithuania Press near Forty-seventh and Wood and the Town of Lake Savings Bank, founded by Juozas J. Elijosius-Elias in 1908.[18]

Other nationalities represented in the ethnic mix of the Back of the Yards before World War I but that lacked significant concentrations included Russians, who scattered themselves about the community with clusters near Saint Michael's Russian Orthodox church on Forty-fourth Street, in the largely Polish neighborhood around Saint Rose's, and among the Slovaks near Saint Mary's Byzantine Catholic Church at Fiftieth and Seeley. A few dozen Italians lived in the aging S. E. Gross tract north of Forty-seventh, while Ukrainians congregated near the Church of the Nativity of the Blessed Virgin Mary at Fiftieth and Paulina. With the exception of several thousand Mexicans who arrived later, the ethnic composition of the Back of the Yards was set for the next fifty years.[19]

Greenhorns arriving directly from Europe and families migrating to

First electric streetcar on Halsted Street, near Fifty-first. Courtesy of Chicago Historical Society.

Chicago from other sections of the United States usually reached the Back of the Yards by streetcar from downtown rail stations. Horsecars along Halsted Street reached the "front" of the yards as early as 1877. In 1896 those living on the eastern edge of the Back of the Yards began to be served by an Englewood to the Loop streetcar running along Racine Avenue. The Slovaks, Russians, and Bohemians who settled at the opposite end of the community had to wait until 1917 before tracks were laid on Damen Avenue. East-west movement was expedited by a line, inaugurated in 1887, along Forty-seventh Street. A second line on Fifty-first Street began service nine years later. At the turn of the century the Union Stock Yards and Transit Company entered the transportation business when it constructed an elevated system, since the surface lines could not come into the yards. Built at the cost of $3 million, the 4.11-mile Chicago Elevated Road circled the pens and wound its way through the buildings of Packingtown making stops at each of the major packers. In 1908 the stockyards branch was linked with the city's mass transit system.[20]

The "jungle" into which these new residents moved had grown with little direction or coordination after annexation of the Town of Lake by Chicago in 1889. In 1901 conditions within the area were so bad that the City Homes Association refused to include the Back of the Yards in its survey of Chicago's housing stock: the situation was deemed not typical of the city. The "unpaved streets, lack of sidewalks, indescribable accumulations of filth and rubbish, together with the absence of sewerage" made for "outside insanitary conditions as bad as [any] in the world." Photographs taken early in this century reveal streets filled with mounds of dirt and what appear to be deep puddles of standing water. Unpaved alleys with piles of garbage served as playgrounds for dirty-faced children. Nothing Jacob Riis captured on film in New York City surpassed the environmental horrors facing Back of the Yards folk.[21]

Housing was primarily of frame construction covered by paint that might once have been white. Residential blocks offered a landscape devoid of color, with "grey streets, grey houses, and smoke-laden air," according to Howard Wilson. Unlike the infamous four- and five-story tenements of New York City, however, residences in the Back of the Yards generally rose no higher than two stories, with two to four "flats" of four rooms in each structure. At first visitors were struck by what appeared to be open space on many lots. Most houses crowded the sidewalk; there were small front porches or stoops and even smaller vacant areas where there might have been lawns. Positioning a residence toward the front of a lot could have left room in the back for an alley house, but there were few such dwellings. Backyards were instead dedicated to piles of redeemable junk, including bottles and metal. Most lots also contained makeshift structures used to house horses and wagons or as coal- and woodsheds. This nonintensive use of backyard space, coupled with an occasional empty lot (usually the result of a house fire), made the area look uncrowded compared with the tenement districts of New York City.[22]

The housing problem in the Back of the Yards, therefore, was not so much a matter of macrolevel density as one of microlevel crowding. The danger to mental and physical health had more to do with the population per square foot of residential space than with the number of inhabitants per square mile. An early twentieth-century survey found that 45 percent of the community's apartments were overcrowded by the standard of one person per room per flat. More than half of the residents surveyed in 1910 slept in rooms that violated the ordinance requiring 400 cubic feet of air space per person. In one instance four people slept in a room containing only 333 cubic feet—a room that could not be legally occupied by anyone over age twelve. Cellar and basement apartments, considered the worst offenders against human decency, were still common. (I found basement rentals still in use as recently as 1985.)[23]

With these conditions prevailing at home, it is not surprising that the community's principal social agency outside—and sometimes in lieu of— the family was the saloon. Before Prohibition, most saloons were close to the stockyards and packinghouses. A string of buildings along both sides of Ashland Avenue north of Forty-fifth Street became famous citywide as "Whiskey Row." A 1911 survey reported forty-six saloons along the three blocks north of Forty-fifth. Some stockyard employees were not permitted to

"A 'back-yard'" accessed "through a narrow passage and surrounded by five small houses" *(above)*. From Breckinridge and Abbott, "Housing Conditions in Chicago."

"A typical alley in the Stockyards District" *(opposite, top)*. From Breckinridge and Abbott, "Housing Conditions in Chicago."

A frame tenement "containing a saloon, a butcher-shop, a milk depot, and nine families" *(opposite, bottom)*. From Breckinridge and Abbott, "Housing Conditions in Chicago."

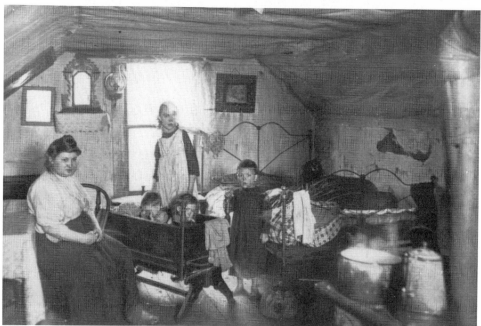

Interior of a tenement, possibly a basement flat *(above)*. From Breckinridge and Abbott, "Housing Conditions in Chicago."

Interior of a tenement, probably an attic flat *(below)*. From Breckinridge and Abbott, "Housing Conditions in Chicago."

eat lunch at their work sites; others eagerly awaited the few moments when they could escape the slaughtering pens for Ashland Avenue. In either instance, within seconds after the noon whistle blew, an army of men and boys surged through the gates at a dead run heading for Ashland to fill their cans and eat their lunches before the thirty-minute break was over. As W. Joseph Grand describes it, "The street, the curb, and the benches, in the sun and in the shade, are lined and filled with men as quickly as they can place themselves."[24]

Visiting social scientists from the University of Chicago, in part because they could not help being, in Gwendolyn Wright's words, "a moral police force" as well as scholars, and in part because they came from entirely different backgrounds, found the saloons particularly offensive. Charles Bushnell, in his detailed study of life in the Back of the Yards at the turn of the century, was more acerbic than most in drawing upon cultural determinism to judge the worth of Back of the Yards residents:

> It means obviously that the people who, either through hereditary advantages or force of character, have advanced in civilization enough to find their places among those who rule the world and direct its enterprises, will not tolerate the saloons near their homes; while those more retarded, who are ruled, want the saloons and give up to them, without any adequate return, but frequently with only added moral and physical depravity, their hard-earned wages.

He argued that the "presence of saloons may be largely accounted for by the absence of decent and cheerful home life." In contrast to local residents, then, these outsiders greeted Prohibition with great relief.[25]

Attitudes like these made the work of Mary McDowell at the University of Chicago Settlement House all the more difficult. Educated, native-born Americans from outside the area were already under great suspicion. If they tried to effect change in the life-styles of the residents, they were certain to meet with firm, even hostile, resistance. McDowell sought to overcome these handicaps, first, by living within the community and, second, by trying to change the lives of the children. McDowell came to the Back of the Yards in 1894, only seven years after Hull House opened a few miles to the north. She demonstrated foresight in choosing to establish her center of operation at the corner of Gross Avenue and Forty-sixth Street, a block from Packingtown and less than a block from Whiskey Point, the location for a second cluster of "day saloons." S. E. Gross's housing tract, built originally in the late 1880s, was rapidly aging by the turn of the century. This residential pocket tucked up against the packinghouses became a way station where newcomers, especially Poles and Slovaks, settled until they got their bearings (and an income) and could move to better parts of the community with their fellow nationals.[26]

The world Mary McDowell came to was much the same as that described earlier: there were no banks, no department stores, no parks, no libraries— and no bathing facilities. As Howard Wilson writes, streets were "only roads

"The noon 'can rush' from Armour's to 'Whiskey Point' for beer" *(above)*. From Bushnell, "Some Social Aspects of the Chicago Stock Yards," 304.

"Typical residence street 'Back of the Yards'" *(below)*. From Bushnell, "Some Social Aspects of the Chicago Stock Yards," 301.

deep with dust which was stirred up in heavy clouds by the feet of horses in the summer time and was converted into a succession of mud holes bordered with dirty pools of stagnant water and littered with trash in the spring and autumn." There was a distinct absence of trees, grass, and shrubbery, and few houses had sewer connections. There was, in the words of Charles Bushnell, "the general appearance of squalor, dirt, and general dilapidation" in the stockyards district. Bubbly Creek was as polluted as ever, and the city dumps still had twenty years' garbage to gather. The settlement house, therefore, was established at a fortuitous moment. It provided a day nursery for working mothers and a medical clinic; language and citizenship classes were available for adults; for children, who probably were more influenced by its staff than were their parents, the settlement house meant playgrounds and sandboxes, garden plots and a vacation school, recreation rooms and a library.[27]

A wariness bordering on pure distrust existed between the non-Catholic social reformers (McDowell attended the Community Methodist Church on Fiftieth Street across from Cornell Park) and several of the local pastors. In 1912 spiritual directors from the three Polish parishes joined together to build their own social service center. Guardian Angel Day Nursery and Home for Working Girls, next door to the settlement house, provided a visiting nurse and a lawyer as well as its most important services, a day nursery and rooms for unmarried young girls. The founders of Guardian Angel resented the patronizing attitude of the settlement house staff. They were also leery of the acculturating influence the settlement house programs had on the youngsters. These Polish pastors were determined to prevent a loss of nationalistic fervor among the next generation.[28]

Living conditions in the Back of the Yards at the turn of the century were deplorable. Ten years later Sophonisba Breckinridge and Edith Abbott, from the University of Chicago's School of Civics and Philanthropy, reported "many changes for the better": "Many of the streets have been paved, a large number of sidewalks have been laid, [and] the sewer system has been expanded." Some improvements made by the city of Chicago were finally evident after twenty years of municipal irresponsibility. Housing conditions, however, continued to create health problems as well as social problems. Moreover, working conditions within the packinghouses (where by conservative estimates over 50 percent of the local work force toiled) threatened workers with new diseases and infirmities.[29]

Nonetheless newcomers, largely unaware of the personal hazards or of the living conditions, continued to arrive—and stay. For some, conditions in the mining towns of Pennsylvania or in rural Europe were even more inhuman than those described in *The Jungle*. They also came because relatives had settled in the Back of the Yards, or because other Slovaks, Lithuanians, Russians, or Poles lived there, or simply because rumors circulated on both sides of the Atlantic that for those willing to work hard, there were always jobs in the packinghouses. Tens of thousands arrived. Every morning they would march six abreast through the side streets of the Back of the Yards, striding with a characteristic "stomp, stomp, stomp" on their way to the back gates of Packingtown.[30] The community continued to expand up to the First World War. It became home to nearly 60,000 mostly underpaid laborers, about half of them born in another country. After World War I this immigrant ghetto matured into a working-class community where the second and third generations took control of their own destinies in the midst of the greatest economic turmoil in the history of America. They survived the Great Depression and began, in the last years before the next world conflagration, to reshape the Back of the Yards to suit their own ambitions.

3

AT HOME
Family Life and the Great Depression

The economic lifeline of the Back of the Yards community in the early twentieth century—the stockyards, packinghouses, railroads, and affiliated industries—thrived during World War I as both government and overseas orders fueled a period of expanded opportunities and steady employment. Profits skyrocketed: the four biggest firms went from a combined gain of $19 million for 1912–14 to $46 million in 1916 and $68 million the next year. Residents also benefited. In one of the largest firms, the number of workers climbed from 8,000 to 17,000 during the war. By 1919, there were 45,000 people working in Chicago's packing plants. Wages also went up. In the twelve months following December 1917, while hourly wages nationwide rose between 20 and 27 percent—and the cost of living climbed 31 percent— packinghouse wages jumped 42.5 percent. Although laborers in the packinghouses continued to earn incomes that produced a shamefully low standard of living, wartime raises were nonetheless encouraging. Equally important, a more consistent work schedule resulted from wartime orders: layoffs were fewer and shorter. There was even the vague hint that a worker's income might someday more closely approximate the sweat expended.[1]

The postwar years, on the other hand, commenced with a period of severely reduced production schedules, in large part owing to domestic surpluses and the constriction of overseas markets. Layoffs followed. Then, in 1921, uncertainty was compounded by confrontation when the packinghouse workers went on strike. The walkout began after packers arbitrarily renounced what remained of the government's wartime guidelines for the meat-packing industry. The strike triggered a community response of noteworthy intensity. Never before had residents representing so many nationalities united in such a public display of labor solidarity. Crowds surged through the streets, congregating around Davis Square Park at Forty-fourth and Marshfield, only a few blocks west of Packingtown. Mounted police sent in to break up one disturbance were met by irate protesters, with mothers in babushkas tossing red pepper into the eyes of both the horses and the policemen. Strikebreakers who lived in the Back of the Yards were warned to reconsider their actions. But the packers had chosen a good time to challenge their employees. In the dead of winter, workers could not afford to stay out indefinitely. Coal was cheap but not free, and the unions could not feed all those who insisted on eating.[2]

The failure of the strike in early 1922 severely damaged the local packinghouse union movement for years. Nevertheless, the economic livelihoods of many Back of the Yards residents stabilized over the rest of the decade. The immigration valve, shut during the war, remained closed as nativistic elements in Congress succeeded in passing the Emergency Quota Act in 1921. When even that legislation failed to stem the flow of new immigrants, Congress replaced it in 1924 with the National Origins Act. By using a 2 percent quota system in conjunction with 1890 census figures, this bill successfully dammed the influx of newcomers from Eastern and Southern Europe. In nine of the ten Back of the Yards census tracts north of Fifty-first Street (typically the areas of first settlement), the foreign-born portion of the population decreased by at least 8 percent between 1920 and 1930; in the Lithuanian neighborhood around Holy Cross Church, it dropped from 59 percent to 42 percent. Immigration legislation split families, leaving members on different sides of the Atlantic. But the dwindling number of immigrants from Eastern Europe (balanced in part by an influx of unskilled workers from Mexico) constricted the labor pool in Packingtown. No longer were there an unlimited number of job-hungry newcomers willing to do anything at any wage.[3]

Even more significant for Back of the Yards residents was a diversification in the occupational and locational patterns of "gainful employment." The number of laborers from the community employed in the packinghouses steadily declined after World War I, shifting from a majority to a plurality by the time of the Great Depression. Workers began to seek—and find—jobs outside the area. Expansion of the Central Manufacturing District along both sides of Thirty-ninth Street promoted this diversification. Within and adjacent to the original tract north of the stockyards were production plants for the Loose-Wiles Biscuit Company, William Wrigley Jr. Company (chewing gum), Pullman Couch Company, Continental Can Company, and American Can Company. There were also pipe- and tool-making firms as well as warehouses for Sears, Roebuck, Spiegel, Goldblatt Brothers, and the Thirty-third Army Air Force unit. Along the new Pershing Road development (where Bubbly Creek once "ran") were other manufacturing concerns as well as the massive army quartermaster depot. Increasingly, daily movement to and from work involved streetcars. Workers broadened their employment horizons—and over time their social experience as well, as they became familiar with

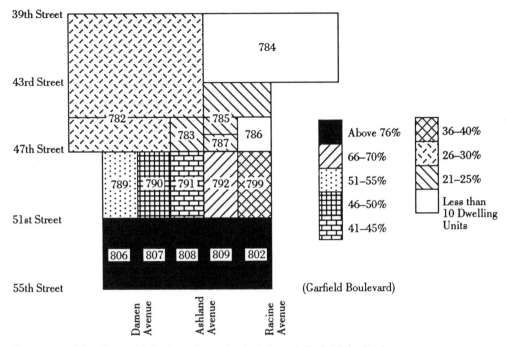

Percentage of dwellings with both a toilet and a bath in each Back of the Yards census tract in 1940. From *Sixteenth Census of the United States: Population and Housing, Chicago.*

different neighborhoods within Chicago and with the diverse populations of the city. In the first years after World War I, this broadening of occupational and territorial experience was most notable among the 78 percent of the work force that was male.[4]

Diversification of employment and reasonably steady work in the packing industry before 1929 promoted incremental improvements in the domestic landscape of local residents. Electricity was installed in flats that still featured the maddeningly fragile gas mantles. Indoor toilets with elevated, pull-chain wooden tanks became a communitywide standard. Some owners raised their homes on concrete rather than wooden post foundations, creating basements at the same time as they mitigated their endless struggles with residential flooding, a perpetual problem in low-lying Chicago. A handful of tenement owners went so far as to install central heating. Even the city made a positive contribution: the remaining cedar-block streets were replaced. Along the main thoroughfares, cobblestones—notorious for the dust, mud, and animal droppings that settled into the crevices—were covered with asphalt. Concrete sidewalks replaced the erratic wooden sidewalks of the nineteenth century. The Ashland Avenue shopping district was markedly enhanced when buildings were moved back and the streets widened as stores and offices replaced saloons driven underground by Prohibition. Streetlights and even sewer lines reached into the residential corners of the community. First-time visitors might have concluded that "the jungle" had been civilized. The settlement house workers, however, would have quickly corrected these first impressions.[5]

Social workers remained concerned over the physical and mental health of those who lived in the cramped apartments common to the Back of the Yards. Most of the area's housing had been built before 1915, and renovations came slowly. After World War I, settlement workers became particularly alarmed about what they viewed as an ominous increase in juvenile delinquency. Reformers warned against what they perceived as the principal causes of this antisocial behavior: poverty that required a family-based economy; a corresponding high-school dropout rate; excessive drinking by immigrant parents; and generational warfare between parents from the Old Country and children who disdained the quaint peasant ways of their elders. Social workers feared that this disdain (which they tended to overstate) was creating a valueless generation that dismissed the past but was too bound by its legacy to fully embrace an American standard of social behavior. They were afraid that a life without adolescence, where the teenage years were filled with cultural strife between ethnic-bound parents and Americanized offspring, was threatening the social order of the neighborhood.[6]

For adults the 1920s were generally a time of adjustment after the turmoil of transplantation to the United States and to Chicago, of the search for halfway decent housing, and of the hunt for work that might provide a marginally stable income. For many immigrant families the decade represented a move toward stability, their *first* stability in the New World. The curtailment of immigration, while painful for some, actually improved life in the tenement flats. Before the First World War interrupted the flow of newcomers from Eastern Europe, Back of the Yards households, especially north of Fifty-first Street, had graciously provided bed space for friends and relatives from the Old Country. During the course of the war and the 1920s, these last arrivals either established their own families and livelihoods or moved on to other destinations. Children who had been born overseas or soon after settlement in America were now old enough to be regular contributors to the family economy, thereby reducing the financial exigencies that underlay the need to take in boarders. Although they continued to demonstrate malleability upon demand, overall Back of the Yards households reverted to a simpler composition. One survey showed that in four representative blocks the number of boarders decreased by 71 percent, 85 percent, 66 percent, and 83 percent between 1910 and 1923. By 1940, 97 percent of the households in the New City area reported no "roomers." Parlors were finally being used for something other than an extra bedroom. Even the settlement house staff could celebrate this development, since middle-class reformers, as cited by Lizbeth Cohen, maintained that "the first evidence of the growth of the social instinct in any family is the desire to have a parlor."[7]

The decline in the number of boarders undoubtedly contributed to a general decrease in the community's population during the 1920s. In total, the fifteen census tracts that made up the Back of the Yards dropped 2 percent in population, from an all-time high of 59,773 in 1920 to 58,528 ten years later. Change was most evident north of Fifty-first Street, where population reductions of between 6 and 34 percent were realized in all but one of the ten tracts. Individual apartments became less congested. Space per household member was less of a problem than in 1910 when Sophonisba Breckinridge and Edith Abbott completed their detailed study of housing in the Back of the Yards. Still, the settlement house staff during the twenties had no trouble finding overcrowded households. The worst case was a four-member Polish family with an equal number of boarders living in two rooms near Forty-fifth and Justine, just around the corner from the settlement house. Yet by 1940 the human density across the community had declined to a more respectable average of one person or fewer per room in three out of four households.[8]

The local housing stock, as the social workers were quick to point out, was aging and becoming more dilapidated with each passing decade. As of 1940, in the combined Canaryville and Back of the Yards neighborhoods ("New City," area 61 in the official statistics), 14 percent of the housing had been built before 1885, 52 percent before 1895, and 94 percent before 1915. Reformers familiar with the health consequences of living in these aging structures lamented the quality of life that the residents, especially youngsters, had to endure. But these same conditions provided Back of the Yards families with the hope of someday achieving what was for many their ultimate goal: homeownership. On the benefits of this investment, reformers and residents could finally agree. Back of the Yards folk had the same burning desire for stability, security, and status through homeownership manifested by their counterparts in other American cities. Moreover, potential home buyers in the Back of the Yards were greatly assisted by the character of the local housing stock. Of the homes in the New City area in 1940, 63 percent were two-story; only 4 percent were higher. Two-story dwellings consisted of at least two flats, often three or four units. A small, block-oriented business (grocery story or candy shop, for example) frequently occupied the first-floor front unit, with the proprietor and family living in the back flat. Rental income from this commercial unit and from the additional flats was usually sufficient to handle mortgage payments on houses that in 1930 tended to be valued between $3,000 and $7,500.[9]

Back of the Yards folk did not become homeowners as rapidly as did Poles in Philadelphia, Slovaks in Cleveland, or Italians in Saint Louis. Nevertheless, by 1930, 34 percent of the residents had been able to buy their own homes. Down payments came from grandparents, other relatives, ethnic-based savings associations, local banks, and even in a few cases the friendly neighborhood butcher. In one instance the refusal of a relation by marriage to provide the down payment backfired to her horror when the

Two-story tenements at Forth-sixth and Paulina in 1959. Courtesy of Chicago Historical Society. Photograph by Clarence Hines. ICHi-22801.

money she would not lend was lost in a bank failure. Particularly revealing about the community was the pattern of homeownership to each side of Forty-seventh Street. North of this main thoroughfare were many of the community's oldest structures. Moreover, these streets were the closest to the stockyards, packinghouses, and railroads. East of Ashland, the aging S. E. Gross housing tract was now squeezed between Packingtown and the commercial developments along Forty-seventh Street and Ashland Avenue. Here the ownership rate was only 19 percent. West of Ashland, where residents had to contend with the Wilson and Company complex, the Chicago Junction tracks, a number of truck and railroad repair shops, and the one-time city dumps, the rate edged upward to 23 percent. On the other hand, some very old dwellings dating back to Edward Dreyer's New City project were south of Forty-seventh Street. But here, the site of 75 percent of the community's housing stock, the ownership rate climbed to 38 percent by 1930. In the Slovak neighborhood west of Damen and south of Forty-seventh Street or the Bohemian tracts south of Fifty-first and west of Wood, the averages rose to 40 percent or more.[10]

As Ewa Morawska pointed out in her study of East Central Europeans in Johnstown, Pennsylvania, steady work was a means to an end, "an instrument to enable their families to survive and at the same time to accumulate some surplus capital to be turned into a life better than in the old country—the 'bread with butter.'" For residents in the Back of the Yards, steady employment provided the income to handle weekly expenses, while rents from one to

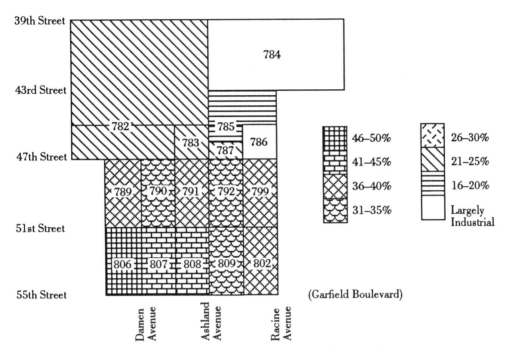

Occupant-owned homes as a percentage of total homes in each Back of the Yards census tract in 1930. From Burgess and Newcomb, *Census Data for the City of Chicago, 1930.*

three extra units covered the mortgage payment. All income, regardless of the source, became part of family-based economy, a system that James Barrett in his study of packinghouse workers effectively characterized for the period before World War I. Although historian Robert McElvaine has suggested that the trauma of the Great Depression triggered a "reemergence of a family economy," among Back of the Yards families this practice had never disappeared. Throughout the 1920s as well as the 1930s, it was customary for more than one family member to contribute to the household income. Barrett uncovered evidence that a significant number of married women entered the packinghouse work force for the first time during the war (perhaps because of declining income from boarders). But this was only a temporary wartime trend. In general, Back of the Yards families followed the pattern of other ethnic working-class districts in urban America whereby married women ceased outside employment shortly after the wedding or during their first pregnancy.

Census figures support the recollections of informants who insist that most married women did not work outside the home. Less than a quarter of all females over age ten (24 percent in 1920 and 22.5 percent in 1930) were "gainfully employed." A substantial majority of these wage earners were unmarried young women who, in the Back of the Yards, usually lived at

Table 1
Gainful Workers (Ten Years of Age and Over) in 1930 by Back of the Yards
Census Tract

Census Tract	Total Number of Workers	Number of Female Workers	Percentage Female of Total Workers
782	3,653	857	23
783	1,810	414	23
784	43	16	37
785	779	94	12
786	0	0	—
787	433	112	26
789	1,387	330	24
790	1,861	436	23
791	1,829	452	25
792	2,105	493	23
799	2,202	442	20
802	491	108	22
806	1,034	212	20
807	1,782	406	23
808	1,952	421	22
809	2,263	547	24

Source: Ernest W. Burgess and Charles Newcomb, *Census Data of the City of Chicago,
1930* (Chicago: University of Chicago Press, 1933), table 8.

home. For the city as a whole, 17.2 percent of married women in working-
class households (with a husband present) earned wages in 1920, while
nationwide 9 percent of married women were in the labor force. Like their
sisters across the nation, however, not "gainfully employed" wives and mothers in the Back of the Yards routinely augmented the family income by caring
for the community's remaining boarders or by taking in extra laundry or
sewing, tasks they could manage while caring for their own offspring.[11]

When Back of the Yards mothers entered the labor force, typically it
reflected an acute financial crisis in the family. Illness, injury, or death of the
principal breadwinner required an immediate revision in a family's normal
routine. All these calamities were commonplace among packinghouse workers, and the last two were remarkably frequent because of automobile accidents. In the case of illness or injury, before mothers with small children
sought outside employment, girls and boys as young as thirteen dropped out
of school and looked for jobs. Such a response drew upon well-established
traditions. Education, especially beyond the eighth grade, was considered
exceptional, a prerogative of "the upper classes." Advanced schooling was
only for males, who would later have to support their own families. Some

parents took the attitude that after eight years of education, regardless of sex, children had an obligation to repay their parents for the care they had received. This point could be made in a harsh, almost bruising fashion, or it could be communicated with a sad shrug of the shoulders that amounted to a reluctant surrender to life's inevitabilities.

Social workers faulted immigrant parents who were willing to sacrifice their children's education to the needs of daily life and to their desire for homeownership. Yet historian Leslie Woodcock Tentler offers an insightful counterpoint to this lament: "Many working-class children were willing, indeed eager, to assume the burden of wage earning at an early age, to dispense with formal education even where parents were anxious for a grammar school or high school diploma. . . . In many working-class communities, moreover, the fact that a majority of children left school at fourteen meant that to do so seemed natural and inevitable." Wage earning was a giant step toward adulthood and status within the family. Furthermore, for many youngsters—and their parents—high-school curricula (with the distinct exception of Tilden Technical High School in neighboring Canaryville) failed to address the everyday demands of working-class life. Both young and old recognized that eight years of training in reading, writing, and arithmetic were more than sufficient to get that all-important first job. On occasion, Back of the Yards youngsters may have envied children from other social classes or in other Chicago communities who enjoyed an extended adolescence through high school, but family obligations tugged at their consciences. Life was filled with uncompensated sacrifices. At least leaving the world of schoolchildren conferred status regardless of a wage earner's sex. Unrealized talents remained hidden within families struggling to get by week to week. Normal financial strains, let alone genuine emergencies, demanded the subordination of individual ambitions and preferences. [12]

Illinois law prohibited full-time employment altogether before age fourteen and forbade it before sixteen without a continuation-school program. Consequently residents had to formulate strategies to circumvent these "middle-class" niceties. Most employers turned away underage youngsters who would have to attend continuation school. Bosses would just as soon not hire young people if they were likely to present any problems. Thus a young teenager who really needed a job had to find a way around state law. For males the problem was easier to solve because packing companies still hired hundreds of errand and messenger boys. In the large firms such as Armour and Swift, continuation schools were conducted in the general office buildings. The "gofers" attended classes one day a week. Other companies sent their office boys to a continuation school near downtown. The obligation to attend classes ordinarily did not interfere with a boy's chances of retaining employment if he could get the job in the first place. [13]

For girls the problem was considerably more difficult. By the 1920s,

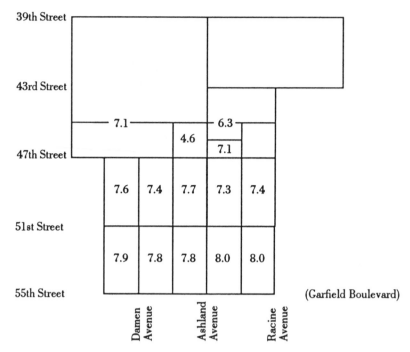

Median school years completed in each Back of the Yards census tract in 1940. From *Sixteenth Census of the United States: Population and Housing, Chicago*.

packing companies were much less likely to hire females under sixteen than they had been twenty years earlier. Young women now had to find employment in industrial or commercial companies outside the neighborhood. Only larger firms, such as the Chicago Mail Order House, the Spiegel Catalog operation on Thirty-fifth Street, or the printing firm of R. R. Donnelley and Sons integrated attendance at continuation-school classes with an employee's work schedule. Consequently girls under sixteen devised other ways around the protective legislation. The principal strategy was to borrow the identity and work certificate of someone older. A sibling of the same sex was ideal. Thus Chicago's work force might include two Mary Jablonskys who just happened to live at the same address. A popular alternative was to borrow the identity and certificate of a good friend who was unlikely to seek employment with the same firm. Once one learned to respond to a new name, the issue was settled until Social Security arrived in the late 1930s. Suddenly every worker in the nation had to obtain an identification number. More than a few times, an anxious employee with five or ten years on the job approached her supervisor and admitted she was not really who she had claimed to be. Seldom, it appears, did these confessions cause problems. More than once the sheepish employee was met by a hearty laugh as the supervisor reassured her she shouldn't feel too bad, since others among her co-workers weren't who they pretended to be either.[14]

The 1920s were transitional years, a calm between the storms of trans-atlantic migration and economic crisis. The economy was so good in some working-class districts of Chicago that one Bohemian *sokol* (athletic club) staged a "'hard times' party which, though stressing poverty, will insist on having good fun." Participants were encouraged to help make it a splendid affair by looking "poverty-stricken." Admission was a nonpoverty-level forty-nine cents. That the calm was behind them and disaster was fast approaching seems not to have been widely understood for the first year and a half after the stock market crash in October 1929. Up to 1931 at least, the effects of what would become known as the Great Depression were still seen as the problems of unfortunate individuals. Layoffs, cyclical employment, and arbitrary wage cuts were familiar events for locals. The last great financial panic followed by years of economic depression had come in the 1890s, before most Back of the Yards families had even arrived in the United States. Their experience with economic disruption on a national scale was scanty and uninformed. More-over, as Jarvis Anderson remarked concerning the impact of the stock market crash on the residents of Harlem, "There was no distance in American life greater than the few miles from the center of wealth and possibility downtown and the black district in uptown Manhattan." Back of the Yards may have been a few miles farther west of the New York Stock Exchange, but its qualitative distance from the market collapse was in fact no greater. Back of the Yards folk reacted at first with as much myopia as did a spring 1930 New Orleans newspaper advertisement, quoted by Roman Heleniak, that asked the reader who "couldn't hold a job . . . was 'B.O.' the reason?"[15]

When local banks began to fail during a seventeen-month period in 1931–32, no longer did anyone suspect that Life Buoy soap was the solution. The crisis was now authentic. Immigrant families had learned that "good Americans" saved their money in banks, not under the mattress. During the 1910s and 1920s they had taken this lesson to heart. The largest bank in the Back of the Yards witnessed a 71 percent increase in total savings deposits between December 1918 and September 1920, while its chief competitor had a 73 percent increase during roughly the same period. The savings habit continued at a moderate pace throughout the next decade. But the election year of 1932 provided a severe test for the newcomers' faith in the American system. An unheeded warning surfaced during 1931 when a small local bank, South West State Bank, closed, only to have its accounts assumed by another local institution, Depositors State Bank. Founded in 1913, Depos-itors operated out of an almost too elegant brick building on the southeast corner of Forty-seventh and Ashland. The bank looked out of place at the principal intersection of "the jungle," with its white stone facade and excessive ornamentation. It seemed better suited to State Street than the main street of Packingtown. Nonetheless it was a popular bank among locals, second only to its across-the-street competitor, Peoples Bank. Depositors assumption of South West State's accounts went largely unnoticed in 1931. To residents, the transfer appeared to be no more than a routine financial rearrangement. That was certainly the attitude taken by *Osadne Hlasy*, a Slovak-language newspaper that proudly trumpeted the involvement of several prominent "Czecho-Slovak bankers" in "the amalgamation." No one panicked. After all, Depositors had successfully absorbed another local bank, Robey State Bank, in 1924 with no disruption in business.[16]

Chicago was hit hard by the bank failures of the early 1930s, as 163 local banks closed in the first four years of the Great Depression. In the Back of the Yards, the rescue of South West State by Depositors turned out to be only a stopgap measure. The following January, Depositors went under. Within the next five months two other banks closed: Sherman State Bank, a small bank at Forty-eighth and Ashland with fewer than two-thousand customers, and Peoples National Bank and Trust Company of Chicago, the most important bank in the community. Peoples had started as a private savings bank in 1903, receiving its state charter the following year. Positioned prominently on a triangle of land between Gross Avenue and Forty-seventh Street and housed in an imposing building that is still used as a bank, Peoples Bank epitomized for many the financial integrity of the American economic system. The economic futures of many families were deposited in Peoples and other banks, which represented the economic order of the new world. Whatever sense industrial capitalism made to transplanted European peasants was tied up with these banks, especially Peoples, as the most widely recognized and visually dominating financial institution in the area. Fear followed uncertainty as Peoples proved unable to return the millions of dollars it owed its customers. Anxious depositors with strained expressions crowded around its front doors. Although Depositors State Bank eventually paid nearly a third of what its customers had coming, the tentacles of the Great Depression had finally taken a firm grip on the Back of the Yards.[17]

The worsening economic crisis began to affect working Chicagoans during the first year following the stock market crash. In April 1930, six months after the panic on Wall Street, the unemployment rate in Chicago stood at 11 percent, with 167,934 workers jobless. By January 1931 that number multiplied to 448,739 (29 percent of the work force), more than three times the national unemployment in 1930. By October 1931, two years after the crash, the jobless rate stood at 40 percent, and there it remained through the following May: 624,000 working men and women in the city were without a regular income! Among major United States cities and industrial centers, Chicago suffered terribly. Between 1929 and 1933, employment in its industrial sector was sliced in half and payrolls dropped by three-quarters. Nationwide, the worst point in the crisis came in March 1933, and estimates differ only on whether 25.5 percent or 29.2 percent of the labor force was out of work. In more direct terms, it meant that between thirteen and fifteen million workers went begging for jobs and millions more had their work hours short-

"New home of Depositors State Bank" on the southeast corner of Forty-seventh and Ashland, 1924. Courtesy of Chicago Historical Society. ICHi-22800.

ened or their wages cut. The nation was stunned by this calamity. In New York City, a couple moved into a Central Park cave. The number of full-time workers at United States Steel fell from close to a quarter of a million in 1929 to zero on 1 April 1933. In Chicago during the 1920s, 227,000 apartment units had been built, including 37,000 in 1927. By 1933 only 137 more dwelling units of all kinds had been erected in the city. Schoolteachers, police, and fire department employees went unpaid for months. By early 1933 the Board of Education owed the teachers eight and a half months' back pay. Those who had viewed municipal employment as a guarantee against hard times were undoubtedly shaken.[18]

In the Back of the Yards (New City) area, unemployment had climbed to at least 29 percent by early 1931. Adjoining neighborhoods fared no better. To the northwest in Brighton Park, 30 percent of the work force looked for jobs. In McKinley Park to the north, Bridgeport to the northeast, and Gage Park to the west, 28 percent of the workers were unemployed. Only in the nineteenth-century streetcar suburb of Englewood to the southeast and in the more recently settled community of West Englewood to the south were the jobless rates somewhat better: 21 and 24 percent, respectively. As late as 1940, with 5 percent of the Back of the Yards work force still on the public

Table 2

Number of Individuals Unemployed in Southwest Side Chicago Communities in
January 1931 and Families on Relief in October 1934

Community	Number Unemployed in January 1931	Unemployed as Percentage of 1930–31 Work Force[a]	Number of Families on Relief, October 1934	Families on Relief as Percentage of Total Number of Families in 1934
Bridgeport	8,576	28	1,906	17
Brighton Park	8,042	30	872	8
Englewood	10,874	21	2,864	13
Gage Park	5,136	28	367	5
McKinley Park	3,022	28	561	12
New City[b]	14,454	29	2,699	14
West Englewood	8,185	24	1,557	10

Source: Edward L. Burchard, *District Fact Book* (Chicago: Board of Education, 1935),
Areas 58 (Brighton Park), 59 (McKinley Park), 60 (Bridgeport), 61 (New City), 63 (Gage
Park), 67 (West Englewood), and 68 (Englewood).

[a]Total work force count combines gainful workers in 1930 with unemployed as of January
1931.

[b]New City, Area 61, consists of the Back of the Yards neighborhood, the Canaryville
neighborhood, which included the territory from Thirty-ninth to Fifty-fifth Street and from
Stewart Avenue on the east to Halsted Street on the west, and finally the rectangle of
land from Forty-seventh to Fifty-fifth Street between Halsted and Racine. This last
district has no special designation.

relief rolls, 15 percent of the 36,767 men and women over age fourteen could
not find jobs.

Yet elsewhere in metropolitan Chicago the depression was more a jour-
nalistic tale than an everyday reality. In the elite North Shore suburb of Lake
Forest, as Frederick Mercer Van Sickle writes, the American Legion reluctantly canceled an annual celebration day "in view of the generally un-
satisfactory economic situation." Expenditure per student at the local high
school had to be slashed by 25 percent, leaving it at only double the "prevailing average cost per student expended throughout the rest of the state."
Extortion, not starvation, "was a constant worry to monied households." It
was all a matter of perspective.[19]

Work in the packinghouses, once the mainstay for locals, suddenly
became unreliable. Many people were laid off; only a few got hired through
family connections. Most hung on to their jobs, dreading the appearance
of a supervisor wearing a scowl. Receipts in the packinghouses reflected the
slow recovery experienced around Packingtown. A survey of twelve typical
Chicago commission firms shows that they handled 14 percent fewer cattle,
46 percent fewer hogs, and 28 percent fewer sheep in 1938 than in the dark

period of 1932. Numbers like these made the depression remarkable and terrifying at the same time. As Alexander Keyssar expresses it, "What was distinctive about the Great Depression . . . was less the frequency of unemployment than the *extraordinary lengths of time* that most jobless men and women remained out of work" (italics in original). The uncertainty whether stable employment would ever return was for many the greatest burden next to the immediacy of hunger and cold. Prolonged unemployment demanded flexibility. A scaler in the pork-trimming room became a door-to-door salesman for a time before moving on to the insurance business. A longtime railroad employee became an undertaker's assistance. Competition for five-dollar poll watcher jobs on election day was frantic. When treks across Packingtown and up and down Ashland Avenue yielded only refusals and signs saying firms were "not hiring," people turned to homemade remedies. They cut pictures from magazines, glued them onto bits of plywood, then carefully cut them into two-hundred-piece jigsaw puzzles that they packed in old candy boxes and sold as cheap Christmas presents. A handful of desperate residents ransacked garbage cans for food, while others panhandled door to door. At Fifty-first and Ashland, the unemployed sold apples near a small workingmen's hotel.[20]

A perfectly reasonable yet pride-smashing alternative to sustained joblessness was applying for unemployment relief. In the state of Illinois the all-time high came during March 1933, when 332,000 families were on the relief rolls. In Cook County, home to Chicago and its suburbs, the figures had peaked three months earlier when 277,000 families were granted assistance. By March 1933 the situation in Cook County had improved to the point where "only" 202,000 families (20.4 percent of the county's population) were on relief. For a time during 1933 and 1934, the numbers continued to drop until, in February 1934, 82,397 families received unemployment aid. The improving percentages were not an indication of better times, however. The decline was due to the elimination of "undeserving families," the expansion of services in other counties, and an increase in Civil Works Administration jobs. Moreover, the figures began to climb again after February 1934. By October the number had reached 134,849 families. At the same time, 14 percent of the families in the Back of the Yards/Canaryville area were on relief. By way of comparison, Bridgeport had 17 percent of its families on relief, while Gage Park had 5 percent. Four years later the settlement house staff estimated that 7 percent of Back of the Yards families were still on direct relief and, in total, 15 percent received aid of some sort including WPA (Works Progress Administration) jobs.[21]

Historically, the Back of the Yards had housed many families suffering from what social scientists labeled "economic distress." At the turn of the century Charles Bushnell mapped these hardship cases and found that they clustered in three areas. One was along the northern edge of the community near the city dumps and the Chicago Junction tracks. Another cluster was in the northeast corner near Packingtown, and finally, the largest concentration was across Forty-seventh Street south to the Forty-ninth Street tracks between Ashland and Loomis. Early in the century, a family of seven on public outdoor poor relief could expect to receive a standard ration of two pounds of soap, five pounds of beans, six pounds of rice, five pounds of rolled oats, two of coffee, and one of tea, and some flour, cornmeal, sugar, lard, and syrup, with a cost per ration of $3.13. Other provisions included shoes and half a ton of coal. Ice was available during the summer and milk year-round. [22]

By the 1930s, little had changed in the substance of relief assistance. The real problem rested in the attitude of the needy, and it was not unique to the Back of the Yards. Across the nation, Americans considered going on relief the ultimate indignity. Too proud to approach strangers for help and too stubborn to admit their own resource systems had failed, only the grim realities of no food, freezing temperatures, and severe medical problems could force some people into what they saw as a final capitulation of family honor. The shame they felt over approaching outsiders for assistance melded with an Old World mistrust for government agents. Families endured hunger that bordered on starvation rather than "go on relief." Instead, they exhausted any savings they might have salvaged from the banks or from under the mattress. Insurance policies were cashed in. Then they turned to relatives and a few choice friends for help. In a pinch, the needy fell back on the sympathy or patience of landlords and nearby grocers. One resident recalls an incredibly kind neighbor who gave her parents half of every dollar the friend's family earned during a particularly difficult time, while another remembers a landlord who lowered the rent to five dollars a month until someone in the family could find a job. To avoid the pain of eviction, families with relatives in the area doubled up or, if they owned tenements, let relatives move into other flats in their buildings rent free. This practice was particularly common with newlyweds, who either lived with in-laws or moved into an adjacent unit. As accepted as this practice was, it imposed severe hardships on the other renters they displaced. The jobless even preferred to ask help from the local precinct captain or ward committeeman rather than become relief statistics. After all, at least they had something to barter with the politicians. [23]

When desperation finally forced the inevitable, a family representative, usually a woman and occasionally accompanied by a child who could translate, journeyed to the local relief station on Halsted south of Forty-seventh Street. Rarely was the wait to be interviewed less than half a day, and often it carried over to the next morning. Applicants answered a series of what proved, despite the best intentions of relief officers, to be embarrassing questions on family possessions, spending habits, work histories, and the sincerity of the applicant's search for new employment. In the later thirties the questioning became more abrasive when assistance workers increased the pressure to have relatives support the needy. The settlement house staff became particularly concerned when this policy reached the point of insisting that relatives join the applicants at the relief office for the interview. What may have been the most painful part of this entire process, however, came when the caseworker visited the applicant's house. To admit a respectably dressed, college-educated, non-Lithuanian or non-Polish stranger into one's flat elicited a jumble of emotions. Embarrassment, defensiveness, respect, and resentment all came rushing out as still more probing questions followed, sometimes coupled with directives that applicants divest themselves of salable items. One informant recalls his very Irish mother chasing the social worker out of the house after the questioning became too prescriptive.[24]

For a brief period in the early 1930s, Mary McDowell and her colleagues used the settlement house as a relief dispensary. During 1932, for example, they were able to distribute $9,292 in aid. The average monthly assistance per family during that time ranged from a high of $18.03 to a low of 78 cents. Funds came from a variety of sources, including the University of Chicago Faculty Relief Fund, the University of Chicago Press, and the University of Chicago Choir as well as from miscellaneous donors and the state of Illinois. The main relief office in the area, however, was on Halsted and served an area almost as large as the original Town of Lake.

Assistance was frequently distributed in kind. Relief boxes came in different configurations based on family size. For a month, for instance, a family of nine would receive ten pounds of sugar, five pounds of soap, flour, and rice, four pounds of lard, prunes, and bacon, three pounds of rolled oats and macaroni, two pounds of coffee, cornmeal, and dried peaches, one pound of split peas, raisins, American cheese, and wheat cereal, nine cans of tomatoes, and eight cans of milk. The most memorable contents of these boxes were the beans: kidney beans, lima beans, or navy beans, but always beans. The boxes were also known to include spaghetti, maybe a head of cabbage, and a few oranges. Sometimes a recipient was unfamiliar with one or more of the items. One Polish family did not know how to use the cracked wheat they received. The concoction their mother cooked from it "could have been [used as] a deadly weapon." At other times relief recipients traded in coupons either at the grocer on their block or at designated grocery stores elsewhere in the community. Even in these circumstances little touches of human kindness were in evidence when, for example, the merchants slipped in an extra piece of fruit or candy. Nevertheless, there still lingered about the needy what one resident called the "smells of poverty." The beans took so long to cook that everyone on the block knew who was preparing "relief beans." Moreover, the soap supplied carried a distinct astringent aroma. And finally, for families whose electricity was turned off, the odor of kerosene lamps was revealing.[25]

In anticipation of winter, relief recipients received a delivery of between half a ton and a full ton of coal. In rare instances the relief agency was even able to provide a cooking (and implicitly, heating) stove for those without one.

As the first harsh winds of a Chicago winter whistled through the city, relief offices distributed any winter coats or new shoes that were on hand. Long underwear was especially appreciated. The settlement house did the same when it could. Occasionally relief recipients received vouchers they could redeem for heavy coats. One place where they could get the most for their pennies in terms of winter apparel was Maxwell Street, Chicago's open-air bargain-basement, you-name-it-we've-got-it market off Halsted near Roosevelt Road (Twelfth Street). Even families who were not on relief but who had to manage their budgets with the greatest care traveled to Maxwell Street to shop for the best buys in large clothing items. Many South Side families survived depression-era winters with the help of dollars saved on Maxwell Street.[26]

Bank closures, an increasing acquaintance with unemployment and relief, and the ever-possible defaults on mortgage payments clarified the situation far better than did stories from other parts of the country or anything happening in Washington. The dust bowl in Oklahoma and press conferences at the White House did not mean a great deal to anxious people traveling up and down Ashland Avenue or across Packingtown looking for work. The stories of heartache in distant corners of America were bits of information that served only to place the real, personal problems at home in a somewhat larger but no more meaningful context. After all, there were no breadlines, no soup kitchens, no Hoovervilles in the Back of the Yards. Yet as the 1930s unfolded, the economic trials facing people ceased to be a matter of individual failure. Increasingly, it was not "their" fault. As one student of the crisis, Clorinne McCulloch Brandenburg, observed in a somewhat startled manner at the time: "The problem which confronted the relief agencies and the [Chicago] community in 1930 was that of caring for families who were becoming dependent upon relief, *not because of their own maladjustments or lack of desire to work*, but because of the slowing down of industry" (italics added). As the crisis worsened, it began to test the ability of all Back of the Yards residents to survive, to cope with something that was supposedly very large, even national and international in complexity, and seemingly unending. Both for those who were on relief and for the majority who were not, how to endure shortages and cope with uncertainty became the real issue of the Great Depression.[27]

The challenges and trauma the depression era wreaked upon Americans, including those in the Back of the Yards, underscored the need for personal havens, for the security and privacy that are needed in stressful times. Home and family provided both psychic and physical security for many Back of the Yards folk. Traditional life-styles, with their roots in Europe and their refinements in America, made it easier to survive when options were so few. Day-to-day existence in the Back of the Yards during the 1930s, just as in the 1920s, could be managed rather inexpensively if a family was willing to "do without." That included doing without variations in diet, doing without schooling, doing without transportation other than walking, doing without doctors and dentists until it literally hurt, and doing without the ability to plan beyond tomorrow.

Enduring the Great Depression required resourcefulness. For example, by 1940 half of the rents in the Back of the Yards ranged between ten and twenty dollars a month. South of Fifty-first, however, rents tended to be at least twenty-five dollars a month, while north of Forty-seventh Street rents below ten dollars were available. If necessary, then, families could search for even more cramped accommodations during difficult periods. In addition, 98 percent of the flats came unfurnished: what a family owned when layoffs, shorter hours, or reduced wages struck was what they got along on during the hard times. Family-owned items in the kitchen included dishware, cooking pots, a table, and some chairs. Bedrooms contained the bedstead, battered dressers, and a cluster of photographs and other mementos. Parlors typically had nothing more than a few straight chairs, a small throw rug, and maybe, if one was really fortunate, a hand-me-down sofa. The material goods of renters were consistently spartan and almost always paid for. As for homeowners, three out of four residential structures in the community were of frame construction. Except for a coat of exterior paint every decade, buildings required little maintenance beyond what families could do on their own or with the help of a more knowledgeable neighbor. By 1940, only 9 percent of the residences were reported to need major repairs.[28]

Inside the typical apartment, a modest life-style helped families adjust to the trying times. By 1940, less than 1 percent of the dwelling units used gas or similar fuels to light the rooms. Electric bills could be kept under $2 a month by an almost exclusive use of the ceiling light in the kitchen. Parlor wall fixtures or floor lamps were used only when a large group of relatives or friends dropped by, and lights in the bedrooms were turned on only to prepare for bed. A standard table radio drew about seventy-five watts of power, and newfangled electric gadgets like refrigerators and washing machines were even scarcer than automobiles on most blocks. On the eve of World War II, only a third of all the dwelling units in the Back of the Yards had mechanical refrigeration. Most people got along with iceboxes. During warm weather, ice was purchased two or three times a week, including payday (Friday in most cases), when meat was bought for the weekend. A square cardboard sign with color-coded markings on its edges was put in a window of the front flats to tell the iceman (with his horse-drawn wagon) how much ice was needed. Those in the back flats had to listen for his characteristic call. The iceman chipped out a twenty-five- or fifty-pound block and, with a leather apron draped over his shoulder, carried it with giant ice tongs up to the flat, where he deposited it in the top of the icebox. In some newer buildings a small exterior door let him put ice directly into the box without coming into the apartment. Younger children, who traditionally had the job of emptying the drain pan beneath the icebox, suffered from chronic forgetfulness. One informant asked rhetorically: "How many times did we get our rear ends spanked because we forgot the

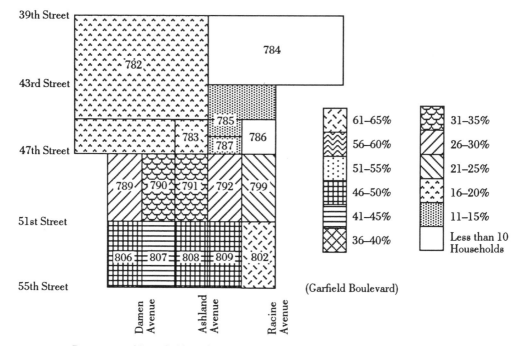

Percentage of households with mechanical refrigeration in each Back of the Yards census tract in 1940. From *Sixteenth Census of the United States: Population and Housing, Chicago*.

damn pan?" A large puddle of very cold water provided many unscheduled opportunities for scrubbing the floor. Thoughtless families drilled holes in the floorboards to let the water run out. (Presumably, they were on the first floor.) During the winter, families saved a few pennies by putting the milk bottle and butter dish between a storm window (if they were lucky enough to have them) and the inside window or on an enclosed but unheated back porch.[29.]

Before World War II, 82 percent of flats in the Back of the Yards did not have central heating. Most had at least two stoves. Poorer families had a cookstove (usually with gas jets for stovetop cooking and a coal- or wood-fired oven for baking) and a potbellied stove in the kitchen. Those who were a little better off also had a parlor stove with a window of isinglass, a thin, transparent mica, through which one could see the glow of the anthracite coal fire. Scrap wood could be obtained from construction sites, railroad yards, or alleys. Coal, which burned longer and was far more reliable, was purchased by the half-ton or ton from the ice company (which was the coal company during the winter). But coal was too expensive for families living on the edge of poverty or worse, so acquiring it took creative measures. Teams of youngsters under age thirteen would take their wagons to the railroad tracks alongside Forty-ninth or Leavitt Street to hunt for broken chunks of coal that had fallen off the trains. Apparently the railroad police understood the economic circumstances of these families, because they rarely bothered the children as long as they stayed on the edges of the railroad property. If the ground alongside the tracks had already been picked over, a more direct approach might be called for. Girls would wave at the train crews, or older ones might perform a little dance while their younger companions stuck out their tongues and made faces. Amused and sympathetic, the crews tossed them chunks of coal. The coal, whether bought or scavenged, was stored in the cellar or, in many cases, in a dilapidated shed at the back of a residential lot. In tenements where two or more families lived, each unit had a bin for its supply of coal. Apparently there was little theft of those precious chunks among families with keys to the same shed.[30]

By choice and custom, the kitchen was the operational—and social—center of the typical Back of the Yards family, as it was in immigrant ghettos across the United States. Moreover, the dampness and cold that came with late autumn and stayed until midspring in Chicago forced them to gather around what was generally the only heating element in the flat: the potbellied stove in the kitchen. The living room was closed off with sliding wooden doors. Bedroom doors were kept shut during the day, and at night were opened to gather the residual heat from the potbellied stove and then the early morning cooking fire. During frigid weather, flatirons were warmed on the potbellied stove, wrapped in towels, and laid at the ends of the beds—which generally held more than one occupant.

Saturdays were a special time, especially during the winter, because then mothers typically baked the next day's pies and the next week's bread. Not only did every corner of the apartment smell wonderful, but the extra heat generated by the cookstove was gratefully savored. The same warmth, but without the olfactory pleasure, was achieved on Mondays, when the wash was done. Most households still used a washboard with two galvanized tubs, one filled with very hot, soapy water and the other with clear water for rinsing. In cold-water flats, mothers awakened well before dawn on Mondays to heat enough water for the entire family's wash. Work clothes that were particularly dirty had to be boiled in a large pot on top of the stove. During the halcyon days of the 1920s, some landlords had installed hot-water tanks in the kitchens, though their burners had to be lit each time hot water was needed. Since bathrooms usually shared a wall with the kitchen, it was easy to run a pipe from the water tank to the bathroom. The wash was dried in a storage attic or cellar during the winter (or in the kitchen, in tenements with no attic or basement) and in the backyard when the weather permitted.[31]

Besides gathering around the kitchen table for warmth or to read the newspaper or do homework, families also pulled up their chairs to listen to the radio. At the onset of the depression, about 40 percent of Back of the Yards families had radios. (Many of these first radios were undoubtedly crystal sets with individual headphones.) Ownership of this new entertainment device varied widely across the community. In one census tract northeast of Forty-seventh and Ashland only 55 out of 370 families had radios (15 percent). Six blocks directly south in an underpopulated tract north of Sherman Park, 68 percent owned radios in the same year. The depression failed to dampen the ever-widening popularity of the radio. By 1940, in every census tract but the northeast corner of the community, at least 91 percent of the occupied dwelling units had radios. The depression changed leisure activities even in the two standard-sized census tracts in that northeast corner. In the tract where only 15 percent of the households had owned radios in 1930, the proportion climbed to 83 percent a decade later, and its neighbor experienced a similar increase, from 17 percent to 75 percent.[32]

Radios were typically used only during specific hours on workday evenings and on Sunday afternoons. News broadcasts were of limited interest. Residents preferred to learn about world events through English-language newspapers such as the Chicago *Tribune* and *Evening-American*. Radios were for entertainment. In families where English was not spoken at home, the radio fare focused on programs that emphasized folk music or religious themes. For Poles the choices were more attractive because Polish-language programs were on the airwaves daily. Father Justyn, a Polish Catholic radio priest who delivered Sunday sermons filled with fire and brimstone, attracted a loyal audience in the Back of the Yards. For Slovaks and Lithuanians, listening hours were limited by day and time. In households that switched back and forth between their native language and English, the evening programs tended to be in English. Laughter brought the entire family together. Particularly popular were comedies such as "Amos and Andy," "Jack Benny," and "Eddie Cantor." The American-born offspring also appreciated dramatic serials such as "The Shadow," "Inner Sanctum," and "Lights Out."

Foreign-born parents seem not to have related as readily to the themes and situations of dramatic programming. Humor, however, was broader in subject matter and within reach of even those who knew little English. Some recent émigrés were known to avoid the radio altogether, but in most households it provided a vital link between foreign-born parents and their Americanized children. Programs in English helped the foreign-born with their vocabulary and pronunciation. More important, the ideas and issues presented in radio broadcasts, even comedies, exposed immigrant parents to the world that was shaping their American-born children. The importance of baseball or the political humor of Will Rogers seeped into homes that were at times replicas of Eastern Europe within the confines of a four-room flat. Historian Liz Cohen has observed that the immigrant home was both an arena for and a refuge from technological penetration. In the case of the radio, technology furthered acculturation by breaching the walls of the tenement through the voluntary participation of its fans. Radio united the generations by its power to entertain, providing a common focus for conversations within the family. It brought a bit of the United States into the Back of the Yards.[33]

Maintaining an apartment's appearance, especially cleanliness, trans-planted Old World habits into an American urban setting. Most kitchens still had wooden floors during the 1930s. Linoleum was found in higher-priced rental units or in newer residences. The practice of scrubbing the kitchen floor on hands and knees until the white pine glistened was a carryover from the peasant culture of Europe. Mops were for the lazy, the careless, or the gentry. Scrub brushes, Fels Naptha soap, and elbow grease were for those who took pride in their homes. In households that followed more rigorous European traditions, this pride traveled right out the door into the common hallway and interior stairwell. Although a few individuals insisted on doing this task more than once a week (besides the interim cleanups of spills from the icebox), Saturday afternoons were generally dedicated to scrubbing kitch-en floors. When the task was completed, newspapers were carefully spread over the wood and not removed until after mass the next morning. Families who did not purchase a daily paper could buy old newspapers in bundles sold just for this purpose. In many Polish and non-Polish homes these floor coverings became known as "Polish carpets," though other families con-sidered such references crass and out of place.[34]

The simple style of tenement life in the Back of the Yards helped families survive the depression decade. They were used to doing without extras, without the latest fads, even without meat, eyeglasses, or intact shoes. This simplicity was demonstrated clearly in the diet of the average resident. The menu lent itself to prolonged repetition. A meal could easily be stretched to accommodate an unexpected visitor or pared to meet a dip in the family's income. In most families, breakfast offered two options: bread and coffee or hot cereal. Both cost pennies for an entire family. The same food seven days a week for years might seem monotonous, but if one expected nothing more, who was to know? A special treat on Saturdays or holidays was pastries from the corner bakery. Oatmeal and farina were breakfast mainstays for the children and, if necessary, could be served for supper.

Lunch for those who were working ordinarily consisted of bologna sand-wiches—five days a week—with an apple or an orange. Ham, salami, and other lunch meats were too expensive for most families. In more difficult times, lunch became a refinement of breakfast: a slab of bread covered with leaf lard. The lard came in a white block, and yellow dye capsules were mixed with it to create a facsimile of butter. To provide variety and to accom-modate tastes, salt, sugar, or an onion might be added. Spread on Lithuanian rye bread, these combinations produced contentment among most working-class folk, and to a few, "Boy, that was heaven!" Coffee with canned milk washed down every meal for children and adults alike.[35]

Because supper was usually soup, it warmed stomachs if not hearts. Homemade soup was cooked fresh several times a week, then warmed over. Beef-based soups were made from cheap parts such as oxtails or neck bones. Every family had its own favorites. There were lima bean soup and potato soup, pigs-tail soup and tripe soup, beet soup and cabbage soup, sauerkraut soup and even prune soup. Many times this was the whole of dinner. On other days, after several bowls had tamed appetites, a small serving of a main course might arrive. Among the tastier delicacies were pigs' ears with boiled potatoes, pigs' snouts with sauerkraut, or brains with eggs. On meatless Fridays, potato pancakes or soups made with vegetables from a small back-yard garden were substituted. Home-grown carrots, string beans, rhubarb, radishes, celery, and cucumbers were either used as side dishes or put in the soup. For families on relief, the soup was usually the only variation from the bread and coffee of breakfast. As noted earlier, relief boxes included all kinds of beans, which were made into different soups. Add a few more cups of water and the soup lasted another day. Many families, whether on relief or just getting by, went to the Loose-Wiles Bakery on Ashland Avenue and stood in long lines to buy a large bag of broken cookies for a quarter. Friends of local bakery owners were sometimes allowed to buy stale cakes and bread, which they wrapped in damp towels and heated in the oven until soft enough to eat.

Sunday was special for those who had a breadwinner in the family. Relatives, employed or not, rotated Sunday dinner after church. By far the most common Sunday meal consisted of chicken soup with homemade noo-dles, followed by boiled chicken (the base of the soup) or fried chicken. Mashed potatoes—dumplings in Bohemian and German families—and a plain vegetable made up the rest of the main course, and homemade pie topped off the meal. A chicken dinner on Sunday represented more than simply another meal. It showed that a family had been blessed with a reason-able income. (Those with more money preferred delicacies like roast pork to the standard chicken.)

Sunday dinner also was the time for renewing family ties. Married chil-dren and other relatives gathered after church and spent the day singing, playing cards, and discussing the past week's highlights and low points. Often the gathering recessed at 3:00, in time for the family to attend Sunday vespers and benediction, after which the children were hustled off with fifteen cents apiece to one of the local movie theaters, while the adults went back to the house for more beer, cards, and conversation. Family members who faced hard times still attended these gatherings, where rumors of job openings were discussed. As evening deepened, leftovers were quietly passed along to struggling family members in an unspoken gesture of sup-port.[36]

The life described above did not differ much from that of other Chi-cagoans or other urban Americans of the same social class during the Great Depression. The furnishings and design of individual apartments may have varied, and the foods served would certainly have differed by location and ethnicity, but the attitudes developed to combat the economic trials of the 1930s probably did not.[37] A study of one hundred Chicago families conducted by Ruth Shonle Cavan and Katherine Howland Ranck in 1938 illustrates this point. The two University of Chicago scholars set out to learn how families had adjusted to an economic crisis beyond their control. The researchers discovered that "well-organized families met the depression with less catastrophic consequences" than others. Such families relied on subordination of personal ambitions to family goals, loyalty to family objectives and ideals, and satisfaction of personal interests within the family group—attributes common to many Back of the Yards families. Cavan and Ranck also found that pride and the fear of compromising the family's honor delayed requests for relief. They pointed out that "families that have felt little disastrous effect of the depression have been those in which the economic condition of the family has changed only slightly." When they described families that had made major adjustments to the depression, the "new" mandates of life resembled ordinary conditions in the Back of the Yards: only the kitchen was heated, there was no electricity, dental work was postponed, baking and laundry were done at home, clothing was repaired over and over again, and less rent was paid. The burden of contributing to family expenses was now distributed over several family members; children living at home turned over all their income to their parents. These were not adjustments made by residents of "the jungle." This was everyday life.[38]

The simple life-style of the years immediately preceding the depression prepared many Back of the Yards families for the turmoil of the 1930s. Extra pennies had been turned into down payments for homes or had been carefully squirreled away in banks. Many times, families had chosen not to spend surplus income. Automobiles, new furniture, higher-rent apartments, and more than two sets of clothes seldom became the target of their few extra dollars. Their expectations had never become elevated beyond their ability to adjust to the new economic depths. As more than one individual recalled, people then just "didn't know any better." Diets had not changed much since the first members of their family arrived in the area. Maybe they ate meat more regularly, but when that was gone there was still bean soup. Clothing styles had changed some, primarily among American-born youngsters, but sewing, tailoring, shoemaking, and barbering skills could still be found in most families or among relatives and friends. Shoes were lined with cardboard, and when the holes became too large for that, folded newspapers filled the gap—literally.

The hardships of the 1930s should never be underestimated. Some of my informants would at first cast a rosy tint over the times. Only sustained questioning revealed their deep-seated hurts and regrets. Others quickly focused on their first memories of "a depression" as always being hungry. But it is clear that the key to enduring the 1930s was that their expectations had never exceeded the immediate possibilities. Graduating from a two-year commercial program in high school, buying a second-hand car, and owning their own homes may have been on their wish lists, but the thirties called for sacrifices, and these dreams, which were just that—things many families had never possessed and might not have until the next generation—were passed over in favor of immediate demands. They were aware of the sacrifices being made; there was simply no choice. Ewa Morawska, in describing Eastern Europeans in Pennsylvania, touched on an important point when she noted that "the Great Depression provided a spectacular confirmation of the immigrants' view of life as *morskoje plavanije*—swimming at sea in an alternation of highs and lows—and strongly brought to the fore their latent fatalism." The reaction of Back of the Yards folk was like that of their counterparts in Pennsylvania: "a mixture of resignation and a determination to hold on and survive despite all." As one of Morawska's informants observed to her: "We were not surprised by hard times. . . . It was normal, it happened to us before." They had to accept shortages and disappointments, but they didn't have to like them. Yet before the Great Depression could be officially declared over, World War II arrived. It extended the period of delayed gratification. For the moment a job, a couple of bowls of soup, and the companionship of family, friends, and relatives were the keys to survival. The rest would have to wait.[39]

4

ON THE BLOCK
Friends and Neighbors

During the interwar years (1918–41), the personal activity space of Back of the Yards residents characteristically varied by gender and generation. A person's activity space, according to John Jakle and his coauthors, comprises "movements taken to and from various activity locations as a part of everyday life." It includes movements in or near one's home as well as trips one makes to work, pray, play, and socialize. During the acculturation process in the Back of the Yards, the first generation's activity space—centered on the home—expanded both in physical range and in social complexity for the next generation. It started with the residential landscape of the block, where streets were both pathways and nodes, and included the many characters who played roles in the daily theater of the street. In time a resident's "home base" came to include social agencies such as parks, dance halls, and movie theaters. Instead of "home" as the hub, the second and third generations enjoyed a collective home base with widened territorial loyalties and broadened social experiences. A gradual reduction in divisions caused by European roots promoted and in turn was nurtured by this integration of activity spaces. Thus, while the Americanization of the Back of the Yards involved traditional elements of language acquisition, educational advancement, and occupational mobility, it also entailed a deepening "sense of place" as residents moved down the block, around the corner, and across the community.[1]

For a married woman living in the Back of the Yards before World War II, activity space outside the tenement flat typically started with the rectangle of open ground behind her home, where she tended a vegetable garden and hung laundry, weather permitting. Back of the Yards tenements were situated

Vegetable and fruit vendor in front of Saint Michael's rectory on cobblestone-covered Damen Avenue, about 1941 *(above)*. Courtesy of R. Gallik.

Vegetable and fruit vendor still at work at Forty-seventh and Wood in 1959 *(below)*. Courtesy of Chicago Historical Society. Photograph by Clarence Hines. ICHi-22802.

toward the front of the lot. Space in the rear was reserved for general storage, with little greenery except for the garden. Even into the 1930s backyards often housed a menagerie, including ducks, chickens, pigeons, dogs, cats, and on occasion a goose or two. Unlike backyards in contemporary suburban developments, rear lots in the Back of the Yards were never intended to accommodate family recreation or neighborly conversations. Yet in spite of the wooden fences that commonly separated properties, clothesline exchanges between women took place in a creative variety of language combinations. At any moment, however, their conversation could be interrupted by the distinctive, heavily accented cry, "Potatoes, onions, carrots, apples, oranges," as the local fruit and vegetable peddler with his horse-drawn wagon called the neighborhood women to their daily rendezvous of bargaining and sisterly camaraderie. When the ingredients for a day's soup or stew had been stowed in their ever-present aprons, women paused to visit with others from their block. The sick and elderly, if they had no offspring to send out to the street, relied on kindly neighbors to pick up their needs from the peddler.[2]

Streets in the Back of the Yards were an integral part of everyone's daily activity space. In suburban tracts today, streets all too often are little more than routes to somewhere else: one's destination is all that matters. In contrast, side streets in the Back of the Yards were at once vehicular corridors, pedestrian pathways, and communal front yards. Front steps in most tenements came right to the sidewalk, leaving a small square of dirt on each side for bushes or perhaps a few intrepid flowers. For most residents, stepping through their doorways placed them directly on the main public thoroughfares of the community—the sidewalks—or, if they happened to have a side entrance, in a dark, narrow gangway that quickly funneled them onto the sidewalk. (Before the Second World War, those who could afford automobiles preferred to park them in structures off the alley.) Curb lines and narrow parkways did not divide private from public space. Thus the space at the front of a lot swept outward from the stoop toward the street in an uninterrupted visual and physical flow. Streets operated as walkways and paved playgrounds, as much a part of a person's residence as the front stairs. And just as their mothers congregated around the vegetable wagon, children waited for *their* favorite vendor, the iceman. When he arrived to make his twice- or thrice-weekly deliveries, children rushed to meet him without a thought for safety, waiting expectantly for him to chip the next twenty-five- or fifty-pound block. They snatched up every sizable sliver of ice and turned them into instant popsicles. The cold, clear taste was so wonderful that at times the iceman's devoted young followers became more a nuisance than a cute sideshow as they nagged him until he turned the corner and moved on to the next block.[3]

The small capacity of iceboxes forced households to schedule at least one trip a day to the local market. "Local" in the Back of the Yards ordinarily meant no more than three or four buildings away from one's apartment for a

Neighborhood store at corner of Forty-ninth and Ashland Avenue. Courtesy of Chicago Historical Society. Photograph by Casey Prunchunas. ICHi-22798.

grocery store and not more than a block for a butcher shop or bakery. In 1934, of the 148 north-south residential (nonstreetcar) blocks in the Back of the Yards, only one in five (22 percent) did not include at least one grocery store. Those with no grocery store were either underdeveloped residential blocks (primarily in the southwestern corner of the community west of Damen) or blocks where churches, schools, and city parks occupied significant expanses of real estate. In the Polish, Lithuanian, and Russian neighborhood northwest of Forty-seventh and Ashland, only two blocks featured just a single grocery store, while one street had nine stores, another had eight, and two more had seven. Overall, in 1934, with a total of 296 groceries, the Back of the Yards averaged one store for every 187 residents and two stores per block.[4]

Grocery stores provided a range of items from fresh meat and bottled milk to flour and sugar in bulk to canned goods and school supplies. They also offered a variety of other services. Earlier in the century, grocery stores had catered to the predominant nationality on a given block. A Lithuanian would never open a shop where only Poles and Russians lived. On streets where three or four nationalities mixed, as many as three grocers might minister to the largest group, with one each serving every other nationality. During the period of first settlement, each national group "looked inward, depending upon its own members for the tastes and aromas of the homeland," according to Alan Kraut. Grocery stores, butcher shops, and bakeries dispensed ethnic foods, with stock chosen to satisfy particular national tastes. To produce the freshest—and cheapest— perishables, merchants left home in the predawn hours for their daily trip to the South Water Street produce market (which during the 1920s was relocated from the Loop to an area near Maxwell Street). Grocers and butchers also stopped at the wholesale meat markets that several packing companies operated. Bakers made sure to keep the right grains and spices in stock so that the different rye breads and national pastries were always in ample supply. Residents came to expect a certain quality in the merchant's stock, some flexibility in payment, and occasionally certain incidental services, including writing letters back home or translating English-language documents. Shopkeepers became mediators between their customers and the larger urban society that surrounded them.[5]

As the years passed and residential clustering by nationality declined, grocers' ancestral heritage became less of a concern than their friendliness and their willingness to extend credit. This last consideration reflected the second—and during the Great Depression, by far the most important—service offered by a family's favorite grocery: it was the nearest credit agency. Some families paid cash for their groceries, but most households bought "on the book." Purchases were recorded in a small black book, noting the general content of the day's purchases and the total cost. By the 1930s these records were kept using an indelible deep blue pencil, which smeared if anyone attempted to erase an entry. Customers kept the books. If a person did not bring the book on a particular day or if a child was sent at the last minute to pick up an item, the grocer would record this exchange on a brown paper bag that was kept near the cash register until the next time the family's book was brought in. Buying "on the book" demanded trust from grocers who, like their customers, survived financially from week to week, if not day to day. It obviously demanded responsibility from each customer.

At the end of each week (defined in the local lexicon as payday—Friday or Saturday), a family was expected to clear the book. During the depression this frequently proved impossible. In many instances grocers extended credit for another week, hopeful that the debt could be settled over time. In many cases merchants carried families for weeks or even months. The patience of these businesspeople depended on a range of factors: How long had they known customers and their extended family? How reliable had members of this family been in the past? How solvent was the merchant? What would happen to the storekeeper's own family if the local economy worsened? For households that cleared their books at the end of each week during the hardest of times, some merchants threw in a bar of soap or a can of peaches (a Christmastime luxury for most people). Inevitably, some customers skipped out on their debts. They may have moved away or simply have changed their routine to avoid passing the store. Embarrassed debtors were known to duck into an alley or up a gangway if they sighted the shortchanged creditor. Legal recourse was useless in these circumstances; merchants accepted bad debts as part of their operating expense. Some were forced out of business by these liberal credit practices.[6]

Grocery stores, meat markets, bakeries, and candy shops served the

Neighborhood store at corner of Fifty-fourth and Wood Street. Courtesy of Chicago Historical Society. Photograph by Casey Prunchunas. ICHi-22789.

neighborhood in another important way. Many of these family-run businesses had been around for decades and were as much part of the local landscape as any dwelling. Indeed, ordinarily they were in the front flat of a tenement—with a somewhat larger than normal, and most enticing, picture window. The look of Back of the Yards streets remained remarkably unchanged over the years. Trees grew slowly, buildings aged a bit, and specific neighbors came and went. But overall the visual composition of a given block remained the same.

Thus small businesses, because they consisted of both structural and human components, contributed significantly to an experience known as a "sense of place." This concept refers to the emotional attachments and meanings people assign to specific locations. Beliefs, attitudes, and subsequent behaviors can be shaped by these spatial loyalties. A sense of place obviously could not have existed for every resident of the Back of the Yards: that would have been impossible among 57,000 people. But the enduring intensity of residents' feelings (as reflected in the oral histories collected for this book and by other scholars) for the people and the cultural landscape of the different neighborhoods within the Back of the Yards community suggests that a sense of place did exist for most individuals. This high-density environment (in terms of dwellings and population) with mixed land uses promoted a close-knit sociospatial association.

Businesses on a given block, whether grocery stores, bakeries, or taverns, promoted interaction among neighbors. In the process of achieving
their economic objectives, these enterprises served as centers of communal
exchange. The entire process of supply, demand, delivery, and credit
focused daily commercial activities upon an area within a block or two of
home, fortifying what at first constituted familiarity with the local neighborhood and later developed into possessiveness toward it. Nearly everyone
walked everywhere. Streetcars were for those who worked miles away, and
automobiles were beyond the means of the average resident. The city of
Chicago was largely an abstraction: the neighborhood constituted a person's
daily reality. To borrow Donna Gabaccia's term, Back of the Yards folk
"capitalized" on their neighborhood. Residents came to know each other as
they made trips back and forth to school, church, work, streetcar stops, and
nearby stores. They developed a knowing confidence about the streets they
traversed daily and an informed trust in the people they encountered within a
particular neighborhood. Familiarity with their environment generated a far
greater concern for what took place on "their" blocks than experienced by
today's suburbanites, who drive miles to grocery/drug/clothing/sports/fast-
food superstores. Mr. Koslowski the grocer had it all over K Mart.[7]

Other vendors also contributed to this integration of residential life with
economic activities. Some of them worked out of the community's alleyways.
The most memorable was the rag collector: as with the iceman, a characteristic call, uttered in a thick accent, announced his presence: "R-rags a-lyin!
R-rags a-lyin!" As the ragman's horse-drawn wagon slowly made its way down
the alley, young men (who dominated this trade) headed for their backyards or
their coal- and woodsheds to fetch carefully accumulated recyclables including rags, scraps of copper and bronze, bits of wire, pie tins, and newspapers.
At one point, rags that were reprocessed into paper brought a penny a pound.
During the 1920s a colleague of the ragman, the greaseman or boneman, also
made the alleyway circuit trading bars of soap for containers of grease (used
to produce soap) and hunks of beef bones (used by Darling and Company to
make fertilizer).[8]

Alleys were considered a benefit in the overall scheme of urban planning
because they routed undesirable functions away from the social center of the
residence, the front yard. By the end of the 1920s, most alleys in the Back of
the Yards were paved, though a few remained pitted, dusty trails during the
summer and treacherous, muddy morasses the rest of the year. In any case,
before World War II refuse of every variety was simply tossed onto open piles
in the alley. Garbage cans as we know them today appeared only in high-rent
neighborhoods, while homemade wooden containers usually identified an
owner-occupied dwelling. On most blocks, however, trash simply accumu-

Ragman in Back of the Yards alley in 1942. Courtesy of R. Gallik.

lated in ever-growing mounds waiting for the city to make its not-so-regular pickups every week or two. Well into the 1930s, Chicago continued to employ horse-drawn wagons with slanted sides to pick up the refuse. Like milk-wagon horses, which were trained to meander driverless down a street and wait at the corner for their masters, horses that pulled the garbage wagons moved slowly down the alleys while men with large shovels (the kind used in coal yards) scooped up the mixed collection of garbage, ashes, and rubbish. When it rained the piles turned into slimy messes, and in the hot, humid days of July and August they became feeding troughs for a multitude of flies. As an example of the tonnage involved, between 1900 and 1920 each citizen in Manhattan, Brooklyn, and the Bronx produced annually 160 pounds of gar-bage, 1,231 pounds of ashes, and 97 pounds of rubbish. A 1912 Chicago survey, however, claimed that "Americans" produced far more waste than their "foreign" counterparts. In terms of the quality of life in the Back of the Yards, that would have been small consolation.

One consequence of this refuse arrangement was that the Back of the Yards was under assault from a legion of rats. After dark these creatures took command of the alleys. Traps had to be set regularly to forestall a full-scale invasion into the tenements. Not until late in the depression did the city finally begin a rodent eradication program in the Back of the Yards. The cumulative combination of smells and scurrying as well as flying pests drove families away from the alleys and toward the front of their tenements. Unlike most of today's suburban households, which use their front yards for orna-mental landscaping and their backyards for family recreation, Back of the

Yards families avoided the rear of their lots whenever possible.[9]

Although alleys were filled with refuse of every kind as well as piles of manure left by horses, they nevertheless became sanctuaries for boys, beginning in early adolescence. These were the youngsters most likely to go "junkin'" in the alleys and to grow familiar with the customs of the back alley. Junking involved poking through garbage piles for redeemable items, particularly metal and soft drink bottles. During certain promotions, labels from Libby food cans brought handsome cash returns. Some boys scouted the alleys on the way to school, carefully hiding their riches until the trip home. Others systematically toured alleyways after school with their coaster wagons in tow. The woodsheds and coal sheds at the back of residential lots provided storerooms for the treasures collected while junking and also served as clubhouses for the boys. Here the youngster learned to swear and to swagger. Here he learned to smoke the popular hand-rolled cigarettes. Machine-made cigarettes cost too much; besides, there was something "manly" about a fourteen-year-old who could roll a tight cigarette.

It was also in and alongside these sheds that the inevitable crap games took place, usually in the early evening on school- and workdays or on Sunday afternoons after church and dinner. Each block had a specific site for the local games of chance. Everyone knew the location, including the police. Lookouts were posted and gates leading to gangways kept open. Occasionally younger siblings who felt left out would lock the gates and then yell "Police!" When Chicago's finest really did cruise by in their distinctive orange roadsters, the warning was sounded and the gang scattered over and through the fences. Sometimes the shooters intentionally left behind the pot on the assumption, borne out by experience, that the police were less eager to harass "criminals" who were willing to give public servants a financial break.[10]

Understandably, girls and younger children of both sexes were discouraged from playing in the alleys and backyards. The curbs and streets were their playground. Whenever the weather permitted, mothers shooed their children outside. The close confines of four-room flats were completely inadequate to hold a swarm of active children while a mother struggled to cook with heavy iron kettles, bake in the big black coal-burning oven, or make homemade noodles, a task that required vast amounts of dust-free drying space on the kitchen table and every bed in the house. During inclement weather, youngsters were confined to bedrooms or to more sedentary pastimes around the kitchen table. But whenever possible, they were sent outdoors.

Older children, especially girls, cared for the younger ones when they played outside. Store-bought toys were few and precious before World War II. Instead, Back of the Yards children exhibited tremendous creativity in making up their own games with whatever odds and ends were available. Popsicle sticks became toy soldiers. Bottle tops were "cash" for playing store. Old inner tubes were made into slingshots. Flattened tin cans made a horsey-sounding "clippety-clop." When streets iced over during the winter, these same cans lashed to sneakers became ice skates. For the resourceful, a wooden crate begged from a nearby grocery store and mounted on broken roller skates became an all-American soapbox car. (A candle in an empty can added a fine finishing touch.) Marked-up sidewalks and streets revealed the popularity of hopscotch. Jump-rope contests vied with sixteen-inch softball games for space along the street. On summer evenings a particular favorite on roadways not made of cobblestones was crack-the-whip. Long lines of youngsters on roller skates trailed behind a larger child who wove up and down the street. Roller skates in various stages of disrepair were generally available either from older siblings or through kindly relatives. Before World War II, bicycles were few but coaster wagons—also used to collect coal from the railroad tracks, groceries from the store, and junk from the alleys—were common.[11]

Front stoops served as the home base from which the younger children moved about the block. In the Back of the Yards, as was true in New York City, Baltimore, Washington, D.C., and elsewhere in urban America at the time, stoops were "communal institutions," "the meeting place and social center" of the block, as John Clark describes it. They provided a unique threshold between private and public space. In the evenings and on Sunday afternoons, adults gathered on their stoops to pass the time exchanging local gossip and rumors of jobs. Politics was seldom the topic of conversation. Whereas Italian women along Elizabeth Street in New York City apparently mingled with their neighbors less than the menfolk and children did, in the Back of the Yards married women moved about their street with great ease, tossing brief acknowledgments toward some neighbors while searching out their friends for longer chats. Back of the Yards mothers often knew the neighbors better than their husbands did because of the daily food shopping. Working-age men tended to stick to their own stoop or one nearby, while their wives casually strolled, sometimes with infants in rickety baby buggies, up one side of the street and down the other. More popular families provided benches for their friends. On occasion a concertina added background music.

Another spate of vendors visited the neighborhood on summer evenings and Sunday afternoons. The balloon man came only on Sundays, and the waffle man, with his trumpet and his magical-smelling waffle maker mounted on a horse-drawn wagon, was popular any night. His products came topped with either honey or plain sugar—customer's choice. Organ grinders made the circuit, some with monkeys on chains, others with parrots on their shoulders. For two cents the animals would pick out slips of paper to tell fortunes. The children—and the host of dogs and cats that lived along the street—raced around the block without fear of automobiles and with a general assurance that most residents looked out for their welfare. Adult-to-adult

Remnant of Whiskey Row between Forty-second and Forty-third Streets on the west side of Ashland Avenue in 1959 *(above)*. Courtesy of Chicago Historical Society. Photograph by Clarence Hines. ICHi-22794.

Children at play on corner of Forty-third and Wood Street in 1959 *(below)*. Courtesy of Chicago Historical Society. Photograph by Clarence Hines. ICHi-22803.

contact within a block was greatly promoted by the boundless energy of the children. Everyone was an aunt or uncle, according to one former resident who lived near Sherman Park. Another person from the Holy Cross neighborhood described each block as having a community of its own. Indeed, some neighbors closed off their streets once a year and held block parties. For young teenagers who were shy and introverted, these celebrations provided a welcome opportunity to learn to dance so as not to embarrass themselves at a lodge or church function. On other blocks, assembling in knots of friends on a stoop was the extent of communal life.[12]

For adults, especially men, an important site for meeting neighbors and friends was the local tavern. Before Prohibition, the Back of the Yards had been famous throughout Chicago for a historic string of saloons along Ashland Avenue north of Forty-fifth Street. "Whiskey Row" catered to the noon-hour "can rush" and to the closing-hour crowd coming out of the packinghouses. Homemade soup, pigs' tails, and sauerkraut or corned beef and cabbage were free for the nickel plunked down to buy a glass of beer. Saloons gladly cashed paychecks, portions of which assuredly never passed out the front door. One establishment along Whiskey Row was known to cash at least $40,000 in checks each month. A smaller version of Whiskey Row sprouted at "Whiskey Point," where Forty-fifth, Loomis, and Gross Avenue intersected across from a main gate of Packingtown. (About 1911, several intoxicated customers wandered out of a Whiskey Point establishment and left their imprint on the adjoining neighborhood by starting a fire that leveled twenty-five tenements.) Prohibition drove these saloons either out of business or underground; most of those along Ashland Avenue closed for good. The buildings were converted into grocery or dry goods stores and even, in one notable case, into a day nursery opened by the packing companies. But other saloons continued to operate along the streets, many in conjunction with lodges or dance halls. Back doors off the alley or side doors off a gangway provided a way out in case of a police raid.[13]

More than driving imbibers into these working-class speakeasies, Prohibition drove them to do their daily drinking inside the tenements. The settlement house staff insisted at the time that many (but not most) locals brewed their own moonshine or homemade beer. The poor-quality ingredients that went into these concoctions could make drinking them life threatening. Moreover, during this "great experiment," hiding makeshift stills and breweries as well as stowing liquor in basement tunnels and beneath floorboards represented the first time many residents had consciously and systematically violated the law since coming to the United States. Most important of all, however, people increasingly drank at home. Those who reported increased alcohol consumption may have been observing more home drinking rather than an actual growth in the number of drinkers or in the amount consumed. The consequences of excessive drinking now took place in the kitchens and bedrooms of the community. Drunkenness precipitated physical violence within families and between neighbors as well as regular calls to the New City police station. Although the packinghouses reported decreases in time lost after paydays (which they attributed entirely to Prohibition), some workers still lost their jobs because of drunkenness. On occasion horses were known, out of habit, to take their wagons—and intoxicated drivers—home to their embarrassed families. Reports that a growing number of women and young people of both sexes were drinking regularly—and even excessively—may also have been related to the site of their indulgence.[14]

Social observers who in the 1920s confidently reported that Prohibition had rooted out the drinking urge within the working class and had removed the notorious corner saloon from America's urban landscape must have been stunned by the events that followed repeal of the Eighteenth Amendment. Their contention that drinking habits had been civilized by the saloon's demise proved only partly correct. Saloons along the main thoroughfares never reappeared in anywhere near the same numbers as before Prohibition, yet the total number of post-Prohibition businesses dedicated to alcoholic beverages must have troubled these same experts. The noon-hour and after-work watering holes simply moved into the residential recesses of the community, becoming a locational compromise between the Ashland Avenue saloons and home consumption. Furthermore, they became "taverns," a term that avoided the disreputable legacy of "saloon" and seemed more appropriate for a business that occupied the first floor of a tenement on a street where the neighborhood children played every day.

The replacement of work-related drinking by neighborhood drinking helped integrate this new enterprise into the life of the block. Taverns became as much part of the local landscape as the nearby grocery store and candy shop. Sometimes they hosted the annual block party, and they could always be expected to contribute to the refreshments. On Sunday afternoons youngsters were sent to the corner tavern for a dime pail of beer. A few secretly slurped the creamy, high-standing foam before returning home. Others anticipated receiving a *shnit* ("short beer") or a "Cincinnati" (a *shnit* mixed with root beer) or simply a nickel for their own root beer, straight up. On weekdays during the worst of the depression, taverns became haunts for the jobless, who sought to escape their melancholy through alcohol.[15]

The "saloon" had also disappeared in terms of its traditional constituency. Although a few of the pre-Prohibition saloons welcomed married women among their regulars, most operated as male retreats, away from work and home. After Prohibition, unmarried men who made regular stops at a favorite bar continued to outnumber single women by a wide margin. Increasingly, however, wives began to frequent the local tavern along with—and occasionally without—their husbands. Later, during wartime, long hours of work, a shortage of datable men, and the bar owners' search for customers encouraged yet another shift in everyday drinking habits as unmarried women joined their married sisters at local taverns. By the postwar period, neighborhood taverns served men and women alike without questions or disapproving stares.

The traditional privateness and exclusiveness of taverns based on sex diminished after Prohibition even as drinking by nationality steadily vanished as a rule of the street. Rather than a pair of Polish saloons, one Slovak bar, and maybe a Lithuanian bar on a given block, one now found multiethnic social centers catering to neighbors regardless of ancestry. Prices, quantity and types of foods, the attitude of the proprietor, and supplementary entertainment became far more important in choosing a regular tavern than socializing with people of the same nationality. This adjustment mirrored the changing character of life on the side streets of the Back of the Yards as residence by ethnicity broke down during and after World War I. The role of nationality in shaping an individual's daily behavior was moderating under pressure from a number of forces, including the dismissal by many American-born offspring of the ethnic straitjackets they viewed as a needless impediment to the social lives of their elders.[16]

Ethnicity previously had played a major role in the drinking habits of Back of the Yards residents, as in those of most ethnic Chicagoans, and when those habits were threatened by the Eighteenth Amendment, ethnic associations came to the defense of their favorite alcoholic beverages. Among the most outspoken critics of Prohibition were Chicago's ethnic newspapers. The Bohemian paper *Denni Hlasatel* decried Billy Sunday's "rabid activities in the field of prohibition." Immediately after ratification of the Eighteenth Amendment, it called for its repeal as "a violation of personal liberty and the States' independence." The German-language daily *Abendpost* (which during the 1930s distributed more than five hundred copies a day in the Back of the Yards) voiced a similar concern: "It means not only the confiscation of property, the destruction of the livelihood and employment of hundreds and thousands, and the restriction of the personal freedom of many millions— which in itself constitutes the gravest violation of the rights of citizens which are guaranteed by the Constitution—but it also means an actual rape of the Constitution itself; a rape . . . which converts it from a solid wall of defense against tyranny and suppression into a convenient tool of tyranny and a means for oppressing the citizens."[17]

The concern these newspapers expressed over the "rape" of the United States Constitution illustrated a growing familiarity with the American political system. More important, it subtly evinced an evolving admission that the future of hyphenated Americans was in the New World and not in the Old Country. Still, this admission came about painfully, at a very slow pace, and it never prevented the ethnic newspapers from lapsing into Old World cultural perspectives. For example, when woman suffrage became a national issue during World War I (Illinois had granted women municipal and state suffrage in 1913), foreign-language papers quickly revealed their cultural and intellectual roots by adamantly opposing the vote for straightforward patriarchal reasons. *Denni Hlasatel* explained that "woman's nature is not fitted for crude and rough public life, especially life in the political arena. This is entirely a man's privilege, a privilege which women should be happy to have escaped so far. . . . it would be for [the] better if they [suffragists] agreed to go on preparing good dishes rather than poor laws." Later this same publication reminded its readers that "the Scriptures say that the woman should follow the man. . . . Man's duty is to provide for wife and children. . . . The average woman does not want anything else but to have a good husband who takes proper care of his family." The Polish-language publication *Polonia* complained that franchise supporters based in charitable organizations were corrupting "our naive women," who "go for advice in case of trouble with their husbands. The role of the self-appointed protectors was played by the suffragettes employed as officers and workers of the institutions. They incited the Polish women against their own husbands by teaching them about the privileges of women and American freedom. . . . In other words, they acted as solicitors for the courts, or as shyster lawyers."[18]

Yet swift ratification of the Nineteenth Amendment appears to have prompted at least a few of these publishers and editors to reconsider their positions. *Abendpost*, which had opposed woman suffrage, adopted a remarkably conciliatory tone during the debate in Congress over the amendment. The paper mused, "We of the old school have always held that political activity would decrease the attraction of, and harm, the woman whom we loved and adored. . . . We fear especially for the peace and order of the home and for the children if women should receive the right to vote, and exercise that right." But in the very next sentence the editors conceded, "Perhaps it will be necessary for us to revise our education, or at least reconsider our former verdict. . . . The War not only required the greatest conceivable sacrifices of woman, but also drew her from the quiet of her home, from her kitchen, and from her children, into commercial and industrial life. . . . Duties confer rights. Responsibility engenders a sense of responsibility. In many women, who gave the matter no previous thought, equal responsibility has awakened and strengthened a desire for equal rights, for the right of self-determination; and all women have a valid claim to these prerogatives." Similarly, *Narod Polski* congratulated Polish women on their enfranchisement, urging them to "plunge into the hard work of enlightening themselves on politics" and inviting women "to work in a larger field!"[19]

Concessions to the political ways of the New World were by no means unqualified. *Dziennik Zjednoczenia* warned that there was "true and false Americanization. The Poles should absorb everything that is good, noble, righteous—but reject all that is wicked and pernicious. Our youth in the large cities do just the contrary, following bad American habits and customs." One "bad American habit" to which women seemed particularly susceptible was turning away from traditional housework for activities outside the family, including unnecessary employment. The most serious shortcoming of American-born youngsters during the interwar period, however, was neglect of the language of their ancestors. This neglect, warned the same Polish paper, would lead to a "denationalization of the Poles in America." Both Slovak and Bohemian publications voiced the same concerns. They complained that, rather than its being the fault of the children, the loss was caused by indifferent parents who acted almost ashamed of their heritage.[20]

Nationality had been pivotal in the original settlement of the Back of the Yards. Each sizable ethnic group had at least one neighborhood where it predominated early in the century, and conflicts arose among the different groups. Newcomers from Eastern Europe were especially envious of the occupational success of the Irish and resented what the greenhorns maintained was the clannishness of the Irish in general. "Turkey birds" was a phrase commonly applied to the Irish. It is not entirely clear whether the term referred only to the reddish hair of some Irish or also mocked their habit of speaking English rapid-fire with a brogue. These sentiments cut across nationalities and may have reflected class strife more than interethnic rivalry. In the case of Poles, these feelings may also have been a reaction to the domination of the church hierarchy by Irish bishops and archbishops.

On occasion, tensions could erupt into violence. During World War I, Poles living around Saint Augustine's joined in the anti-German bigotry then common nationwide as they accused their German neighbors of installing a radio antenna in the church's belfry. Verbal clashes were common during the war. At least one German family had its windows broken by vandals, and the strain was enough that one Polish man bought a gun to protect his family. Again these conflicts may have masked the envy Polish laborers felt toward the, broadly speaking, more successful Germans. Hard feelings based on Old World animosities also erupted between Poles and Lithuanians in the neighborhood they shared near Sacred Heart Church and Holy Cross Church. Shouting matches could escalate into rock throwing. The must sustained potential for violence, though, came from a Canaryville-based Irish gang known as the Ragen's Colts, who were known to tour the Polish area around Sherman Park looking for fights.[21]

The ethnic press did little to ease these strains. In the eyes of the self-proclaimed protectors of ethnic purity, allegiance to one's own traditions must never be compromised by identifying with other customs. In 1903 Bohemian children who sported green on Saint Patrick's Day were castigated as pretending to be from Ireland. After all, "Our Bohemian nation with its culture, maturity, and history surpasses by far the Irish nation." Two decades later *Dziennik Zjednoczenia* condemned the city council when it declared Saint Patrick's Day a holiday and angrily reminded Poles that the Irish (who allegedly constituted 75 percent of employees at city hall) were the same people who supported immigration restriction legislation and "sneer[ed] at the Poles." In 1921 *Narod Polski* worried that too many of "our girls [are] strolling around the city, lingering at hotels of a questionable character, and their [sic] frequenting all kinds of Venetian gardens in company of the worst type, young Jews, Greeks and other underworld scum."

In the same year, the paper commented on "a band of Lithuanians saturated with a mad hatred against Poland; and who, most probably for German money, are spreading defamation against Poland by means of English pamphlets." Meeting this last challenge, *Naujienos*, a Lithuanian publication, charged that "Poles are Polanizing Lithuania," but then what could a person expect "from the Poles, because they have no honor and no character"? The Old World resentment and mistrust of Slovaks for Czechs simmered in Chicago in spite of efforts by the Bohemian press to highlight the accomplishments of Slovaks over the centuries. Tensions worsened in anticipation of the 1930 federal and 1934 city censuses and during the Century of Progress Exposition held in Chicago during 1933 and 1934. When the first Slovak Catholic Day was celebrated on 28 August 1931 at Saint Michael's parish hall on Forty-eighth Street, *Osadne Hlasy* pointedly reminded its readers that the campaign to expand this event into a National Slovak Day was not an effort to promote a *Czecho*-Slovak celebration.[22]

Although ethnic origins may have been central in the social relationships of the immigrant generation, they still had their place in the lives of their offspring as well. In the Back of the Yards, every nationality had its own folk music groups, benevolent societies, and national religious sodalities as well as local building and loan associations. For many residents ethnic pride lay just beneath the surface, ready to spring forth at a moment's notice. Thus, when the very first contingent of Polish-American troops who had served overseas during the First World War returned to Chicago early in 1920, the Citizens' Committee from the Town of Lake managed to recruit enough automobiles to pick up the returning heroes at Union Station. Small, multipurpose auditoriums such as Pulaski Hall at Forty-eighth and Throop or Slowacki Hall at Forty-eighth and Paulina (the latter also housed a library of works in Polish) were always filled by the ethnic organizations, from Group 2448 of the Polish National Alliance to Division 18 of the Polish Youth Society, which presented a three-act musical comedy on peasant life. Field houses at the three local parks provided additional space for music and choir recitals as well as holiday folk festivals. Saint Michael's parish, the largest Slovak parish in the United States, supported ten branches of the First Catholic Slovak Union.[23]

For Bohemians the most important ethnic center, other than Saints Cyril and Methodius Church, was a building known simply as School Hall. Here the Czech language was taught after school and on weekends. In 1934 the tuition was only one dollar a year, yet some parents still had trouble paying the fee. Nonetheless, many managed to send their children to School Hall: the education of the next generation in the heritage of Bohemia was too important for money to interfere with the inculcation of the homeland's culture and traditions. Adjacent to School Hall was a building where the local *sokol* (athletic club) met several times a week. When the club celebrated its fiftieth anniversary in 1938, a crowd of five thousand attended the celebration, including the attorney general of the state of Illinois, Otto Kerner. Businesses with clear ethnic allegiances prospered during the interwar years. Building and loan associations were scattered about the community, usually serving persons of a specific nationality. The Lituva Building and Loan Association at Forty-sixth and Paulina near Holy Cross Church took care of Lithuanians, while the Sherman Park Building and Loan Association at Fifty-second and Racine worked with Poles in that neighborhood.[24]

Change was under way, however. In the years that followed the restrictive immigration legislation of 1924, the intensity of nationalistic feelings, without a continuous reintroduction of Old World culture, showed signs of waning at the grass-roots level. Residents did not lose their ethnic allegiances overnight, to be sure, but over the years, as native-born offspring grew up and established their own families, they went about their daily lives without being preoccupied with ethnicity. Among organized ethnic agencies such as the press and even the church, this tempering of nationalistic loyalties took much longer. These organizations had a vested interest in upholding ethnic loyalties, in constantly reminding members of the differences that separated them from their neighbors. For second- and third-generation residents, however, by the mid-1930s pride in one's nationality was no longer the criterion by which a person judged a next-door neighbor, baseball teammate, school chum, or dance date. Differences based on where in Europe one's parents or grandparents had originated did not matter nearly as much by the middle of the Great Depression. The mixing of nationalities on a residential block and within the tenements of the community played a significant role in loosening ethnic ties and reducing interethnic hostilities.[25]

The Back of the Yards, like immigrant ghettos across the United States, had been settled by families who preferred to huddle with compatriots from the Old Country. But unlike urban districts where a single group dominated, the Back of the Yards housed so many different nationalities that "ethnically pure" streets vanished within a relatively short time. Even streets characterized as "Polish" or "Lithuanian" in the early years of the twentieth century always included other nationalities. This is the point James Barrett makes so well in his study of the packinghouse workers. He questions the level of ethnic segregation that earlier studies emphasized. Barrett argues that even before 1920 there was "a striking degree of ethnic diversity" in a community where even "Poles, the most highly segregated foreign-born group in the city, were less segregated." During the early years of this century, families who were not members of the predominant nationality on a given block undoubtedly experienced some distancing or, in the words of one resident, a "certain coolness" from those who refused to associate with a stranger from another country. Ethnic agencies fostered these divisions. The churches, though primarily Roman Catholic, often isolated residents from each other. One

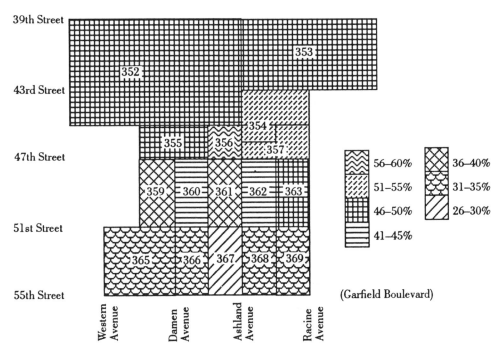

Percentage of foreign-born in each Back of the Yards census tract in 1920. From Burgess and Newcomb, *Census Data of the City of Chicago, 1920*.

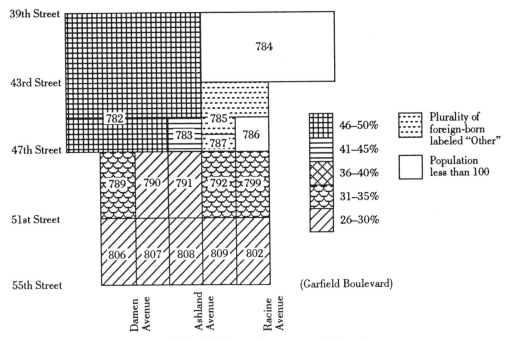

Percentage of foreign-born in each Back of the Yards census tract in 1930. From Burgess and Newcomb, *Census Data of the City of Chicago, 1930*.

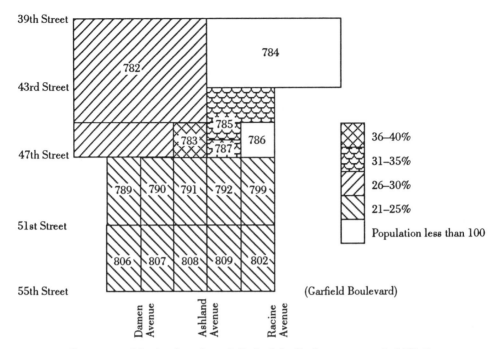

Percentage of foreign-born in each Back of the Yards census tract in 1940. From *Sixteenth Census of the United States: Population and Housing, Chicago.*

young German-American girl experienced the intensity of these divisions in a memorable episode. Her family lived almost next door to Saint Joseph's Church (Polish). Nonetheless, she was driven from the confessional when she innocently explained to the priest that she could not make her confession in Polish. She was immediately ordered out of the church and told, in a tone she never forgot, to go "to her own church." Robert Slayton relates how priests from different Catholic churches avoided greeting each other when walking down the sidewalk: one of them would cross the street to avoid his "rival."[26]

Barrett correctly argues that, even before the First World War, though diversity "was not typical, *some* degree of mixture was quite common" (italics in original). Moreover, Barrett's concern here is not so much the presence of different nationalities on a certain block as whether ethnic groups had contact with one another. Caroline Golab has described how Poles in Philadelphia shared neighborhoods with other Eastern Europeans but did not necessarily share their lives. This appears not to have been true in the Back of the Yards. Informants unequivocally maintain that, except for a mistrustful attitude toward the Irish, there was tolerance and acceptance toward neighbors of other European ancestries between the wars. Settlement house documents written during the 1930s certainly reflect less preoccupation with interethnic strife. By the time of the depression, verbal exchanges including name calling ("Lugan," "Polack," "Krauthead") were largely barbs thrown on the spur of the moment. A hard slide into home plate during a ball game could generate an epithet that referred to the runner's nationality, but no one took it seriously as an *ethnic* insult. Neighbors who did not get along might use nationality to frame their dislikes, but again the underlying clash was personal, not ethnic. Informants openly acknowledge that friendliness was definitely slower to develop among those of the immigrant generation than among their children. By the 1930s, however, the former were a large but aging minority. For their American-born offspring, national heritage was demonstrably less important. Yet as Donna Gabaccia has insisted, this cultural assimilation by the second generation was not complete, nor did it mean that the younger cohort had "lost respect" for their elders. Whether a person spoke Polish or Lithuanian at home mattered very little on the street, in the alley, at school, or on an assembly line. In these activity spaces only English was spoken, and everyone was the same. What mattered increasingly, aside from loyalty to one's family, were ties to one's neighborhood. Place ties bound families in a *geographical*, not an ethnic, unit. What block they lived on or what park they played at, rather than what country their parents—or by now even their grandparents—came from drew people together. Friendship, including dating and spouse selection, was increasingly based on considerations other than lands that most younger people had only studied at school or heard stories about at home. More and more, parents surrendered to their children's choice in dates—and subsequently their choice of spouses—even in instances involving partners of different nationalities. Adjectives describing nationality steadily vanished from daily conversation.[27]

The growing recognition of where one's homeland lay became part of Americanization not only in the Back of the Yards but also in other communities across Chicago. This was illustrated in the appearance of a new Lithuanian newspaper, *Juanimas*, in 1936. The paper's title means "We the Second Generation." Its purpose was to acknowledge "the beginning of a new era for the second generation of Lithuanian-Americans—an era of patriotic enlightenment of closer contact with their nationality, fatherland, their language, and the history and traditions of the nation." Whereas the Lithuanian language was indispensable in the lives of the immigrant generation, it "is not so for us . . . simply because we were born and grew up in America and because our minds have been so thoroughly permeated with the English language that it has become part of our nature." The publishers expected to be accused of lacking Lithuanian patriotism, but they insisted it was not their "aim to destroy or hinder the work and influence of the present Lithuanian agencies. . . . It is a Lithuanian paper, dedicated to every Lithuanian in this country, and to the proposition that every one of Lithuanian parentage should be proud of that distinction." In its pages, *Juanimas* routinely used the term "American-Lithuanian." It promoted contests that involved persons of Lithuanian extraction but refused to require participation through the Lithuanian language. It also promoted naturalization classes, urging "mothers and fathers who have not become a citizen of this country" to take advantage of these opportunities.[28]

If tolerance—even friendship—for those of different European ancestries characterized acculturation in the Back of the Yards after World War I, the same was not generally true for people of other races and ethnicities. Only a mile and a half separated black Chicago's western boundary, Wentworth Avenue, from the eastern edge of the Back of the Yards. For the thousands of unskilled and semiskilled Back of the Yards residents who toiled at Armour, Swift, and their competitors, their first sustained contact with African Americans came during World War I when packing companies recruited thousands of black laborers. Previously the two races had encountered each other only when Back of the Yards folk took the streetcar to lakefront parks and beaches or to the Loop. Immigrants from Europe quickly adopted American racial habits. Prejudice built upon racial differences was an early lesson of acculturation. The immigrants' propensity to judge people based upon ancestry fueled racial attitudes that flourished in the workplace and seeped into the residential community.

That the first African Americans had entered Packingtown as strike-breakers in 1904 guaranteed that racial tensions would fester over time. A layoff of fifteen thousand workers in spring 1919, even though a large proportion were African Americans, aggravated the situation. Efforts by labor unions to overcome racial divisions on the killing floors were uneven and of questionable effectiveness.[29] Chicago's bloodiest race riot then compounded the situation. It began on a sultry July afternoon in 1919 when a black youngster drowned at Chicago's Twenty-ninth Street beach after being stoned by whites. The police refused to arrest his attackers. African Americans who witnessed the tragedy clashed with officers and assaulted white beachgoers. Word of racial violence spread quickly across the South Side. That same evening, white gangs beat, stabbed, and shot thirty-eight African Americans. The next afternoon, mobs carrying baseball bats and bricks waited for black packinghouse employees to board streetcars at Forty-seventh and Halsted after work. A few laborers never made it to the streetcars. Others who did were no luckier, as the crowds yanked trolley poles from the electric lines, idling the cars. The targets of these attacks leaped off the cars and ran for their lives. Some escaped, others did not. A black worker named John Mills was beaten to death. In the Back of the Yards proper, African-American streetcar passengers were attacked along Ashland Avenue. Several bodies may have been dumped into Bubbly Creek.

Then, suddenly, six days after the violence began, a terrifying early-morning fire roared through the Polish and Lithuanian neighborhood near Sacred Heart and Holy Cross Churches. Forty-nine buildings were destroyed. Property losses totaled a quarter of a million dollars, and 948 residents were left homeless. Rumors flashed through the neighborhood nearly as fast as the fire. The colored did it! No, the Poles did it! No, anarchists did it! When suspected arsonists appeared the next night, they were beaten off. Pastors from local churches joined in a startling display of cooperation; they denounced both the violence and the unfounded rumors concerning the arsonists' identity. The clergymen asked for calm and urged their congregations to avoid falsely blaming either their neighbors or African Americans. Instead they accused the Ragen's Colts—a Canaryville gang known to have incited the streetcar assaults along Forty-seventh Street—of starting the devastating fire. It was ironic that it took such a painful episode to inspire this token accommodation between the Polish and Lithuanian religious leaders.[30]

One indication that racial and ethnic attitudes among Back of the Yards residents were going to change slowly, if at all, was their infrequent (except for some packinghouse workers) and largely unfriendly encounters with African Americans. A more sustained test came during the 1920s and 1930s with the migration of several thousand Mexicans into the community. Chicago's Mexican population jumped from 1,200 in 1920 to over 19,000 ten years later. The first Mexicans in the Back of the Yards area arrived during World War I. Others followed as strikebreakers during the 1921–22 walkout. For the most part they came from the western and central states of Mexico, including Jalisco, Zacatecas, and Michoacán. They made this migration in stages, stopping along the way to work in agriculture or building railroads. At first Mexican laborers in the Back of the Yards were forced to live in railroad cars and in large boardinghouses operated by labor contractors. When they tried to find more suitable housing, the only flats available to them were in the most dilapidated section of the community: the congested pocket wedged between the businesses along Forty-seventh and Ashland and Packingtown—the very same enclave where the poorest European greenhorns had settled upon their arrival.[31]

By the middle of the 1930s this neighborhood, which included the University of Chicago Settlement House, had become an intriguing mix of Poles and Slovaks and the newly arrived immigrants from south of the border. During the 1920s, the local Mexican population was predominantly male. The few businesses catering to them were primarily male-oriented social centers: small restaurants, barbershops, and a disproportionate number of pool halls. Later, wives and children arrived. By the early 1930s the family-based character of this Mexican enclave allowed the settlement house staff to assist their neighbors more effectively. Although programs were scheduled for all ages and both sexes, social workers had their greatest success among the women and younger children. A Mexican Mothers' Club met for years. In the beginning its activities centered on courses in basket making, knitting, and other crafts. Later its members were urged to use English, and field trips to radio stations in the Loop broadened their spatial and cultural horizons. The settlement staff was less successful in attracting working-age males, although for a brief period during the mid-1930s El Frente Popular Mexicano, an anticlerical labor organization, worked out of the settlement house. Its original goal, Louise Año Nuevo Kerr reports, was to "achieve the social and economic betterment of the working class . . . [and] to protect the Mexican who returns to his own country." The club's meetings regularly attracted between twenty-five and seventy-five members. By late 1937, however, El Frente had worn out its welcome.[32]

During the first decade of settlement, Mexican communities of modest size developed on the Near West Side (almost 7,000), in South Chicago (4,300), and in the Back of the Yards (about 3,000). With expansion came the usual assortment of cultural and social activities. Spanish-language newspapers were established, and by 1930–31 there were at least two hours a week of Spanish-language programming on the radio. Like their Eastern European counterparts, Mexican residents in the Back of the Yards learned—to their later regret—to trust Peoples Bank with their savings. They were lured to Peoples by the appointment of a countryman, Juan de Geraldo, as an officer of the bank. During the 1930s a few families cautiously tested the residential waters west of Ashland Avenue, streets dominated by Lithuanians, Poles, and Slovaks. This move brought them into contact with Davis Square Park. By 1934 the Pro-Fiestas Patrias Committee felt comfortable enough to host an afternoon of sporting events at the park. Visiting soccer teams from Mexico were invited, and the Mexican vice consul presided over the celebration. Mexican youths began to use the playing fields at Davis Square for soccer matches. When a confrontation developed between these youths and some local toughs, the park director suggested a boxing match to sort things out. The troublemakers backed off. Although most Mexican immigrants to the Back of the Yards were Roman Catholics, the archdiocese of Chicago failed to provide a national church for them until after World War II. To attend Sunday services in Spanish, the faithful had to travel by streetcar to Saint Francis of Assisi Church on Roosevelt Road (Twelfth Street). Not until the late 1930s were religious services offered locally in a series of storefront chapels. One site, previously occupied by a butcher shop, had been left in a wretched state. Nonetheless, volunteers repaired the store, transforming the giant icebox into an altar. Finally a permanent location for Immaculate Heart of Mary Vicariate was found on Ashland Avenue near Forty-fifth Street. The existing building, which had originally housed four stores, was renovated in a Spanish motif and dedicated in 1945. Between the wars, several Pentecostal and Baptist missions ministering to the Spanish-speaking population opened and subsequently closed, including a Baptist church on Gross Avenue near the settlement house.[33]

In May 1942 Sue H. Perry from George Williams College conducted an in-depth study of Mexicans in the Back of the Yards. Her goal was to compare fifty families living in the United States with those from the same social class in Mexico and to evaluate the social and economic problems of the less privileged Mexicans in Chicago. She deliberately looked for subjects from

For the Spanish-speaking residents of the Back of the Yards, **Immaculate Heart of Mary mission on Ashland Avenue** (seen here in 1966) **was finally dedicated in 1945.** Courtesy of Chicago Historical Society. Photograph by Casey Prunchunas. ICHi-22799.

the lower middle class: "laborers, barbers, bakers, small shop keepers, etc." Breadwinners from several families in her sample worked in the packing-houses and railroad yards, usually in menial jobs. Of fifty families, only five lived west of Ashland Avenue. The rest lived in the northeast corner of the community between Forty-fifth and Forty-seventh Streets, from Ashland to Loomis. Forty-nine of the fifty families reported their health as "good in general." Seven said they had problems, though these were not detailed. In terms of education, Perry's sample resembled their ethnic predecessors at the turn of the century. Three times as many fathers had never attended school as had gone beyond the sixth grade (6:2). A slightly better ratio (10:7) held true for women. About half of both the men and the women could read "only a little Spanish," while a third could read it well. More men than women could speak "a little English," although nineteen of the women as opposed to sixteen of the men could read some English. Of the married women, 29 percent worked, a rate slightly higher than for their European neighbors. And like their neighbors, Mexican families cited visiting friends as their favorite form of "recreation," and 80 percent reported owning a radio. Nearly the same percentage of families as owned radios also went to the movies or attended club meetings at the settlement house when they were not visiting friends.[34]

When these residents identified the ethnicity of their friends, only one family reported that most of their friends were not Mexican, and overall only seven said some of their friends were not Mexican. The researcher herself identified the "greatest problem in life here" as "the attitude of prejudice toward them on the part of us Americans and also of other nationality groups like the Poles." Twenty years earlier Robert Redfield, the noted sociologist from the University of Chicago, had reported similar problems after conducting interviews in the Back of the Yards. Conflict between these newcomers and longtime residents, however, appears to have been unorganized and personal. An occasional mugging may have been racially motivated, although the evidence is not entirely clear on this point. Still, attitudes dripping with distrust separated Poles from Mexicans. As early as 1928, *Dziennik Chicagoski* announced a special meeting at Pulaski Hall because "persons of other races are establishing their homes in the township of the Town of Lake," which had "depreciated real estate." Property owners were "requested to weigh the problem carefully." For the most part, by 1941 open expressions of hostility had diminished markedly. Subtler forms of prejudice continued to surface, such as rent gouging. Despite being neighbors along streets such as Marshfield and Laflin, adults seldom mingled. Children, on the other hand, were known to ignore the prejudices of their elders. In general, however, Mexicans and Eastern Europeans kept their distance from one another. Estimates vary as to the number of Mexicans within the community by 1940; the figure most frequently cited is two thousand. (Some voluntarily returned to their homeland because of the depression.) Although historian Thomas Philpott is probably correct in suggesting that "gradually, grudgingly, the people [of the Back of the Yards] were coming to regard Mexicans as another white group," tolerance may have been more an accident of avoidance than a positive step.[35]

5

AROUND THE CORNER
Home Base Expands

During the interwar period, a better-developed, more inclusive street life brought those living on a particular block together as never before. Shopping for food became the basis of a social network among married women who did not work outside the home. Regular pedestrian routes encouraged residents to establish strong ties to the block where they lived, and these ties to *place* were reinforced by frequent social interaction with neighbors on the stoop. For young children, the street was a playground. Even ethnic differences, at least among Euro-Americans, diminished with generational succession.

When activities moved around the corner onto nearby streets, however, sociospatial patterns took on gradations of complexity. Around the corner—but still within the local neighborhood—residents confronted bureaucratic institutions that bridged the gap between the intimacy of "home base" and the impersonality of a metropolis like Chicago. The Roman Catholic church, the municipal parks, and the local schools (whether parochial or public) provided intermediate sociospatial—or mesospatial—experiences. Although the Catholic church was closely linked to the nationalities of Back of the Yards folk, nonetheless its ultimate administration was conducted by individuals whom most residents would never encounter except in the newspaper. Although agents of this institution (the pastors and their assistants) were well known to residents, the sanction for their authority still came from outside the local community. Popular clergymen who angered a pastor or the archbishop might suddenly be reassigned without warning, with no consultation with parishioners. On occasion sharp differences arose between managers of these local religious centers and their congregations. Pastors, in particular, developed reputations that at times went beyond their religious institutions. And during the interwar years, the church and its affiliated schools were forced to adjust to the changing habits—and expectations—of their constituents.

The city park system and, to a lesser extent, the public school system also constituted part of this bridge between the microspatial activities of home and block and the macrospatial associations related to work, to some forms of shopping and recreation, and eventually to a sense of community. As in the case of the churches, the civil agents of authority (park directors or school principals and their teaching staff) were for the most part well known, yet they also remained aloof from the residents by virtue of their titles, their responsibilities, and often enough their socioethnic backgrounds. Spatially and behaviorally, then, these institutions were *for* the people but not really *of* the people in the same sense as interactions with family and neighbors. Nonetheless, in combination these mesospatial establishments were keys to broadening activity spaces, keys to the evolution of "home base" into the more complex relationship I will refer to in the next chapter as the "home range."

Sue Perry, in her study of the routine life of Mexicans in the Back of the Yards (discussed in chap. 4), remarked that forty-seven of the fifty families in her survey were Roman Catholic. She found it puzzling that only three families said they would go to the church for help in time of need. More than anything, this attitude reflects the absence of a Spanish-language church in the Back of the Yards, but it may have also shown that the faithful understood that institution's self-defined role much better than outsiders did. Although they inevitably became much more, parishes were founded solely as centers of worship: for a given geographical area if they were territorial (Saint Rose of Lima and Saint Basil locally) or for a specific ethnic group if they were national (the remaining Back of the Yards Catholic churches, representing several rites). Their ministry focused first on the spiritual needs of the faithful and second on a refinement of that first duty: the education of the young. All other activities including festivals and sodalities were aimed solely at discharging these first two responsibilities. Several parishes sponsored small fund-raising carnivals and occasionally parishwide dances. Saint Augustine's had a multilane bowling alley in the basement of its church hall that was especially popular among young adults. Both Saint Joseph's and Saint Michael's opened their church halls to youngsters for evenings of roller skating. Before World War II, however, Catholic churches in the Back of the Yards could not envision themselves in roles any more temporal than those they were already filling. In Richard Linkh's words, "American Catholic leaders tended to look askance at the type of social work which placed paramount importance on the material and social well-being of the immigrant," even when agencies outside the church, including settlement houses, were involved. As for the church itself, material advancement by the faithful was incidental to the institution's true mission on this earth.[1]

If any effort was made during the 1930s to assist the needy, a parish's Saint Vincent de Paul Society (the centuries-old international organization dedicated to helping the poor) could be expected to carry out the assignment. Of all the local chapters, none was more active than the one at Saint Augustine's. Every week during the 1930s, members carried boxes of food and clothing to the needy of the parish. Some of my informants criticized the churches for not doing more, whereas others absolved them, insisting that the pastors had little to give. Even Saint Basil's, known as the "rich people's church" among those living north of Fifty-first Street, suffered a 41 percent decline in its annual income between 1929 and 1934. The pastor, Father John Bennett, made several donations to the central office of Catholic Charities, including $4,500 in 1931. At Sacred Heart, probably the poorest of the three Polish parishes, the pastor sent out emissaries to report on the needs of those who had requested help from the rectory. These investigations were designed as much to ensure that applicants actually were in need as to determine what items might be of the greatest use to them.[2]

As I noted in chapter 2, many of the local pastors remained at their posts for decades. Several had founded their parishes. The personalities of these men became inseparable from the operation of "their" churches. Gruff demeanor, abrupt manners, and autocratic ways of handling church affairs can be linked to the pastors' European backgrounds and to the traditional training they received at the seminary. These men held themselves to be guardians of the ethnic consciousness of their congregations and viewed acculturation as a danger to the faith of their flocks. They were, in the words of Victor Greene, "religionists" who "insisted that their faith . . . and their nationality were synonymous and exclusive." For these men national patriotism could not exist without the faith. As a result, church practices generally blurred the line between ethnicity and religion. Sermons and Gospel readings on Sunday were offered in a foreign language throughout the 1920s and well into the following decade. Vespers, the Sunday afternoon service that families often attended as a unit, was partly in Latin and partly in the mother tongue. This convergence of ethnic and religious expression was particularly significant for the immigrant generation (a cohort that often included the pastor) and was simply "the way things were done" for later generations.

Within a relatively short span of time, individual identity in terms of nationality and in terms of religious affiliation fused with a third element: where one lived. Families generally preferred to live within a few blocks of "their" church. As sociospatial attachments to particular areas within the community grew stronger after decades of residence in the Back of the Yards, life on the block often became inexorably linked with a nearby church. A combination of nationality, religion, and territoriality became integral to the emotional content of everyday life in the Back of the Yards. These were the issues that consistently mattered, though the preeminence of any one of them changed over time and varied with the individual. Class, politics, education, and even labor unions were generally incidental factors that meant less day to day.[3]

Nevertheless, the original fusion of nationality and religion was buffeted by the very same challenges that were attacking secular aspects of ethnic identification as American-born generations grew up during the twenties and thirties. The religiousness of Back of the Yards residents, immigrant and native-born alike, never waned during the depression, at least as measured by church attendance. If anything, Sunday masses may have been better attended during the early 1930s. But some church leaders were not content with that. They joined forces with the ethnic presses to ensure that the association between the faithful's obligation to their God and to their ancestral home remained unchanged.

From the time of the First World War, this struggle over ethnic loyalties focused in particular on the younger generation. *Narod Polski* warned that if "American chauvinists were allowed today [1919] to throw the Polish language out of parochial schools, then tomorrow they will be allowed to throw out from these schools the Catholic religion." As time passed, the struggle increasingly focused on the parochial school as the agency of socialization responsible for cultivating ethnic loyalty among the young. In 1921 the Bohemian paper *Denni Hlastel* alerted "Bohemian Catholic parents to the fact that it is their duty to send their children to Catholic schools. A preference for Bohemian parochial schools should be given by them." *Osadne Hlasy*, the Slovak paper, was no less clear: "We should bear in mind, that an apple seldom falls far from a tree, and, if our offspring is to inherit some of our traits, why not select good ones? Let us, therefore, once more be reminded of our Christian Catholic obligation and send our children to Parochial Schools." The challenge became how to merge ethnic loyalty with learning. As Catholic leaders saw it, "public schools teach, but do not rear children. They educate the mind, but not the heart of the child. . . . religious principles are necessary to educate the hearts of children. It is here that our Catholic schools come to the rescue. To send children to Catholic schools demands sacrifices and self-denials. Nevertheless the moral bliss of your children is worth the price." Public schools, warned *Dziennik Zjednoczenia*, do "not take into consideration either religion or the mother tongue of our children, subjects which are so near to our hearts." In addition, a parochial school education meant training in self-control and personal discipline as much as tutoring in a classroom subject. A subtle yet effective mechanism used to instill moral control was adherence to an ethnic culture.[4]

Within Chicago, the number of parish-based elementary schools had grown from 62 in 1890 to 235 by 1930. Attendance at these schools soared from 31,000 to 145,000 during the same period. In the Back of the Yards, parochial schools (with the exception of Saint Rose's and Saint Basil's as territorial churches) historically held classes both in the Old World tongue and in English. Polish schools may have been the most determined on this

For Lithuanians, Holy Cross parish was established at Forty-fifth and Hermitage in 1904. Courtesy of Chicago Historical Society. Photograph by Clarence W. Hines. ICHi-22788.

point. There were daily classes in Polish grammar, speech, and history. Religious instruction was in Polish. Although mathematics and social studies were taught in English, the nuns used Polish in their classroom conversations, and when a parish priest visited the classroom, all exchanges had to be in Polish. Failure to exhibit complete loyalty to one's ancestral traditions was met with severe disapproval. Nuns and priests sternly admonished their charges never to enter a Catholic church other than "their own" except as part of the Holy Thursday liturgy when, as a body, they visited a total of nine churches. (These visits reinforced the children's place ties because they visited only the nine churches in the Back of the Yards and not those in neighboring communities.) Furthermore, the role of tradition in combination with Scripture as the twin foundations of the Catholic faith was inculcated at an early age. Reverence for the past, then, had both a spiritual and an ethnic expression.[5]

These religious institutions and pedagogical systems notwithstanding, daily habits were evolving between the wars. As Josef Barton has pointed out, measuring these changes is an "elusive problem" for the historian. Yet it is clear that language played a key role in promoting change. During the 1920s, English became entrenched as the language of the streets and alleys. It was the language of the parks and movie theaters. It was the language of Ashland Avenue and the Loop. It was the language of a young person's world in the Back of the Yards. It gave members of the second generation an advantage over both their parents sometimes, and over their mothers often. As children grew up, they used language to express their independence from their families. And when English broke through the wall of ethnicity surrounding the church, Americanization was accelerated.

Influenced perhaps by wartime anti-German prejudice, Saint Augustine's followed the pattern of other German Catholic churches in the city when in 1918 it became the first national church in the Back of the Yards to preach Sunday sermons in English. It took the other parishes more than a decade to follow suit. Even then English was normally used at only one mass on Sunday—usually the last. (The first generation preferred the early masses in any case.) Nonetheless this change took place, however reluctantly, in every parish before the coming of World War II. The composition of the congregation was changing, and at some point the churches had to acknowledge this. The situation would not be quickly resolved, yet the adult membership within the parishes was shifting in favor of those whose only home had been the United States. This transition was sharply reflected in the birthplaces of the young adults who were preparing to start their own families. At Saint Michael's (the Slovak Catholic church), in seventy-eight of the eighty-eight marriages performed in 1914 both partners had been born overseas while in only two were both bride and groom native-born. Ten years later, in eighteen of forty-one marriages both partners were foreign born while in sixteen both had been born in the New World. By 1934 in only five of the marriages did both partners come from Europe, while thirty-nine of the couples were both American-born. The churches had to respond to this Americanization among the faithful, and inevitably the change diminished loyalty to what increasingly were foreign cultures.[6]

A new style of religious leader was needed to guide the church through this transition. In Chicago, the example for progressive leadership came from the top down. Under Cardinal George Mundelein, after 1916 the archdiocese of Chicago underwent a major reorientation of its policies toward national churches. Mundelein ran the archdiocese with a general's disposition, insisting that his clergy was to "cover up my mistakes, not to expose, to discuss, or to criticize them." Although a liberal in terms of the church leadership in the United States, at first Mundelein stepped carefully through the religious minefield known as national churches. Any incident could trigger a crisis involving, especially, the well-organized Polish clergy of Chicago. In the beginning Mundelein sought to couch his Americanization program in the context of a reluctant adjustment of the faith to the New World. Later he became bolder as he sought to bring control of the parish and school administration, including finances and staffing, under the central authority of the archdiocese.

Leaders of the national parishes, including Father Louis Grudzinski from Saint John of God (Polish), protested Mundelein's adamant refusal to copy the obliging stance his predecessors had taken toward ethnic pluralism. The cardinal's policy emphasized territorial rather than national churches. His program received a warmer welcome among some of the younger priests, including Father Joseph Kelly from Saint Rose's, Father Edward Plawinski from Saint John of God, and Father Roman Berendt from Sacred Heart. These men saw their spiritual duties as taking them beyond the static confines of the church and school buildings directly into the side streets and meeting halls of the community. A brief biographical sketch of one of these assistants will illustrate how the character of the local churches slowly changed during the course of the 1930s. [7]

Ambrose Ondrak was born in Chicago in 1892. His parents had migrated to the United States from Bohemia during the 1880s and settled into a working-class life on Dekoven Street near the legendary Chicagoan Mrs. O'Leary. Later the family relocated to Fifty-fifth and May Streets, a move that permitted Ondrak to attend school at Saints Cyril and Methodius, the nearest Bohemian parish. As a youngster, he rose at 4:30 A.M. to sell papers before going off to school by streetcar. He attended DeLaSalle High School for a year before dropping out at age fourteen to work as a delivery boy for a printing firm in the Loop. Young Ambrose then decided to become a priest. While studying at Saint Procopius Academy and College in nearby Lisle, Illinois, he returned home during the summers to work in Packingtown as a scaler with Morris and Company. In 1918 he was ordained by then Archbishop George Mundelein. During his priestly studies, Ondrak attended classes at both the University of Illinois and the University of Chicago, studying what, for a priest of that era, were very nontraditional subjects: mathematics, physics, and astronomy. In 1924 he was appointed assistant pastor at the Slovak parish of Saint Michael's at Forty-eighth and Damen. This was the beginning of a twenty-two-year assignment in the Back of the Yards.

Father Ambrose, as everyone called him, came to the parish at a time when tensions between Slovaks and Bohemians continued to simmer. Slovaks were quick to feel that Bohemians were patronizing them. But Father Ambrose's personality never permitted differences in ancestry to become an issue. He was known as the "kids' priest," always moving about them in the schoolyard, joining in their games, laughing loudly and enthusiastically. Teenagers and young couples approached him rather than the stern, rough-voiced pastor Father Charles Florek. Ondrak directed Saint Michael's Young Men's Club, an active organization involved in summer softball leagues as well as in distributing Christmas food baskets to needy families. But Father

For Slovaks, Saint Michael the Archangel Church was erected at the corner of Forty-eighth and Damen in 1900. Courtesy of Chicago Historical Society. 1971 photograph by Casey Prunchunas. ICHi-22792.

Ambrose moved beyond the property lines of Saint Michael's. He expanded his ministry into other parts of the community, helping to create the Neighborhood Council and directing summer classes at both Cornell and Davis Square Parks. Ondrak was a new kind of priest, one who ignored ethnic divisions and whose background was steeped in the American experience. For his faithful service, he was elected abbot of Saint Procopius in 1946. His parishioners cried when they saw him in later years and begged him to return. Parishioners knew him as "a darling" of a person and a man "ahead of his time."[8]

Father Ambrose's linkage of activities at city parks with his priestly ministry demonstrated a perspicacious understanding of the evolving importance these municipal facilities (in addition to Sherman Park) had for Back of the Yards youngsters between the wars. With little room for energetic diversions inside their families' four-room flats, children drifted—and were pushed—outside as often as possible. Children socialized each other in the Back of the Yards just as they did in other parts of immigrant America. Alleys, as I noted earlier, were a male-dominated retreat for teenage boys much as saloons had been for their fathers before Prohibition (and as the taverns were, in a somewhat altered state, after 1933). For younger children of both sexes and for girls entering their teens, the community's residential streets and sidewalks served as playgrounds. But as these youngsters grew up, their activity spaces after school expanded to include locations beyond their home blocks, as they searched for their own types of recreation.[9]

City parks, more so for boys than for girls, became a favorite place to meet with peers away from both parents and siblings. These peer groups generally came from the same block, though exceptions were easily made for schoolmates who were good at team sports. Parks became activity centers that reinforced peer-bonding based on residence and gender. They became a physical and social extension of the place ties that first developed when a young child had to stay close to home. "Gangs" of youngsters (boys especially) formed on each block and became rivals of youths from neighboring streets. Thus, by the twenties and thirties it was Marshfield Avenue versus Paulina or Winchester versus Wolcott, not Polish versus Lithuanians. Unlike the parks in other sections of Chicago, Back of the Yards parks solidified interethnic harmony rather than strained it. By and large, "gangs" were spatially linked agglomerations of similar-aged boys who came to identify one of the parks as "theirs" much as their immigrant parents or grandparents had claimed a national church during an earlier period. Until gang members began either to date or to play baseball in leagues that used fields in adjoining communities, these gangs customarily avoided other parks, regardless of how convenient they might be. Another park was not "theirs," and those whose park it was could be expected to confront "strangers." When families moved, youngsters usually became absorbed into one of the ongoing clusters within the new block and cut off communication with their former chums. Youngsters understood the territorial rules pertaining to different neighborhoods within the community and abided by them, requiring others to do so as well. They seldom tarried long outside their own neighborhood. And in contrast to the delinquency habits that Frederic Thrasher found so common among Chicago neighborhood gangs, block-based groups in the Back of the Yards during the interwar period did not have a reputation as troublemakers.[10]

The city had established Davis Square and Cornell Square Parks early in the century as two in a series of nineteen "neighborhood squares." Mary McDowell had lobbied intensely for Davis Square Park. When at the last moment a politically motivated change threatened to relocate the park in another community, McDowell stormed into the office of the park commissioner in charge of the new playgrounds and countered his excuses with a political threat of her own: she promised to stir up every labor union in the Twenty-ninth Ward if he did not restore the park to its original site. At the gala opening of the park in 1904, the president of the Park Board credited Miss McDowell and other settlement directors for the idea of a park and playground system. Sherman Park operated as both the local playground and what in other settings might have been labeled a "public garden" but in Chicago was known as a "community park." Situated on six square blocks that had been a cabbage field, Sherman Park was a modest link in the park-boulevard chain that stretched from Jackson Park at the lakefront west along

Midway Plaisance (south of the University of Chicago) to Washington Park and then west again along Garfield Boulevard (Fifty-fifth Street) to Western Avenue. The green-belt (or greenway) system then zigzagged northward until it reached Garfield Park on the city's West Side. Along the route were several community parks familiar to Back of the Yarders, including Sherman, Gage, and McKinley.[11]

Chicago's dream of a continuous ribbon of green encircling the older core of the city became a reality only with the implementation of numerous plans prepared over many decades. Still, Sherman Park provided more amenities than were available at neighborhood squares. For one thing, it was six times as large as either Cornell Square or Davis Square Park. A gracefully sweeping lagoon surrounded the playing fields. On Sunday afternoons young adults on a "serious" date might consider paying the rather steep fee of twenty-five cents for an hour of leisurely drifting around the lagoon in a rowboat. Above all, Sherman Park introduced a note of exuberance into the lives of local residents. On Sundays families would bring "a little picnic basket and sit up on that hill [behind the fieldhouse] and enjoy that park." "It was a big treat when we'd go to Sherman Park . . . [it] was a *beautiful* park, a gorgeous park." Few weekly activities could bring such a thrill and so uplift the lives of these people.[12]

Between the lagoon and the streets that surrounded the park was a buffer consisting of lawns and rows of trees reinforced by an eight-foot-high fence made of three-quarter-inch iron bars. (The neighborhood parks once had similar fences, but they came down during World War II for use as scrap iron.) These barriers delineated the boundaries of each park both physically and psychologically in a sharp, clear-cut manner. The fences and huge gates that guarded the street-corner entrances served as edges that clearly separated the sidewalks, streets, and tenements from the parks. They were a form of social control. According to recreational professionals of the era, as cited by Cary Goodman, the "greater the congestion, the higher and stronger should be the fences . . . so that roughs could be kept out, property not destroyed and boisterousness and obscenity made difficult." The staffs at Back of the Yards parks worried less about trouble in and around the field houses than about gangs who were known to harass younger children at the gates. These troublemakers were often the same groups who victimized unaccompanied youngsters outside movie theaters along Forty-seventh Street and Ashland Avenue. For the most part, however, parks were remarkably safe, and they provided the same green spaces among the vast tenement areas as did their counterparts in New York City. They were an interruption in the flow of the commercial and residential landscape that added distinctive color amid the gray streets and houses.[13]

They also were centers for both organized and unorganized play. Inside the park grounds, space was divided according to age and sex. There were playgrounds with swings, slides, jungle gyms, and large sandboxes for the

Looking north across a Sherman Park baseball diamond with fieldhouse in front of Saint John of God Church (Polish) *(right)*. Courtesy of E. Niez.

Looking north across a portion of Sherman Park's lagoon with Saint John of God Church in the background *(below)*. Courtesy of E. Niez.

younger children. Softball fields (for Chicago's distinctive sixteen-inch, gloveless variety) were away from the playground and close to the hardball diamond, which for safety was enclosed, at least in part, by a chain-link fence. The center of park activity, however, was the field house. In this huge concrete building, complete recreational programs were scheduled for boys and girls aged six to sixteen. An auditorium on the second floor was used for choir, dance, and theater recitals as well as for scout meetings and puppet shows. Classes in rug making, crocheting, weaving, punch work, embroidery, and woodworking were held in smaller "crafts" rooms. The game room was for checkers, Ping-Pong, chess, dominoes, and card games, while the boys' and girls' gyms were used for calisthenics, volleyball, indoor baseball, basketball, and boxing. During the summer the outdoor pool could be used in one-hour blocks of time. To stay in the pool longer, youngsters learned to dry their hair with extraordinary speed so they could get back in line and join the next hour's contingent without appearing to have just left the water. Swimsuits and towels were lent by the park district. Like military clothing during the war, these swimsuits came in all-purpose sizes. Slim-waisted boys had to take extra care in cinching their trunks to avoid embarrassing moments after cannonballing into the water. [14]

A popular corner in every field house was the local branch of the Chicago Public Library. Staff librarians had a challenge on their hands, especially at Davis Square Park in the community's poorest neighborhood. During the winter children used the library nearly as much to keep warm as to read the books. Nationwide during the depression, public libraries reported adding almost four million borrowers between 1929 and 1933. But in the Back of the Yards, all three of the libraries suffered a drop in annual circulation. Davis Square had a decrease of 41 percent between 1931 and 1933 (57,802 to 34,176). Cornell Square declined from 130,000 volumes circulated in 1929 to 79,000 in 1933, while Sherman Park dipped only from its all-time high of 159,776 volumes in 1928 to 140,008 in 1932. All the libraries devoted a substantial portion of their holdings to children's literature. They sponsored reading clubs for the older set and held story hours for preschoolers. (At Cornell Square an African-American librarian known as "Grandma" ran the storytelling program.) Because young people were the libraries' principal clientele, the staff acted as social workers as well as library professionals. Children came into these buildings undernourished, shivering from the cold. Others held the books up to their noses as they tried to read without sorely needed eyeglasses. Only after the appearance of the Back of the Yards Neighborhood Council in 1939 did park officials finally have an ally in their extracurricular child-care chores. [15]

Once a week, parks managed to entice a significant number of adults into the field houses. As late as 1940, depending on the neighborhood, between 13 and 79 percent of the dwelling units still lacked both indoor toilets and bathtubs. During the relatively stable period of the 1920s some homeowners had introduced both toilets in apartments (as opposed to those shared in a hallway or back porch) and private bathtubs. The bathtubs required hot-water tanks, usually installed in the kitchen with pipes running to the kitchen sink and the adjoining bathroom. As historian Jacqueline Wilkie has pointed out, the average working-class American did not have the luxury of a bath-room in the home until after World War I. As late as 1910, new tub models cost upward of two hundred dollars, the equivalent of a year's rent for a four-room flat. Throughout the interwar period, on Saturdays Back of the Yards residents of all ages marched in two waves (one male and one female) to Davis, Cornell, and Sherman Parks for showers in the late afternoon and early evening. The closing of Cornell Square's bathhouse for nearly a year in 1937–38 while the park district switched from coal- to gas-fired boilers undoubtedly caused considerable inconvenience for families living north of Fifty-first Street. Males bathed in large open rooms with as many as forty shower heads, while females washed in a room divided into small individual stalls. By the end of the 1920s the city had stopped providing free towels and soap. During the winter the number using the park showers dwindled as families made do at home with a rotation system (from youngest to oldest) employing galvanized steel washtubs. Earlier in the century, under pressure from Mary McDowell, the city had opened a public bathhouse on Gross Avenue across the street from the settlement house. Territorial habits prevailed even here, however. Few adults living west of Ashland made regular use of the municipal bathhouse.[16]

During the coldest weeks of the year, the park's ball field was flooded and allowed to freeze. Park staff erected a "hot house" with a potbellied stove to warm skaters during their periodic breaks. Skating was a "safe" activity where boys and girls could meet without fear of teasing from their peers. Similarly, during the summers free park shows gave teenagers opportunities to meet the opposite sex on neutral ground. On a rotating basis, each park showed free silent films once a week after dark, a practice that had started back in the 1920s and continued until World War II. Of all the events at the parks, these may have been the most important; they were certainly the most memorable. Giant canvas sheets were draped between the flag poles near the front of the field house or from the edge of the field house roof. The audience sat on the ground, though a few benches were placed near the front, sup-posedly for older people. Even parents who did not associate much with their children beyond the stoop joined them at these park shows. Families would bring straight-backed wooden chairs and large bags of broken cookies from the Loose-Wiles Bakery and spend three hours together in sing-alongs fol-lowed by several movies. Adventurous young film buffs might even consider cautiously mixing in with the crowd at a neighboring park if they were desperate to see a particular film again. The Methodist church across the street from Cornell Square also showed films once a week during the summer. A large sheet was suspended from the roof of the parsonage, and the children sat on a small grassy lot next door. Those who attended Catholic schools had to keep an eye out for priests from their parishes. Before the ecumenical era, the priests would definitely take exception to the youngsters' visiting a non-Catholic religious center.[17]

City parks began as sites for specialized activities. In time they became part of a collective "home base." From one point of view, parks might be perceived merely as public territory characterized by temporary occupation and no long-term jurisdiction by individuals. But from another perspective, parks became a shared element within the local landscape. Young people drew city parks into their everyday activity space and thereby linked these municipal facilities to the residents' family, commercial, and religious lives. Yet at the same time that children drew parks toward their homes, parks drew the youngsters away from the family circle. Parks became agents of Americanization as they socialized children both to teenage life and to the life of native-born Chicagoans. Park staff scheduled events that moved the children about the city. Park-sponsored scout troops took overnight camping trips to suburban forest preserves. Free tickets permitted park staff to take Back of the Yards youths to nearby Comiskey Park to witness the exploits of the always-struggling Chicago White Sox. (Professional sports remained a foreign experience for many immigrant parents.) From jump-rope contests on the street to crap games in the alley to the swimming pool at the park, the recreation of young Back of the Yarders was public in nature. It moved them about their neighborhood and brought them in contact with youngsters from other blocks. Their parents, meanwhile, especially if they were immigrants, preferred to entertain themselves in the privacy of their own homes, their own stoops, or their favorite taverns. Children's activities broadened their world, whereas those of adults, through free choice, generally confined them to a smaller space and a more exclusive group of friends.[18]

In other cities across America, public schools performed a role in acculturation equal to if not greater than that of the municipal parks. In the lives of Back of the Yards youngsters, schools played a surprisingly minor part. Five public grade schools served the community between the wars. (In 1934 the combined enrollment at the four schools for which data are available was 4,769 compared with 7,415 for the nine Catholic grammar schools in the Back of the Yards.) The schools were systematically distributed across the community, yet their collective impact on community life was remarkably slight before World War II. Part of the problem may have been with school personnel. A University of Chicago researcher who conducted interviews at the various schools remarked on the sharp cleavage between the principals, who were primarily Protestant, and the largely Catholic faculty. In addition, many of the teachers were Irish, the only European nationality that, before 1941, continued to earn the mistrust of Back of the Yards residents. Furthermore, the schools offered only a few after-school activities, among them violin and piano lessons at the heart-stopping price of twenty-five cents a lesson.[19]

The immigrant generation's suspicion of the public school system as a secular Americanizer of its offspring undoubtedly hampered the work of the local schoolteachers. Ever since the turn of the century, professional educators had been intensifying their efforts, in John Bodnar's words, at "using the classroom to inculcate American values and beliefs in the foreign-born and having them abandon their former traits and beliefs which were often perceived to be strange, often radical, and simply undesirable." In addition, substantial portions of the curriculum still seemed irrelevant to the requirements of the industrial work force, a condition made all the more obvious to some families by the depression. Long-term attitudes toward postelementary-school education notwithstanding, by the 1930s changes were evident in the Back of the Yards. Economic conditions discouraged some youngsters from leaving school for the workplace. More important was the grudging admission by a growing number of Back of the Yards parents that a high-school education might gain future generations more secure employment. But this glacial movement toward acceptance of secondary education as the proper method for raising children was countered during the interwar period by the fact that Chicago's educational system was a mess. During most of the 1920s under Mayor William Hale Thompson, from the Board of Education down to the local schools, an old-fashioned spoils system complete with scandals and cronyism dominated public education in the city. Then, throughout the early thirties, financial insolvency rocked the school system as teachers went unpaid for months and draconian plans for slashing a wide range of programs and services dragged down morale and crippled whatever effectiveness the system could muster. The school system was so preoccupied with its own problems between the wars that any contributions it might have made to improving life in the city's working-class districts, including the Back of the Yards, were never realized.[20]

The autonomy that the parks gave younger folk and that location-based employment patterns provided their older siblings set the stage for the creation of a communitywide council in 1939. The Back of the Yards generation that came of age about the time of the Great Depression acceded to a perception of the community that was broader and more inclusive than their predecessors would have granted. The second and third generations had a different understanding of the local area than did their parents and grandparents. Younger people walked the streets with greater assurance, gave a wider geographical scope to what they called "home" in Chicago, and after the formation of a neighborhood council, even embraced a new name for their community. The origins of this sense of community lay at the level of individuals—in their social and spatial relationships with the nearby block, church, and park, and even in their status as hyphenated Americans.

6

ACROSS THE COMMUNITY
Place Ties Deepen

The daily routine of youngsters in the Back of the Yards took them away from their homes and residential blocks as they spent time at school or in the nearest city park. Older siblings who joined the work force during the 1930s through either design or desperation, also experienced a sociospatial tug outward from their families and the activity space of their childhood. The unrelenting search for steady employment familiarized them over time with more and more of Chicago. In addition, the recreational habits of adults, especially young adults, drew them away from home and family as they traveled about the community and the city in search of leisure pursuits. They crisscrossed the Back of the Yards and nearby parts of Chicago with a notable absence of fear for their safety. An expanded but integrated sociospatial network, known as the "home range," linked home and block life with workplaces, with the Town of Lake shopping district, and with recreational centers throughout the city. The concept of home range envisions a noncontinuous area that J. Douglas Porteous describes as incorporating "a network of public paths and public or semipublic nodes." Back of the Yards residents began to feel "associated" with an expanded territorial zone and, less intensely, with other people who also "belonged" to that area. As geographer Yi-fu Tuan notes, it takes time "before we can feel at home in a place."[1]

In the aftermath of layoffs, bank failures, and draconian wage cuts, unemployed family members relied on relatives and neighbors for guidance in the frustrating search for work, full time or otherwise. A network of friends listened for news of any job openings. For the immigrant generation, the first place to look for work would have been the packinghouses. For their American-born offspring, Packingtown was further down the list of options.

116

As I noted in chapter 3, during the 1920s a growing number of male workers from the Back of the Yards had turned to companies outside the Union Stock Yards for steady employment. The Central Manufacturing District was a favorite alternative. Unlike the unskilled work in the packinghouses, jobs in the CMD varied widely. They required many different skills and levels of experience, sometimes including a high-school education.

Job diversification during the 1920s proved to have been fortunate in the face of the economic maelstrom brought about by the depression. When hard times arrived, they hit the packinghouses just as hard as they did other employers, but layoffs and slowdowns affected different industries to differing degrees. With more diversified employment habits, workers from the Back of the Yards managed to survive more effectively than they might have twenty years earlier. They had become accustomed to finding work in other parts of the city, and they were willing to travel long distances by streetcar to reach these jobs, having broken out of their little single-industry enclave after World War I. In the 1930s, when jobs cropped up here and there across the city, workers were ready to take them. Back of the Yards residents endured because during the 1920s they had learned about a metropolitan-based economy that required spatial and occupational flexibility.[2]

These new employment habits had particular meaning for the community's young women. The mothers of these depression era women would have searched for work only in Packingtown, preferring to find jobs close to home. Family, ethnicity, church, and job were all tied together in a single locality. Their daughters, on the other hand, avoided the packinghouses. The younger generation casually traveled out to the western suburbs, to industrial plants in South Chicago, or into the Loop. They were far more likely to go to the Crane Company (a metalworking firm specializing in plumbing fixtures and pipes) at Forty-first and Kedzie or to Western Electric at Twenty-second and Cicero—at least an hour's ride each way by streetcar. They were willing to travel to any part of the city where they could find work. Jobs in the far corners of Chicago permitted them to leave for the first time the immediate neighborhood where they had grown up, unaccompanied by a parent, sibling, or peer.

Confidence grew as they traveled about the city. For young women, occupational mobility was related as much to spatial behavior as to skill level or economic advancement. They now had the freedom to frequent strange parts of the city at all times of the day and night, making new friends who came from different backgrounds, held different values, and dreamed different dreams than those common to the insular world of the Back of the Yards. This territorial independence laid the groundwork for other unorthodox behaviors, including unchaperoned attendance at local dance halls, marriage to men of different nationalities, and a relatively easy adjustment to the demands of wartime work. There was nothing particularly exhilarating about standing on an assembly line eight to ten hours a day soldering parts for radios at twenty-five cents an hour. But freedom from parents' apron strings provided a sense of self-worth that could mature into levels of independence.[3]

The fragile economic lifeline that let inhabitants of the Back of the Yards survive the Great Depression obviously mandated vigilant budgeting for commercial entertainment. Pleasure always had to yield to the insistent demands for shelter and sustenance. By the 1930s movie theaters became increasingly popular as an affordable distraction, a cheap retreat from everyday problems. Indeed, "movies were *the* preeminent form of popular culture in the 1930s," remarks historian Robert McElvaine. A weekly average of sixty to seventy million tickets was sold in the United States during the early years of the depression. For Back of the Yards residents on tight if not survival-level budgets, four storefront theaters along Ashland Avenue between Forty-sixth and Fiftieth Streets offered hours of relaxation for twenty-five cents or less. The Olympia Theater, as a case in point, had a capacity of 550. Built in 1915, it offered two features daily, with the program changing every other day except on Saturday, which was devoted largely to serials and cartoons. To use the second week of April 1939 as an example, *Off the Record*, with Pat O'Brien and Joan Blondell, was paired with *Charlie Chan in Honolulu* on Thursday and Friday. On Saturday the theater offered a single feature with four serials and cartoons. The fare on Sunday and Monday turned to *Woman Doctor*, Walt Disney's *Mother Goose Goes to Hollywood*, and an installment of the fifteen-part serial *The Lone Ranger Rides Again*. Tuesday and Wednesday finished off the week with *Next Time I Marry* and *Out West with the Hardys*, starring Mickey Rooney. Down the street, the Crystal often featured Polish-language films, whereas the Cornell Theater on Fifty-first Street established a reputation for something considerably less appealing. The Cornell was known as "the Dumps." Insects and rodents scurried about underfoot in the accumulated clutter. Moreover, the theater's regular clientele exhibited a form of theater etiquette distinctly different from that witnessed in downtown movie houses. Customers brought jars of olives to munch with their popcorn, and in one instance a limburger cheese sandwich nearly emptied the building.[4]

The architectural triumph among local movie houses was Peoples Theater on Forty-seventh Street, half a block west of Ashland. Said to have been built at a cost of $600,000 in 1918, Peoples was of fireproof construction, with a steel and tile roof, an ornate facade worthy of a Loop theater, and a seating capacity of 2,200. Peoples offered vaudeville shows in addition to feature attractions. The local newspaper rented its stage to sponsor classes in American cooking. There were amateur nights and family nights, but its most memorable attraction was "dish night." On one midweek evening, Peoples offered a free piece of china to every full-paying female customer. Young women intent on building hope chests carefully scheduled trips to the theater among a network of friends and family. (The serving platter required atten-

Northwest corner of Forty-seventh and Ashland in 1965. Peoples Theater can be seen at the left, with its partially dismantled water tower at the center. In recent years Peoples has been subdivided into several small clothing stores. Courtesy of Chicago Historical Society. Photograph by Sigmund J. Osty. ICHi-22795.

dance on dish night for three consecutive weeks). Thanks to this long-standing tradition, many young women came to possess at least a few pieces of the gaudy red-and-gold-flowered china. Theater dishes were a touch of class in an otherwise materially deprived existence.[5]

With the exception of Peoples Theater, Back of the Yards movie houses were small, crowded, and inelegant. When they could afford it, couples preferred more tasteful establishments in the Loop (such as the Oriental and the Chicago Theater—both of which featured vaudevillian opening numbers) or establishments such as the Southtown Theater at Sixty-third and Halsted. With its ornate interior and first-run film selections, the Southtown also provided a child-care center and featured a pond complete with live goldfish in an expansive, deeply carpeted lobby. Back of the Yards couples struggled to finance these evenings of entertainment on limited budgets. Fourteen cents a person for a round-trip streetcar ride and a one dollar admission fee (in the Loop) dictated that trips be planned with the greatest care.

During the summers, rides atop the open double-decker buses on Garfield Boulevard were refreshing, though it was always "rider beware" as the vehicles narrowly missed the underside of railroad viaducts. Sunday afternoons might be spent at Municipal (Midway) Airport watching the airplanes. Streetcar excursions took couples to Chicago's presidential parks: Washington Park near the University of Chicago, Jackson Park along the lakefront, and Lincoln Park north of the Loop. During 1933 and 1934 the options became far more intriguing when the city hosted a world's fair on the centennial of Chicago's cityhood. After a slow beginning, attendance averaged over 100,000 daily, and by its closing in late 1934, more than thirty-nine million people had visited the fair. The fair provided desperately needed jobs and also gave a general boost to the city's collective psyche. Best of all, the "Century of Progress" offered Chicagoans wonderful entertainment at modest prices. Each attraction, however inexpensive, was greatly diverting. Furthermore, it often drew young adults beyond the confines of family and neighborhood. The settlement house staff noted in its 1927–28 report that Back of the Yards "young people prefer to leave the district and seek their recreation elsewhere" because there "is more adventure in visiting new places and meeting new faces than in staying so near home that you know nearly everyone you may meet at the hall."[6]

After moviegoing, dancing was probably the next most popular form of recreation among young adults, and enthusiasts roamed the community and city in search of the right dance halls. Dancing was especially popular among women in their late teens and early twenties. Some attended dances three or four times a week before they were married and went frequently even afterward. Unless they had a date for the evening, young ladies went to these events with girlfriends, who provided companionship and support while they scouted the dance hall for likely partners. According to the settlement house staff, Prohibition had driven morally reprehensible dance halls out of business. By the time of the Great Depression, weekly dances were held at local lodge and union halls, at School Hall (the Czech cultural center), and at church halls. Saint Michael's Young Men's Association regularly attracted several hundred to its dances. In addition, small commercial dance halls along Ashland Avenue, including one on the second floor over Depositors Bank, provided additional opportunities to unwind during the workweek.

On weekends a favorite gathering spot was Paradise Inn, on Damen Avenue south of Fifty-first, which offered free dancing in a large pavilion with a live orchestra until two in the morning on Saturday and nine at night on Sunday. Fish plates were available for fifteen cents on Fridays. The Inn

---

One of the South Side's most popular entertainment centers during the interwar years, especially for its dance bands, was White City at Sixty-third and South Park (*opposite, top*). Postcard of White City, postmarked 1913.

One block north of the Paradise Inn was "Brebec's Block," on the northwest corner of Fifty-first and Damen, with a popular bowling alley on the second floor next to several medical offices (*opposite, bottom*). For years Brebec's Department Store, well known in the nearby Bohemian and Slovak neighborhoods, was on the first floor (beneath the bowling sign). Several oral histories used in this book were collected in a successor to Gus's Restaurant. This venerable structure was recently leveled and replaced by a fast-food establishment. Courtesy of Chicago Historical Society. 1971 photograph by Casey Prunchunas. ICHi-22793.

featured a beer garden and a two-lane bowling alley, but it was most famous for its unscheduled entertainment. The "Bucket of Blood," as the Inn was known locally, tended to attract young men who, after a long week at work, were quick to take umbrage at the slightest insult: fistfights became a colorful part of its weekly routine. For more elegant but less thrilling evenings, South Side working-class couples took the streetcar to White City at Sixty-third and South Park or to the plush, "architecturally innovative" Trianon Ballroom at Sixty-second and Cottage Grove, which featured a young conductor named Lawrence Welk.[7]

Movie theaters and dance halls provided young adults, married and otherwise, with amusement among people of their own age and social perspective. In contrast, immigrant parents seldom attended films regularly, although there were exceptions. Some fathers, after a day's labor in Packingtown, were known to leave the family dinner table for an evening at the Crystal watching the latest Polish film. On occasion a child had to be sent to bring the wayward parent home after he had fallen asleep in the dark theater. For the most part, however, public entertainment, including trips to the beach or to Riverview (Chicago's famous amusement park), constituted the leisure activity of American-born generations. They enjoyed the freedom from family traditions and valued opportunities to meet members of the opposite sex from different backgrounds and different parts of the city.[8]

Everyday excursions across the Back of the Yards and the city, whether related to employment, to family business, or to recreation, inevitably entailed travel after sunset, and such journeys could usually be undertaken without risk to personal safety. Couples and individuals alike routinely moved along streetcar thoroughfares and residential side streets in the early morning hours. Echoing the sentiments of an overwhelming majority of informants, one resident recalls that Back of the Yards streets were ordinarily safe and quiet: "Nobody bothered you." Another insisted that you "could walk in the neighborhood during the day or even in the evening without any fear." Violations of the Prohibition laws aside, crimes against property appear to have been the most common unlawful acts in the Back of the Yards between the wars. Attractive clothing, and even bedding, hanging on a clothesline was known to disappear. Fresh bread that the deliveryman placed in a grocery store's storage box in the early morning hours sometimes vanished. Whether the thieves were "taking" because they were poorly clothed and underfed or simply stealing for entertainment or financial gain is not entirely clear. Shoplifting, however, was clearly a special problem during the 1930s in urban communities across the United States as well as in the Back of the Yards' largest department store, Goldblatt's. A massive seven-story white brick edifice with large "Chicago style" windows, situated on the southwest corner of Forty-seventh and Ashland across the street from both Peoples Bank and Depositors Bank, Goldblatt's maintained its own security force to counter shoplifting. A store detective interviewed in 1934 repeatedly commented on the problem, especially in reference to juvenile thieves.[9]

When apprehended, suspects were whisked away to the New City police station, two block west on Paulina. A small two-story building built in 1897, made of pressed brick with stone trimming and copper cornices, the station included holding cells and an auto patrol garage. From its earliest days, it had been kept busy on weekends handling the steady stream of disorderly conduct cases associated with excessive drinking. In 1900, 61 percent of the recorded arrests were for "disorderly" conduct, whereas only 4 percent were for burglary and robbery. From 1919 to 1921, of the Chicago communities with over fourteen murders—fifteen of the city's neighborhoods including Bridgeport, Englewood, Canaryville, and Brighton Park—the area served by the New City station ranked third lowest in the murder rate by population. Although this may not be a testament to the community's quality of life, that ten of the twenty murders were perpetrated by "blows" rather than by shooting, stabbing, or strangulation suggests that these violent crimes can be attributed more to the area's quarrelsome saloon life than to premeditated violence. (Note that these data were drawn from a territory that included a large expanse of southwest Chicago beyond the Back of the Yards.) Crimes of passion did occur, however. Twice in 1929, for example, Mexican residents were attacked by conationals, once with a revolver and another time with a rock or bottle. Residents on Winchester Avenue near Saint Michael's Church were horrified—and have never forgotten the day—when a man murdered his wife after accusing her of adultery.[10]

By the late 1920s and throughout the 1930s, though, the principal law enforcement problem for the community was juvenile delinquency. In the neighborhoods north of Fifty-first, the delinquency rate for 1927 to 1933 was 5.3 for every hundred males between ages ten and sixteen, placing the community eighteenth in a study of twenty-five communities. Overall, in a survey of 140 areas in Chicago, 74 percent had lower delinquency rates than the "stockyards" district. From 1935 through 1941, the percentage of petitions filed in juvenile court from the New City station ranged from a high of 1.04 percent of the city's total in 1937 to a low of 0.45 percent two years later. (At the time "New City"—Back of the Yards and Canaryville combined—housed 3 percent of Chicago's population under age nineteen.) But again, in terms of the type of offense, the crimes were primarily against property. "Violence or injury to person" accounted for only three out of fourteen petitions in 1935, none out of fifteen the following year, one in each of the next three years, and none in 1940 and 1941.

Between 71 and 100 percent of the petitions were for "property crimes." Nonetheless, these actions carried the potential for great harm. For instance, in 1932 "some vicious malcontents" broke into the basement of Saint Augustine's School and connected a long fuse to a jar of kerosene. The fuse burned its way up to the neck of the jar, then sputtered out. Five years later a nineteen-year-old arsonist was seized after setting Seward Elementary

School on fire. Damage totaled $20,000. Most crimes against property, however, involved theft. In 1939 five youths were arrested after smashing windows along Ashland Avenue in the early morning hours. Several bottles of liquor, two dozen pork loins, and $25 worth of men's pants and leather jackets were stolen. Armed robberies probably committed by older individuals rocked the community in 1939, including a time when two armed men briefly kidnapped a local judge after he stopped his car at the intersection of Forty-seventh and Ashland. They forced him to drive to the western suburbs, then took his car and $45 in cash. In other cases, a shoe store was robbed of $75 in September, and two months later Goldblatt's reported a daylight robbery by five men who stole $8,000.[11]

The most common type of personal assault within the Back of the Yards was the jackrolling of drunks. Chicago had a long, sad tradition of this form of mugging. (Clifford Shaw wrote a revealing account of it in his sociological classic *The Jack-Roller*.) In 1933 journalist Edmund Wilson noted that across Chicago jackrolling had "become conspicuously more common lately." Typically, young men waited outside Ashland Avenue saloons and later outside taverns along the side streets for their inebriated victims to stumble by. Some victims may have been dumped into Bubbly Creek. Junior versions of these small gangs occasionally harassed younger children outside movie theaters and at entrances to the city parks. But this was still better than what was taking place in nearby Canaryville, where the Ragen's Colts controlled street crime.[12]

With one notable exception, Chicago's international reputation as the center of organized crime in America barely touched the Back of the Yards. The community's contribution to Chicago's heritage of gangsterism was Johnny "Dingbat" Oberta. Oberta ran his operation out of a florist's shop on Forty-seventh Street. He openly sported a large revolver prominently tucked inside a shoulder holster. He socialized with off-duty cops at speakeasies and was important enough to be invited to an underworld summit meeting that included Al Capone, Bugs Moran, and Joe Saltis, Oberta's one-time crime boss. A square-faced Pole with a self-imposed "bobbed" name, Oberta could display a disarming smile that masked a gunman's view of the world. He worked at maintaining a Robin Hood image among his neighbors, distributing baskets of food at Christmas and, like a stockyards version of John D. Rockefeller, handing out coins to the youngsters who trailed after him. In time Dingbat became restless and tried to move out of the small-time theater of "the jungle" by running for state senator and alderman, the latter against an incumbent who two years earlier had received 99 percent of the votes cast. A dismal showing after his "boys" had campaigned throughout the area from a flatbed truck did nothing to dampen Oberta's ambitions. Soon thereafter, Dingbat met the same end many Chicago hoodlums have reaped over the years: a quick death on an abandoned roadway in the western suburbs.

The most famous criminal case ever to come out of the Back of the Yards, however, was partly authentic and partly Hollywood. In 1932 a delicatessen at Forty-third and Ashland was robbed and a police officer was killed. Joseph Majczek and a friend were convicted of the crimes and sentenced to ninety-nine years in prison. Convinced of her son's innocence, Tillie Majczek scrubbed floors at night for eleven years to raise enough money to offer as a reward to anyone who could prove her son was a victim, not a criminal. Evidence uncovered by Chicago *Times* reporters revealed that the prosecution had suppressed a statement made by the only eyewitness saying she could not identify either of the convicted men as having participated in the robbery and murder. After Majczek passed a lie-detector test administered by the developer of the polygraph, public sentiment prompted Illinois governor Dwight Green to grant the Back of the Yards resident a full pardon after thirteen years in prison. Five years later, in 1950, a court overturned the original conviction and his name was finally cleared. A movie version of this tragedy (*Call Northside 777*) starred Jimmy Stewart.[13]

In spite of the crimes described above and the occasional violence associated with labor organizing, residents felt remarkably safe when walking the streets at night or sleeping on their porches, in their backyards, or even in the parks on muggy summer evenings. For summertime ventilation, exterior doors were kept open if someone was at home, and they were often left unlocked when the family was away. Rules of the street, even if not faithfully followed by criminals, stated that no one stole from friends or neighbors. This may be one reason the Goldblatt Brothers' Department Store had so much trouble with shoplifting. It was the only major chain store operating in the Back of the Yards during the mid-1930s. As for the locals, they had little that was worth stealing. In addition, the beat cop who knew residents along the block reinforced feelings of physical security for people who had never experienced much financial security. The level of crime reported in the settlement house records, in weekly issues of the local newspaper, and in the oral histories suggests that residents were relatively safe as they moved about the community. By 1928 the settlement staff noted an improvement in the "rowdyism and petty crime once very characteristic" of the gangs. Conditions were described as having "improved very markedly." A widely experienced feeling of personal security, coupled with a host of school, church, work, and recreational pursuits as well as normal street life, promoted the "sense of place" discussed earlier. The historical moment was ripe for an initiative that would transform these place ties into something larger and more organized—a communitywide association.[14]

If leadership for such an adventuresome undertaking was to come from within the community itself, at first glance Mary McDowell appears to have been a likely choice. After all, in 1906 McDowell had finished second to the internationally famous founder of Hull House, Jane Addams, in a poll that asked, "Who is the best woman in Chicago?" Ever since her arrival in the Back of the Yards in 1894, McDowell had fought the good fight. Her most notable success had been the campaign to close Chicago's sprawling garbage dump at Forty-seventh and Damen. She had battled the city's political establishment over the ultimate disposition of Davis Square Park. Her support of the packinghouse workers during the 1904 strike earned her accolades as "angel of the stockyards." The University of Chicago delivered dozens of eager young scholars to her doorstep. Their research, ethnocentrically limited though it may have been, provided documentation that McDowell used to badger the city's political establishment into making some improvements in the local area.[15]

These successes had their limits, however. McDowell's major accomplishments came downtown: in the mayor's office, before the city council, and within various municipal departments. Furthermore, her greatest successes came during the first decade and a half of this century when Progressive reform was at its apex. McDowell and her associates came to the Stockyards District at a time when college-educated young people had been stimulated to aid the victims of poverty. Settlement house staff wanted to undo the harm brought about by the country's headlong rush into industrialization and urbanization. But as Allen Davis has pointed out, Jane Addams and her colleagues were unclear on what they would do "after they had moved to the house in the 'slums.'" Moreover, reformers, including those in the Back of the Yards, "betrayed a sense of paternalism, a feeling of *noblesse oblige* as they viewed the crowded slums." At the same time that they were grappling with municipal authorities to eradicate local environmental hazards, the settlement house staff exposed their not-so-hidden agenda of imposing middle-class propriety on the downtrodden.

One objective of these reformers was to acculturate the foreigners as quickly as possible. The settlement house papers are replete with remarks tinged with nativist generalizations: "The Irish with their rare social nature are found to be a distinct factor in the progress of a community," while "Bohemians desiring as they always do space for grass, trees and flowers moved away from the immediate vicinity of the Yards." Many of "the Italian women were clean" but it was more important that "the Sicilians we know have not led us to believe that they are in any way criminally disposed but are quiet peace loving neighbors." The personal prejudices of the settlement house staff received constant reinforcement from the continuous stream of college-age students who visited Gross Avenue. The situation sometimes resembled a human zoo where a subspecies was observed for purposes of "higher" education. In 1941 students still came from as far away as Berea College in Kentucky, from Judson College in Alabama, and from the University of Oklahoma in Norman to see what the big city could do to the oppressed and, presumably, how high-minded individuals could ease the situation. Despite McDowell's best intentions, the settlement house remained both physically and culturally detached from much of its surroundings.[16]

In addition, the University of Chicago experiment "had a very limited effect on the neighborhood," according to Robert Slayton, because the "important institutions in the community were opposed to it." To the South Side Democratic politicians, these reformers were incessant troublemakers, unwilling to work within the system. To the local Catholic pastors, settlement workers were "not of the faith." A child of the Social Gospel movement, Mary McDowell understood her calling to have a Christian underpinning. She innocently underscored her religious distinctiveness by attending Sunday services at the Methodist church on Fiftieth Street across from Cornell Park. Perhaps most damning of all, the settlement accepted hundreds of dollars each year from the packers. As the intellectual descendents of Progressivism, Back of the Yards social workers in the 1920s and 1930s focused their efforts on the young people of the community—and rightly so. Older residents, in many cases still European in their world-view, were suspicious of anyone who did not speak their language or who appeared to represent religious heresies, let alone the upper class.[17]

This is not to say that the University of Chicago Settlement House failed to provide useful services to its neighbors. When the great influenza epidemic of 1918 struck, the staff turned their building into an emergency hospital and field kitchen. The deadly impact of this epidemic within the Back of the Yards is evident in the Parish register at Saint Michael's. The parish typically averaged about seven deaths a month in October. In 1918 the total for October was fifty-six. The timing of this deadly assault can be pinpointed even more precisely. In the twelve days between 16 and 28 October, forty-five people died in Saint Michael's parish. Even Saint Basil's parish at the upscale "suburban" edge of the community south of Fifty-first Street experienced a 58 percent increase in deaths from 1917 to 1918, largely owing to the epidemic. In the face of such a crisis, the settlement house's six nurses and four physicians labored determinedly. They were able to save all but one of the victims who were brought to the center. In addition, the hastily organized soup kitchen served about three thousand meals during the influenza siege.[18]

Although these extraordinary efforts undoubtedly deserved—and earned—the appreciation of neighbors, the center's contacts with adults remained marginal. For many years a Bohemian Women's Club, "Klub Svoboda," met at the settlement; its membership reached 150 by the early 1920s. The settlement house also sponsored citizenship and English language classes, and the staff organized a club for unemployed Polish men during the worst period of the depression, though agitation by labor organizers and leftists disrupted meetings and forced the settlement to curtail the club's activities. The center also operated for a brief period as a relief station, and it repeatedly sponsored clothing drives, distributing donations to the needy, especially during the harshest periods of Chicago's infamous winters. Whenever possible the staff also found jobs for unemployed neighbors, though the social workers were limited in what they could do in this regard.[19]

On behalf of preschoolers and school-age youngsters, though, the settlement staff worked tirelessly and to great effect. There was a nursery school for two dozen children between ages two and a half and four, after which they could "graduate" to the settlement's kindergarten for two more years. From midafternoon until ten at night, the game rooms were open. Classes in drawing, painting, cartooning, woodworking, toy making, clay modeling, piano, violin, harmonica, dancing, sewing, knitting, cooking, typing, shorthand, boxing (and first aid), roller skating, photography, and Spanish were all available. There were basketball and baseball leagues as well as vegetable gardens and free movies on the roof of the boys' gymnasium. Boy Scout and Girl Scout troops used the building, and an elite group joined the Mary McDowell Discussion Club. A representative from the club even traveled to Washington, D.C., to participate in a national youth congress. A library holding two thousand volumes had an annual circulation of nearly seven thousand.[20] Probably the settlement's most memorable undertaking was its summer camp in Chesterton, Indiana (a few miles south of the famous Indiana Dunes on Lake Michigan). Originally, a $3,000 gift from Miss Shirley Farr had permitted the purchase of ten acres with a small lake. In 1929 this land was exchanged for forty acres with a stream. Camp Farr had a swimming pool, a recreation and dining hall complex, an infirmary, a crafts house, and residential cabins. Boys and girls could spend one to two weeks at this rural retreat. For many it was their only adventure outside Chicago during the difficult decade of the 1930s.[21]

If Camp Farr was the settlement house's most fondly remembered project, the center's most successful efforts were among its Mexican neighbors. As early as 1931, the schedule of "Mexican activities" filled the week, from an adult cultural club on Sunday to a drama club on Wednesday to a junior boys' gym class on Saturday. In the absence of a Spanish-language church, the settlement became the center of Mexican culture in the Back of the Yards. Cinco de Mayo festivities were held at the settlement. A Mexican orchestra played at the weekly movies, probably the first time many Poles and Slovaks had ever heard Mexican music firsthand. By 1936, over half of the children in the settlement's kindergarten were Mexican. McDowell's determined efforts to eliminate barriers between the neighborhood's Eastern Europeans and the newest arrivals earned her a special place in the hearts of Chicago's Mexican population. A translator's note scribbled in the Chicago Foreign Language Press Survey heralded Mary McDowell's "great contribution to the social welfare of the Mexican people," for which she appropriately "received an honorary medal from the Mexican Government in appreciation of services rendered to the Mexican people in the Stock Yards District." Her death in 1936 was described as "a great loss to the Mexican people of Chicago." Known for her unwillingness to tolerate "goofing around," Mary McDowell was "a god," in the words of one resident who still "prays for her every day." As a final tribute to her memory, in early 1937 the Chicago city council approved the renaming of Gross Avenue as McDowell Avenue.[22]

The death of Mary McDowell removed the settlement house's only "legitimate" representative who had any chance of pulling together the community's disparate elements. Shortly before her death, McDowell had attempted to "secure the cooperation of representative professional and business men" for a "more detailed discussion of neighborhood needs." Supervisors from the local parks, several school principals, and the New City police captain were invited to a meeting in 1935, but after early pledges of support for a neighborhood council, the fifteen participants soon began to go their separate ways. McDowell sought to enlist their cooperation through the Stockyards Community Council. Organized in 1918, the Community Council consisted of at least fifty social service, religious, and business groups whose aim was to coordinate recreation for the youngsters in a ten-square-mile area around the Union Stock Yards and Packingtown. The council was divided into sub-councils including the "New City" Community Council.

The Stockyards Community Council's intentions may have been honorable, but the organization failed to take any real action. Funds to run the summer camp program and the playgrounds came from the packers, local banks, and other businesses in the area. Religious leaders from the local Catholic churches were invited to participate but refused, which left the council with no contacts at the grass-roots level except park directors, who had little influence beyond the park gates. Appeals by the settlement house for support from the local pastors, including Father Grudzinski of Saint John of God (Polish), a longtime foe of the social workers, went unheeded. Meanwhile, throughout the 1920s the figurehead president of the council was a Methodist Episcopal minister. For its part, the settlement continued to have trouble maintaining contact with Catholic residents; in a survey of 233 junior girls (grade-school age) associated with the center, only 69 (30 percent) attended Catholic schools, while 2 attended Saint Martini's (Lutheran). Until the cooperation of church leaders could be guaranteed, efforts at building a communitywide association were doomed to fail.[23]

A second, unrelated effort to unify the community was undertaken by the local newspaper. In 1937 the *Journal Town of Lake* spearheaded a union of "senior young people's clubs in the community" to promote "greater harmony and understanding among the various groups in the neighborhood, to work for co-operation in the scheduling and sale of tickets in the case of social events and harmoniously to work out athletic meets and leagues." The initial response was impressive. Several dozen athletic associations, social clubs, and religious societies said they were willing to cooperate. After this initial burst of enthusiasm the effort flagged, however, and by early August the council was still announcing "definite arrangements" for a picnic in September. It is unclear whether the event was ever staged, but by the end of that year the council of clubs had disappeared from the pages of the *Journal Town of Lake*. The paper's initiative was shot through with problems, some typical of these early attempts at organizing the community. The first problem was that the council met at the settlement house. Moreover, its "temporary" president was the news editor of the *Journal,* the vice president was the director of Davis Square Park, and the treasurer was the owner of Goldberg's Credit Store on Ashland Avenue. The council's leadership, in short, consisted largely of adults who were not associated with the clubs that made up the council. And then there was the basic question whether such a coordinator of grass-roots events was necessary at all. [24]

Business leaders from the Forty-seventh and Ashland shopping district constituted yet another network of individuals actively involved within the community during this period. Invigorated by improvements in the local economy by 1938, the agenda of the Town of Lake Chamber of Commerce called for a series of improvements in traffic safety and flow along Ashland Avenue. With the cooperation of local aldermen, an expensive project paved over two blocks of "wastelands" on Marshfield Avenue where stores fronting on Ashland were building their parking lots. For years the residents had tolerated a gutted roadway consisting of broken stones and dirt, but after pressure from the business community, the Works Progress Administration and the city joined together to grade, pave, and install sewers along the two-block stretch behind Ashland Avenue. (The WPA was a New Deal relief agency dedicated to federally financed construction projects.) Similarly, the troublesome bottleneck caused by the Forty-ninth Street tracks as they passed over Ashland prompted businessmen, aldermen, and the WPA to join together to replace the old steel viaduct with a wider concrete overpass that still stands today. After repeated injuries to pedestrians, traffic lights were finally installed along Ashland north of Forty-seventh Street. The merchants also initiated a campaign in late 1937 "to publicize Town of Lake through the mediums of the foreign press, the radio and the *Journal* as the 'Bargain Center of Chicago.'" This promotion urged residents to "Shop in Town of Lake," where everything was at the lowest prices and where stores offered personal service and courteous treatment. [25]

A senior partner in the revitalization of the local shopping district was the *Journal Town of Lake.* The close relationship between the paper and the merchants of Ashland Avenue (and Forty-seventh Street) was illustrated in a combination platform and editorial published on 30 September 1937. The platform listed seven community projects needing work and one agency the paper singled out for special recognition. The projects included plans to improve the roads and traffic patterns around Forty-seventh and Ashland, to remove litter from the streets, and to eliminate old overhanging wooden signs. For emphasis, the last plank declared the paper's support for the Town of Lake Chamber of Commerce. Immediately below the platform was an editorial that offered a somewhat broader perspective on the *Journal's* role within the Back of the Yards. The paper called itself "the speaking image of

Looking south along Ashland Avenue from near Forty-fourth Street in 1941.
Packingtown is behind the billboard and gas station on left. Courtesy of Chicago
Historical Society. ICHi-22796.

the neighborhood." The text remarked that "intrinsically, a community is
inarticulate. Its voice is its newspaper. The news printed in the Journal is
YOUR news. Its advertisements are those of YOUR merchants. And the causes
for which it fights are YOUR causes." Readers were reminded that "you are
unquestionably part of your community and that the community causes are
your causes. Then the Journal becomes your heart as well as your voice."[26]

If the *Journal* was the heart and voice of the community, the soul was still
the business sector, at least as envisioned in the pages of the *Journal*. "We
Believe in Our Community" became the banner that headlined a regular
section of advertisements for firms and individuals who provided services to
local residents. An "Editorial" paragraph proclaimed, "We are proud of our
small parks, our schools, our playgrounds, and, of course, we are especially
proud of our many churches, which are responsible for the moral and spiritual life of our community." Norman Geyer and Company, a real estate firm
at Forty-eighth and Ashland, frequently ran a little piece entitled "Geyer's

Community Comment." After a *Farmer's Almanack* style thought for the week, it always ended with the reminder, "We are interested in this community."

In addition to typical advertising by service and retail establishments, the *Journal* used its headlines and news stories to highlight the doings of the Chamber of Commerce, specific shopping promotions, and various remodeling projects undertaken by different merchants. In a newspaper noted for very few photographs other than head-and-shoulders snapshots of individuals, the *Journal* consistently included pictures of renovated storefronts. Finally, the paper also featured a column titled "Who's Who in Town of Lake." The "who" was always a businessman or businesswoman. Not once did the *Journal* consider a local park director, park librarian, Boy Scout troop leader, settlement house head resident, church pastor, or school principal qualified for inclusion in the column. Morris Janowitz, in his classic study of Chicago's community newspapers, observed that many of these papers owed their origins to "the development of the satellite business center in the metropolitan district" because it "made possible a base of advertising revenue." For the years before 1940, Janowitz perceptively portrayed the *Journal*'s role in the Back of the Yards.[27]

This campaign to promote the Town of Lake shopping district and the *Journal*'s attempt to establish a council of clubs reflect the modest but growing pride, and even confidence, that various elements within the community felt for the local area—sentiments largely absent before this time. These campaigns would have been unlikely ten or twenty years earlier. Instead, the Stockyards Community Council, a reformist coalition controlled by nonnatives and influenced by such untrustworthy elements as the packers, was the best that could be accomplished before 1930. Whatever the "loss of community" literature may assert about the interwar years, historian Patricia Mooney Melvin is correct in arguing that "local life and neighborhood attachment persisted during this period"—and beyond. Communities, she says, "do not exist in a vacuum but instead are shaped by the particular historical context in which they operate." In the 1930s, Chicago possessed, according to Edmund Wilson, "much more a true community than New York." Whereas ethnicity held the community together during an earlier period, the same factors that historian Kathleen Neils Conzen suggests helped foster ethnic identity (common residence, "shared lifestyles, work experiences and class interests") could also come together to promote an attachment not just for the geographical territory that delineates a community but also for its residents and indeed its distinctive local culture as well. And as Yi-fu Tuan points out, "the awareness of the identity" of one's own neighborhood may be increased by exposure to the outside world. "Neighborhood," he says, depends "on knowledge of the outside world. . . . Residents of a real neighborhood do not recognize the extent and uniqueness of their area unless they have experience of contiguous areas."[28]

In the Back of the Yards, the sense of place that had been nurtured at the block and neighborhood levels now began to blossom into something larger—indeed, potentially momentous. This growth was fueled by contact with other communities within the city. The Back of the Yards was evolving as a distinctive "place" in the midst of the greatest economic crisis in the nation's history. After decades when the area was the poor cousin of the South Side, a pride in its character began to manifest itself under different guises. Absent from these new efforts were references to that earlier day when the area was nationally known as "The Jungle." Instead, by the late 1930s the emphasis was on a commitment to valuing what had been accomplished over time while also working to upgrade social and economic conditions. The use of "Town of Lake," a historically neutral term, instead of "Stockyards District," "Packingtown," "New City," or even "back o' the yards" reflected this new attitude. When Saint Michael's Young Men's baseball team played Saint Simon's, its Slovak rival from Gage Park, the intensity of the game went beyond mere athletic competition. According to Back of the Yards Slovaks, Saint Simon's was home to the "rich bitches," the Slovaks who had money—in fact, to Slovaks who were no longer Slovaks once they moved beyond Western Avenue. A few families who thought they had escaped the area's poverty and blight after moving to housing developments west of the Back of the Yards returned to their "old neighborhood" when they found they missed more than the stench of Darling and Company. It was probably no coincidence that in 1937, at the same time the *Journal* was striving to solicit the communitywide cooperation of young people's clubs and the Town of Lake Chamber of Commerce was boasting of its shopping district, the area's "old-timers" were called together at Davis Park Library to "talk over the good old days" of Armour's Patch and Henkle's Farm. Both organized and unorganized elements within the Back of the Yards were all moving from different directions toward a common point: acknowledgment that ties involving history and geography bound residents of the area together. The question then became how this unity might be revealed in a concrete way and who would successfully envision the correct form.[29]

7

THE NEIGHBORHOOD COUNCIL
Space and Time Intersect

In 1939, as the changes described in the previous chapters became part of the everyday routine of Back of the Yards residents, a handful of energetic individuals emerged from within the community. These leaders successfully pulled together the ties of territorial and ethnoreligious loyalties under the aegis of a community council in an effort that in all likelihood would have sputtered to an inglorious halt only a decade earlier. Rather than confronting a population constrained by spatially restricted spheres of activity and split by differences over ancestral homelands, organizers of the Back of the Yards Neighborhood Council found residents, clergymen, the Chamber of Commerce, and the local newspaper receptive to an agency of purposeful community action. The Council's early success in upholding common values, in championing commonly valued local improvements, and in attracting federal relief funds into the area strengthened its hand within the community and ultimately within the city's political hierarchy.

Two individuals—one a "foreigner" by education, residence, and religion and the other a neighbor from an adjacent community—set this communal enterprise on its course. Like so many social scientists before him, Saul Alinsky came to the Back of the Yards with a mission. Professor Clifford Shaw had sent him there as part of the University of Chicago's project to organize neighborhood youth committees. Alinsky had been born in Chicago in 1909 of orthodox Jewish parents who had emigrated from Russia. He was raised three miles north of the stockyards, not far from Hull House. After an adolescence and young adulthood that he admitted were devoid of social conscience, he graduated from the University of Chicago cum laude in 1930, having become involved with several social action clubs. He subsequently worked as a research associate at the university until in late 1938 he arrived in the Back of the Yards. Within a few months he made contact with the director of Davis Square Park, Joseph Meegan. A native of Canaryville, Meegan graduated in 1928 from DeLaSalle High School and four years later from DePaul University in Chicago. He taught at two local high schools for a few years and then in 1936 took the supervisor's examination for the Park District. After a brief stay at a new park in the far southeastern corner of the city, he was transferred to Davis Square as director in March 1937. The Works Progress Administration had recently refurbished the field house, so Meegan turned his attention to the park's programs, a challenge he embraced with typical enthusiasm and self-assurance. One of his first projects was to integrate young Mexicans into the park programs. When some local youths balked, Meegan's threat to have it settled in the boxing ring forced the troublemakers to back down.[1]

Alinsky and Meegan met in late February 1939 after attending a meeting of the Packingtown Youth Committee held at the recently opened YWCA center of Fifty-first Street. The Youth Committee was a spin-off of the Packinghouse Workers Organizing Committee (PWOC), which in turn was an affiliate of the Congress of Industrial Organizations. The union, as it recruited in Packingtown, wisely extended its campaign into the surrounding residential neighborhoods. The Youth Committee was a group of young unionists ostensibly working to improve local recreational facilities and secondarily to help unemployed men of their age group to find work. As with the *Journal Town of Lake*'s Council of Clubs, the first response to the Youth Committee's program was enthusiastic. Resolutions, passed with unanimous support, called for administrators of the National Youth Administration (a sort of "junior Works Progress Administration" for young people between sixteen and twenty-five) and the WPA to be apprised of conditions in the community and urged support for all political candidates who pledged to bring a "New Deal to Packingtown." Those attending also urged improvement in the community's recreational opportunities, medical care, and housing conditions. But a meeting called by labor organizers at the headquarters of the YWCA, without the presence of church leaders or representatives of ethnic clubs, was sure to be questioned in spite of the presence of Joe Meegan and two local aldermen.[2]

Sometime after the meeting Alinsky approached Meegan, and a warm though brief friendship ensued. Alinsky would go on to establish a national reputation for his tireless efforts at organizing grass-roots community groups. At the time he first visited the Back of the Yards, Alinsky's guidelines for neighborhood organizing were still being formed. But he had notions about what was needed and, above all, about the role communication would play in solving the social ills of urban America. Meegan, in contrast, was less of a theorist; he was the insider who was familiar with the people and culture of the Back of the Yards. Alinsky, in spite of his long association with academics, was contemptuous of their paternalism, while Meegan carried a local's mistrust of do-gooders from the outside. Alinsky was fascinated with union organizing and thus felt far more comfortable working with PWOC leaders, whereas Meegan was not enamored of the unionists and felt far more at home with the parish priests. This talent for working with the community's religious leaders was immeasurably assisted by the fact that Meegan's brother was the priest-secretary to Bishop Bernard Sheil, the archdiocese's social action specialist and a man beloved for his dedication to youth. Alinsky and Meegan balanced each other's interests and character strengths. That they became close friends for a time surely made what seemed nothing less than a Disney-style fantasy easier to discuss and plan.[3]

Their vision was to organize a council that would unite all the disparate local elements and seek to cure the area's social and economic ills. Even before the first communitywide meeting on 14 July 1939, the suggestion of a community organization awakened a response from these "disparate elements." While most of the pastors remained cool to the idea of a broad-based association, several younger colleagues, including Ambrose Ondrak (who opened the first meeting with a prayer), became enthusiastic supporters. Unqualified endorsement of the council by Bishop Sheil added the archdiocese's unofficial imprimatur. The *Journal* (which mistakenly labeled the organization the "New City Neighborhood council" in its first reference to it) sounded an optimistic note in a piece published the day before the opening meeting. A headline announced, "Neighborhood Council Seeks Remedy for Community Ills," while the following column mentioned that 109 organizations had promised to send delegates. Scheduled to attend were representatives from the Packinghouse Workers Organizing Committee and the Packingtown Youth Committee as well as the Lithuanian Olympic Committee, the Saint Michael's Young Men's Club, the Polish National Alliance, the Knights of Columbus from Saint Augustine's, and businessman Barney Goldberg. Nearly every sector of the community was to be represented at this "community conference."[4]

The Council's organizers understood in their unsophisticated way the importance of symbolism in such an undertaking. They sensed that territorial loyalty, if properly promoted, had far greater potential to elicit cooperation than, say, ethnicity alone. But they also understood that ethnicity and religion as well as class and place had to be united if their venture was to succeed. The call for that first meeting shrewdly played upon both local history and current developments as it listed some of the problems besetting the area. It admitted that for "fifty years we have waited for someone to offer the solution—but nothing has happened." So now "we ourselves must face and solve these problems. We know what poor housing, disease, unemployment and juvenile delinquency means; and we are sure that if a way out is to be found, we can and must find it." "We churchmen, businessmen and union men have formed the Back of the Yards Neighborhood Council" with the intention of uniting "all the organizations within that community known as the 'Back of the Yards' in order to promote the welfare of all residents of that community regardless of their race, color or creed." Urban neighborhoods by their nature possess an organizational hierarchy based on population size and composition. Different intensities of cooperation and loyalty typically flow from the different orders of neighborhood groupings, and generally the greatest loyalty is found on the smallest scale. The Back of the Yards Neighborhood Council's organizers aimed to connect microscale (family) and mesoscale loyalties (neighborhood and church) to a macroscale unit (the Back of the Yards) through ties of landscape, individual behavior patterns, and social values. The Council sought to inform each resident that he or she was a part of this larger whole, this community. So it appealed to the "entire neighborhood" to submit items for the Council's newspaper even if they were "of interest to you and your friends only" and reminded its readers, "This is a Community, in every sense of the word. Ties of church, work and many other interests bind us together. Our problems are the same. As we come to realize this, our community-sense, we can work together to solve them." Believing they could extrapolate individual spatial behaviors and social loyalties to a more complex level of cooperation was a crucial gamble by the Council's leaders.[5]

Equally strategic was the repeated reference to churchmen and churches to lead off the list of people supportive of the Council and the list of ties binding residents together. Having a dominant religion that was in a transitional phase of moving away from the divisiveness of nationality helped Meegan and the Council gain legitimacy with the local population. Alinsky, who soon left to found the Industrial Areas Foundation, appreciated this circumstance, as evinced in a piece he wrote for the National Conference of Juvenile Agencies in early 1940. "More than ninety per cent of the population of the 'Back of the Yards' community are Catholic in religion," noted Alinsky. "It is the Catholic Church which serves as the medium through which these people express their hopes, desires and aspirations. The Catholic Church is an integral and dynamic factor in the experiences and lives of the people of 'Back of the Yards.' It brings them into the world, gives them a large part of what little feeling of security they possess and presides at the ceremonies when they depart this life." In his subsequent work, Alinsky recognized the power that religious agencies inherently possessed for moving parishioners toward a "higher" good. This alliance between the local centers of spirituality and the Back of the Yards Neighborhood Council was so strong that parishes from neighboring areas, including McKinley Park, joined the Council. So did Saint Martini's Lutheran Church. Congratulatory advertisements placed in the 30 April 1941 issue of the *Journal* by various parishes (and even Bishop Sheil) reveal how quickly the bond between the Council and the churches was cemented. The advertisement from Saint Michael's parish read, "Back of the Yards Neighborhood Council Is Consistent with Real Catholic Action." The one sponsored by Sacred Heart Parish stated,

"Catholic Social Teaching Presupposes the Union of Church, Labor and Business. Because We Have the Back of the Yards Neighborhood Council This Program Is Being Carried Out." The church-Council bonds became enduring.[6]

Another effective strategy was the subtle introduction of the term "Back of the Yards" as the new designation for the community. Residents' recognition of a neighborhood name is understood to foster unity and identity. "Back o' the yards" had a long history along the streets to both sides of Ashland Avenue north of Forty-seventh Street. A song with thirteen verses (aptly titled "Back o' the Yards") had been written in 1924 heralding the grand old days of the 1870s and 1880s. But as noted earlier, by the late 1930s "Town of Lake" had become the common name for the area. It was a neutral, even benevolent term compared with designations that resurrected images of *The Jungle*, Bubbly Creek, the city dumps, and the wretched poverty that had existed south and west of Packingtown during the early years of the century. "Town of Lake" was historically more accurate than such alternatives as "New City," the university-assigned designation that, for residents, referred only to the police station on Forty-seventh Street. But Meegan and his associates at the Council gambled on a designation that made an almost boastful reference to the stockyards and packinghouses. They used it as a badge honoring endurance, resilience, and stubbornness. Residents were heralded for refusing to succumb to the industrial and environmental elements weighing them down. Meegan admitted to me that he used the term intentionally to break away from the more familiar "Town of Lake." He wanted to give the Council a forceful moniker that relied upon pride to make it work. And residents admit Meegan's plan succeeded. Even those who lived on the southwestern edge of the community and had become comfortable with the "Town of Lake" designation capitulated to the salesmanship of Joe Meegan. "Back of the Yards" amalgamated the place ties that residents already felt for particular neighborhoods and for specific recreation centers (parks, movie houses, dance halls, and the like) and projected them onto a larger plane—the plane of the entire community. The stockyards, packinghouses, and railroads marked the community off from adjoining areas and eventually came to represent symbolically the "inner world" of the Back of the Yards.[7]

Differences between the Back of the Yards Neighborhood Council and predecessors such as the Stockyards Community Council were numerous, but two important ones center on leadership and goals. Although Joseph Meegan was technically from the other side of the tracks (east of Halsted—and rest assured, residents knew where he came from), he was still a native South Sider who, in spite of his Irish ancestry, was accepted as a local boy with some rather impressive ambitions. If in later years Meegan had used his position as the Council's executive director (a post he was appointed to from the beginning) to run for political office, the Council probably would have disappeared within a few years, if not months. Instead he remained in the neighborhood to become a very big fish in a rather small pond. When it turned out he did not use the Council merely as a stepping-stone, Meegan earned the grudging appreciation if not always admiration of the locals. They eventually came to recognize that his success meant they too benefited in some manner. His gains, even in terms of reputation, ultimately had positive consequences for the community at large.

From the beginning, the Council's goals reflected residents' concerns. The first announced agenda contained little fluff or abstract posturing. The Council wanted an infant welfare station, low-cost medical and dental clinics, a large day nursery (a backhanded slap at the settlement), elimination of disease-breeding conditions, local extension of National Youth Administration programs, conversion of empty lots into outdoor recreation sites, purchase of a summer camp, establishment of "play streets" where no automobiles would be allowed, support of "adequate relief standards," and improved housing conditions. Only the demands for "priority rights of local residents to local jobs" and a "federal housing project" were unlikely to be met within a reasonable time. (And the Council did coerce the business community into supporting the former.) Within five months of the Council's first communitywide meeting, an infant welfare station had opened in the field house at Davis Square Park, home to the Council until wartime. Following up on a suggestion first promoted at the Packingtown Youth Committee meeting, the Council immediately set out to acquire the railroad land at Forty-seventh and Damen—the old city dumps—to build a playing field. In February 1940 fill-in work started, and by July donkey baseball games inaugurated the "Back of the Yards Community Field." For the next forty years the field was home to softball and hardball leagues as well as the Council's most spectacular annual affair, the Back of the Yards Fair, which was staged for the first time in September 1940. The carnival/festival remained the community's most important annual event for decades.[8]

The Council's successes during its first decade of operation were legendary for the time and have been chronicled in both popular and scholarly accounts.[9] The organization's attention at first focused primarily on improving the quality of life for the community's school-age youngsters. This included, by 1941, a free milk program using surplus milk from the United States Department of Agriculture. The program continued during the war as the government took over its operation. The Council's success at improving nutritional, medical, and recreational services for the area's children depended on cooperation from the many "disparate elements" within the Back of the Yards. Support from the local Catholic churches grew stronger as the Council carefully avoided projects that might trigger the clergy's opposition. The participation of several assistant pastors in the Council's work during 1939 and 1940 eventually won over even the most cynical of the clergy. The business community fell in step even faster. Four months after the Council was officially established at its July 1939 communitywide assembly, a subcommittee obtained an agreement from several Back of the Yards businesses to hire local people first. The *Journal* headlined the cooperating merchants and even ran a six-paragraph article in late November detailing the enthusiasm of Star Credit Clothing Store on Ashland for hiring "local people." The paper urged its readers to "Buy Back of the Yards" because merchants were sympathetic to residents' employment needs. By the following April the Chamber of Commerce had joined the Council, setting the stage for years of friendly cooperation and mutual support.[10]

The *Journal Town of Lake* managed to outdo even the business community in its rush to endorse the Council. The publishers' enthusiasm for the Council spilled over the front page in every issue beginning in September 1939. Two months later an incredible event took place as the paper's owners, John Haffner and Aaron Hurwitz, turned over control of the *Journal* to the Council. Without warning, Haffner and Hurwitz changed the paper's name from *Journal Town of Lake* to the *Back of the Yards Journal* in its 16 November 1939 issue. In a front-page editorial, Joe Meegan invited readers to "Meet Your Newspaper." He claimed that under its new banner the *Journal* was "the first community paper in the nation written by its readers and acting truly as the mirror of life in our Back of the Yards. Its purposes are to unite all organizations within the Back of the Yards to try to better conditions. We are especially interested in church, labor and business. Besides being educational, all articles are newsy and timely. They are of interest to school children as well as adults. . . . Every person, regardless of race, creed or color, is a potential reporter."

The entire paper, from its front page to the advertisements inside, reflected the new policy. "Parish Notes" listed church activities, both spiritual and social. There was even a rare entry titled "Mexican News Notes." The Council followed through on its interest in bridging the gap between the Eastern Europeans and the Mexicans by including the latter in the leadership of the Council. The Council under Meegan became an outspoken supporter of the Mexican population's request for its own church. The renovated *Journal* embraced ethnicity in general, lauding the assimilation of "Poles, Bohemians, Lithuanians, Germans, Irish" in "the Great Melting Pot That Constitutes Back of the Yards." The paper applauded the cooperation of all sectors within the community: "Church, labor and business sitting around the Back of the Yards table; Poles, Lithuanians, Germans, Irish, Czechs sitting together." The tone was upbeat and self-congratulatory as the *Journal* became the voice of the Council, even donating a week's proceeds to the organization. The year-end summary of local achievements in 1940 reads very differently from its predecessors in prior years. By 1940, though the Chamber of Commerce and improvements in the commercial landscape around Forty-seventh and Ashland continued to receive some mention, the emphasis had switched to the achievements of the Council and to church projects such as the new high school under construction at Saint Joseph's or the celebration of Lithuanian

Day at Holy Cross. The *Journal* had clearly become a representative "voice of the community."[11]

The two local agencies that failed to fall in behind the Council were the settlement house and the Democratic party establishment. With Mary McDowell gone, the settlement house lacked an influential leader who might have ensured its role in the Council's opening campaign. Instead the settlement stood by while Meegan and Alinsky assembled a strong grass-roots coalition that could ignore the settlement house entirely. The settlement staff clearly appreciated the incipient community spirit apparent in the late 1930s. In a September 1939 data sheet, the settlement's goals were uncharacteristically expanded to include promoting "neighborhood unity." The document went on to note that the new "Back of the Yards Community Council" and its interaction with the settlement were "a matter of importance for the settlement's future relationships in the community." But the Council wanted nothing to do with the settlement. Meegan viewed the social service center as an outpost for do-gooders who did not accept the residents' folkways and values. He insisted that the settlement had done "nothing" for the community west of Ashland Avenue.[12]

On the other hand, the Democratic party did wield considerable influence within the local area. The party's initial reluctance to support the Council arose from the bosses' suspicion about Meegan's personal ambitions and the Council's ultimate purpose. The Back of the Yards, as defined for this book, made up the northeastern third of the Twenty-ninth Ward until 1921. After that date it was divided between the Thirteenth and Fifteenth Wards. (A sixteen-block strip from Forty-seventh to Fifty-fifth between Loomis and Racine was partitioned off as a piece of the Fourteenth Ward.) In 1931 the political boundaries were once again redrawn, and this time the community was partitioned among three aldermanic districts, the Twelfth, Fourteenth, and Fifteenth Wards. Gerrymandering never interfered with the handsome Democratic majorities posted in every election after 1921. With one exception in each case, wards in which Back of the Yards residents voted delivered a minimum of 61 percent majorities to the Democratic candidates for alderman from 1925 to 1939 and 58 percent majorities (or better) to every Democratic candidate for mayor from 1923 to 1939. Several Democratic aldermen were virtually unopposed, and in his 1935 landslide, Mayor Edward Kelly garnered between 79 and 91 percent of the votes in the Twelfth, Fourteenth, and Fifteenth Wards.

In presidential elections, Back of the Yards wards were only slightly less routine in their loyalty to the Democratic party. After supporting Woodrow Wilson's successful reelection campaign in 1916, the community's voters (Twenty-ninth Ward) followed the national trend toward Republican Warren G. Harding four years later by an overwhelming vote of 14,547 to 6,186. In the next presidential contest, the new Thirteenth Ward returned to the Democratic fold with a 61 percent majority, while the Fifteenth Ward, representing

South Side "suburbanites," backed Republican Calvin Coolidge by a slightly larger margin. Political normality returned by 1928, however, when Al Smith attracted 81 percent of the Fourteenth Ward's vote and 58 percent of the Fifteenth Ward's count. In the next three elections, Franklin D. Roosevelt won the support of 74, 80, and 77 percent of the voters in the Twelfth Ward, while the Fourteenth Ward reported 82, 83, and 77 percent majorities for the former New York governor. The Fifteenth Ward chipped in with victory margins of 71, 76, and 67 percent. Back of the Yards voters held FDR in the same esteem as did many other Americans. He was a "savior" and a "redeemer." This adoration permitted him to amass majorities in Back of the Yards wards that exceeded his margins across both the city and the state.[13]

In spite of their strong sympathies for the personality and programs of Franklin Roosevelt, politics in general did not excite Back of the Yards residents. Only a small segment of the population regularly concerned itself with the political process. Some immigrants never became citizens; others who did voted only when it was financially prudent or politically necessary. Politics was seldom discussed around the kitchen table or on the stoop even in the 1930s. The one exception was the career of Anton Cermak, a Bohemian from the Pilsen community who became Chicago's "complete ethnic politician" and its mayor during the early 1930s. For people from the Back of the Yards, Cermak proved that an immigrant could climb to the top of the political pile. When he was killed in a failed assassination attempt on President-Elect Roosevelt and was replaced by a South Side Irishman, Edward Kelly, however, it took the edge off the political excitement of Bohemians and Slovaks in the Back of the Yards.

Although residents commonly blamed Herbert Hoover, the Republicans, and the bankers for the depression, these accusations seem to have been almost perfunctory. Hard times during the 1930s did not trigger rebellion or political unrest. Instead an underdeveloped, even immature, political culture existed in the Back of the Yards. Politicians were seen as remote figures who wielded great power but, like the depression, were beyond the influence of individual citizens. Among local Democratic chieftains, Fourteenth Ward alderman James J. McDermott maintained his public presence among the common folk by sponsoring splashy events such as the annual Young Men's Jefferson Club Softball League and by appearing at Fourth of July celebrations in Sherman Park. His principal contribution toward the betterment of the local community centered on the needs of the Town of Lake business community. For example, McDermott and his Twelfth and Fifteenth Ward colleagues, Bryan Hartnett and James Kovarik, backed the widening of the Forth-ninth Street railroad viaduct on Ashland Avenue and the repaving of Marshfield Avenue—but only where it gave access to rear-lot parking for stores along Ashland. McDermott promoted the construction of a separate library building at Sherman Park by the WPA, and with Alderman Kovarik he pushed through the project for an enlarged water main under Forty-seventh

Street. Expensive projects that looked out for the interests of the business community or promoted the local patronage system received the complete attention of local politicians. Programs to ensure weekly garbage pickup or eradicate rats seldom engendered comparable enthusiasm.[14]

In part the disdainful attitude the Democratic party leaders demonstrated toward the Back of the Yards arose because ward committeemen like McDermott did not live in the community; nor did Bryan Hartnett, alderman of the Twelfth Ward, which included the Polish and Slovak areas west of Wood Street and north of Forth-ninth. James Kovarik, on the other hand, had lived in the Back of the Yards since the early 1890s. He served as alderman for two terms until 1923, when the city switched from two aldermen per ward to one. Kovarik, with grace, surrendered the Twenty-ninth Ward office to his colleague Thomas Byrne and instead took a position with the Board of Election Commissioners. He returned to the city council in 1931 and remained on it until his death in 1947, when he was replaced by Frank Micek, another Bohemian from the Back of the Yards.

Ethnicity continued to influence voting behavior in Chicago during the 1920s and 1930s, though with diminishing intensity over time. The ethnic press in particular continued to promote fellow nationals without regard to party. *Denni Hlasatel* urged support in 1922 for Joseph Sabath, a Bohemian Jew, by arguing that "all Bohemian voters should especially regard it their duty to go to the polls Monday and give him their votes. He is the only countryman of ours who has gained such a high office." Twelve years later the German-language *Abendpost* was no less clear on this point: "This newspaper has always advocated giving preference to candidates of German extraction without regard to party affiliations." It qualified this sweeping endorsement by later inserting the proviso that voting by ethnicity should follow only if "these candidates are trustworthy and are capable of filling the offices to which they aspire." Although groups like the Slovaks and the Lithuanians embraced the Democratic party wholeheartedly, by the 1930s residents had begun to expect repayment for their loyalty in currency more meaningful than Fourth of July hot dogs. Regular refuse collection and enforcement of housing codes were more deeply appreciated. Thus, when the Back of the Yards Neighborhood Council offered a concrete program whose enactment would improve neighborhood life along each street, residents reacted with general assent and support. They would no longer be bought off with fine speeches and softball leagues.[15]

For this reason, at first the politicians were wary of Joe Meegan and his associates: with characteristic brashness and self-assurance, Meegan looked like a ready candidate for political office. Although in the end he did not harbor such ambitions, the Council's executive director knew how to work both sides of the political fence. When Republican Dwight Green was elected governor of Illinois in 1940, Meegan arranged to have himself and another member of the Council invited to the inauguration. He even managed to meet the governor and his family, although Green had won only 34, 30, and 42 percent of the votes in Back of the Yards wards. (The lifelessness of the local Republican party after Mayor Kelly's landslide of 1935—followed in the next year by the Roosevelt deluge—was so readily apparent that an irate Republican from the Fourteenth Ward felt compelled to write to the *Journal* and protest, "Yes, We Have Republicans in the 14th Ward.") In general, then, the Back of the Yards Neighborhood Council confronted a political environment that was dominated by the Democratic party. Only after Meegan had proved his sincerity as a noncompetitive promoter of "his" community did the Democratic machine finally agree to establish first a tentative and later a warmer relationship with Meegan and the Council.[16]

The Council finally provided the Back of the Yards with a sufficient "squeak" to be heard in the political back rooms of Chicago. Even as New Deal programs shrank, during its first two years of operation the Council aggressively solicited additional federal funds for the area through the Works Progress Administration and the National Youth Administration, both of which had already been involved with the unemployed in the community. As it was for Americans in other hard-hit corners of America, work relief was always preferable to handouts. Nationwide, 78 percent of WPA funds supported construction in the public sector. Thus Back of the Yards men labored on the Illinois and Michigan Canal, on a major renovation at Municipal Airport, and on smaller WPA projects, including repainting local schools and cleaning up city parks.

New sidewalks were installed throughout the community, as were streets and sewers along several blocks. (Forty-five years later the city still had a backlog of nearly five hundred WPA streets that had not received major improvements since the New Deal.) By late 1938, over fifty-nine miles of streets had been rehabilitated within the Twelfth, Fourteenth, and Fifteenth Wards. In addition to the Forty-ninth Street viaduct construction and the paving of the Marshfield Avenue "wastelands," a major WPA project was the construction of seven miles of major sewer lines along Ashland Avenue. Public Works Administration funds partially financed a new pumping station north of the stockyards that was intended to work in conjunction with the new sewer system to combat flooding on the South Side. Several dozen WPA and National Youth Administration (NYA) workers were employed by the settlement house during the course of the 1930s, mostly as recreation and crafts assistants. Significantly, they do not appear to have been local youths. The settlement also participated in vocational guidance programs conducted by the WPA, including one ill-fated effort to influence young women in the Back of the Yards to enter the domestic service sector of the economy. The Civilian Conservation Corps (CCC), which eventually enlisted over three million recruits nationwide, also recruited youths from the Back of the Yards. The CCC, perhaps more than other programs, added a touch of worldliness to the work relief experience; Back of the Yards men were assigned to downstate

One Works Progress Administration project in the Back of the Yards was this modern library in Sherman Park, fronting on Racine Avenue. Courtesy of Chicago Historical Society. 1952 photograph by Mildred Mead. ICHi-22790.

Illinois, to the Upper Peninsula of Michigan, and even to California. The geographical parochialism that was inevitable among these youths was, if not entirely eliminated, at least diminished as a result of these opportunities. The CCC experience may have also eased their transition to military duty during the upcoming war. [17]

The Council also persuaded the National Youth Administration to invest in Back of the Yards youth. Up to that time, NYA job funds (other than money assigned to the settlement house) had been distributed through the local high schools as part of the Roosevelt administration's campaign to encourage youngsters to complete their educations by providing jobs. However, this program was less than effective in a community like the Back of the Yards, where many teenagers had already dropped out of high school to look for work. A second NYA program, intended to offer job training as well as placement for those not attending classes, was far better suited to Back of the Yards youngsters. Joe Meegan became friends with Michael Howatt, director of the NYA in Chicago and subsequently succeeded, first, in having Davis Square Park named a recruitment center and, second, in freeing up job assignments for local youths. During a week in late November 1939, 150 residents received NYA jobs through the Council's intercession. By March of the next year 875 young men and women had received such jobs, and even

Alderman Bryan Hartnett had to admit that Council had done "a splendid job in doing something in a practical way for local youths." Over the months, the Council continued to post job listings, and normally within a week's time it was able to place every person who registered. By 1941 the program was paying off as young people with NYA work experience found regular employment.[18]

The influx of federal money came at a time when the local economy finally showed signs of improvement. The Index of Factory Employment for the city of Chicago rose during 1936 from 68.7 (with 1925–27 = 100) in January to 80.2 in November. By April 1937 the settlement house noted "some re-employment at Armour's . . . and also some openings in factories." Early in the next year the local employment outlook was described as good compared with the previous year, and by late 1938 several hundred workers at the International Harvester tractor plant on Thirty-first Street had been called back. A year later the monthly settlement reports repeatedly remarked on the "decided upturn in employment" communitywide. By late 1941, five weeks before the Japanese attack on Pearl Harbor, the staff complained about too many job opportunities! Jobs were allegedly enticing both men and women into the work force, leaving their children unsupervised. Although the *Journal* continued to run a heartbreaking column titled "I Need a Job," the worst effects of the Great Depression were decidedly behind the community by 1938–39. Undoubtedly part of the reason the business community launched its "Buy in Town of Lake" campaign in 1937 was its awareness that residents had a few more pennies to spend. How long it took for the depression's more insidious effects to fade from memory is harder to measure. World War II came along and disrupted community life so thoroughly that the economic difficulties of the 1930s were swept away by the immediate task at hand. As elsewhere in the United States, the depression was not so much solved as overwhelmed.[19]

8

POSTSCRIPT
After World War II

World War II suspended routine community life just as effectively in the Back of the Yards as it did across the country. For example, at Saint Basil's Church the number of weddings in 1943 was half that in 1941. At Saint Michael's, nuptials performed in 1943 were one-third the number in 1941. Plans for tomorrow were once again put on hold. Lives filled with uncertainty, thanks to the Great Depression, had only begun to ease when along came wartime. Although the lingering economic insecurities of the depression were subsumed by the war, social and cultural habits from the interwar years did not vanish so readily. If anything, spatial patterns related to occupation were reinforced as women working in the war industries and associated manufacturing concerns in the early 1940s became even more familiar with "their city" and more confident in moving about it for employment and recreation. When normality returned after the war, some young families migrated to the city's southwestern communities of Marquette Park and Mount Greenwood or to western suburbs like Cicero: but most Back of the Yarders reestablished family life in a community that possessed new self-awareness and confidence.[1]

The success of the Back of the Yards Neighborhood Council in the postwar period, widely chronicled in the popular literature of that day, came about because the organization continued to promote projects that made sense to residents. A complete history of postwar Back of the Yards—including its Council, churches, and parks and the Forty-seventh and Ashland shopping district, as well as the eventual shutdown of Packingtown by the early 1960s—remains to be told. The setting, a one-time immigrant slum, was transformed over the first half of the twentieth century. It developed—in spite of the powerful consequences of the Great Depression—from a poverty-

147

ridden, ethnically divided "jungle" to a struggling blue-collar, inner-city community. The values and habits of the postwar era were shaped during the tension-filled years of the Great Depression, when nothing was taken for granted and little hope was placed in the future. Residents became cautious, defensive, and parochial. They were proud of what they had accomplished in spite of obstacles placed in their—and their parents'—paths, and they became particularly stubborn over the thought of surrendering their slice of Chicago to the next generation of newcomers. The communal equilibrium achieved between the wars could not sustain dramatic change.

In its role as representative for the community at large, the Neighborhood Council became the social order's most outspoken defender. So when the Council provided garbage cans to any residents who needed them, persuaded local financial institutions to make low-interest loans for home improvements, prosecuted landlords who violated housing codes, resisted attempts by industrial developers to effect zoning changes that might damage the quality of residential life, and even promoted a middle-income, single-family, suburban type of housing project on the prairie west of Damen, residents supported the organization wholeheartedly. Pride in the community intensified when a 1953 campaign led to the repair or improvement of nine thousand houses within ten years. Residential conservation became not only a slogan but also a financial and emotional investment for the locals. Anything that might jeopardize the new social order would not be welcomed after the sacrifices made over more than a half-century of "surviving."[2]

In his last years, Saul Alinsky became intensely critical of Back of the Yards residents in general and of the Council in particular. He insisted that at first he had considered the community a "David of equality for all mankind against the Goliath of prejudice, segregation, and the repression of the prevailing *Have's*." He quoted Governor Adlai Stevenson's flowery praise of the Council: "If I were asked to choose in all America a single agency which I felt most admirably represented all that our democracy stands for, whose aims most faithfully reflected our ideals of brotherhood, tolerance, charity, and the dignity of the individual, I would select the Back of the Yards Council." But praise shifted to condemnation as Alinsky began to characterize residents as "segregationists" who feared change and the loss of material possessions. He had not always felt so repelled by the Back of the Yards. In one of his few comments on the Neighborhood Council in the period immediately after its creation, the Council's "technical consultant" observed, "I fully agree with your proud conviction that America should look at you. The spirit of democracy probably burns brighter today in the Back of the Yards Chicago, than anywhere else in the nation." From founding fathers and mothers who pioneered a new spirit of democracy that "is truly a torch of hope in a world today torn by distrust, bigotry and hatred," his characterization changed to "segregationists" who had become "part of the city's establishment and are desperately trying to keep their community unchanged." What

In 1956, a portion of Packingtown (including the double-decker cattle run) was demolished in preparation for new construction *(above)*. Note Wilson and Company plant on west side of Ashland with Belt Line tracks between Wilson complex and the Central Manufacturing District's Pershing Road development. Courtesy of Chicago Historical Society. ICHi-22797.

Demolition of Wilson and Company buildings in 1959 *(below)*. Courtesy of Chicago Historical Society. Photograph by Clarence W. Hines. ICHi-20647.

Abandoned packinghouse in the late 1980s. Photograph by P. Jablonsky.

happened between 1940, when Alinsky held the Back of the Yards and its Council to be "truly historic," and these last remarks written a little over a quarter-century later?[3]

Part of Alinsky's disillusionment may have stemmed from personal reasons, but the key factor was undoubtedly the community's unwillingness to accept racial integration during the 1960s—a reaction typical of Chicago in general. As late as 1970, the "New City" area was 95.6 percent white. By 1980 it was 57.5 percent white as black Chicago expanded into the southeastern corner of the community and, later, the Spanish-speaking population increased dramatically, especially in the oldest corner of the community near Packingtown and the Belt Line tracks. Today estimates place the racial composition of the Back of the Yards at less than one-third white, with the rest divided between African Americans and Hispanics. Each group has its own community organization. After 1970 the Back of the Yards experienced a dramatic demographic shift reminiscent of the turn of the century, when tens of thousands of other "outsiders" poured into the four-flat frame tenements, only to create their own community in the years that followed.

The stockyards are gone, removed by the brute strength of earthmoving equipment during the 1950s and 1960s. Not the slightest evidence remains of an incredible complex that processed millions of cattle, hogs, and sheep

Davis Square Park's fieldhouse in the late 1980s. Photograph by P. Jablonsky.

during nearly a century of operation. Abandoned packinghouses, frayed remnants of the greatest meat-packing center the world has ever seen, sit amid weeds, garbage, and streets with crater-sized potholes. Conrail still uses a good portion of the Belt Line tracks, whereas the Central Manufacturing District along Pershing Road struggles to keep itself from becoming yet another in the string of empty-shell factories so common throughout the Near South Side of Chicago.

The Back of the Yards itself remains a distinct residential district with clear vestiges of its past. The housing stock sags a bit more, but then it is now a century old in many areas. Abandoned tenements, once an anomaly, are more frequently seen, as are empty lots where house fires have acted as a force of urban renewal. But along other streets homes are rehabilitated by owners as another generation of working-class folk settles into the community. Children still fill the streets around Davis Square Park, much as they did when Mary McDowell first came to "save" the residents from their environment—and their own cultures. Fire hydrants are still opened on muggy July afternoons, and neighbors still squat on front stoops in the heavy air of summer evenings. Vendors hawk their wares along the community's residential blocks, though now the language of the street, if not English, is Spanish rather than Polish or Slovak.

As noted in chapter 7, the former city dumps received a much-needed facelift in the months before Pearl Harbor. During the 1950s and 1960s, once a year these softball fields were transformed into fairgrounds for the biggest of the community's festivals, the week-long Back of the Yards Neighborhood Carnival. The Council managed to bring together not only residents of the community but also suburbanites whose families might have once lived in this "jungle." The scarred remains of the community's fairgrounds sat abandoned for many years, until the recent construction of yet another uninspiring shopping mall. The intersection of Forty-seventh and Ashland, the great shopping district, continues to attract crowds of pedestrians during the course of a day, though Peoples Theater has been subdivided into clothing stores and the first floor of Depositors State Bank now bears the tired facade of a Walgreen's drugstore. A visitor who takes the time to look above the first floor, however, will frequently find pieces of the community's history etched in stone—the names of former (usually the first) commercial residents. A poignant example is on the southwest corner of Forty-eighth and Ashland, where a dirty stone banner above a window filled with posters advertising discounts on shoes, dresses, and fanny packs identifies the site of Sherman State Bank.

Historian Olivier Zunz has asked the searching question, Is the sense of community best expressed within a spatial context?[4] Leaving aside for the moment the issue of "best," it is clear that community spirit in the Back of the Yards was dependent upon—indeed, was generated by—spatial forces. The culture of the community evolved in part from spatial habits and territorial loyalties. But the arrival of yet another contingent of newcomers during the 1960s and 1970s was a challenge that has unfortunately not been met. Both individual and collective defenses against the "new outsiders" were evident throughout the sixties and seventies, and it is unclear whether an updated "sense of community" can be rediscovered. I hope that this story of geography, ethnicity, community, and everyday life in the Back of the Yards demonstrates that inevitable change need not destroy what has been built with such pride and determination. The past can serve as a foundation if it is seen as a beginning and not as an end that becomes enshrined and thereby forever resistant to the newest "scouts."

Notes

Works that are cited in the notes using only the author's last name and a short title can be found listed in full, with publication information, in the References.

Introduction

1. Sanders, *Professional Radical*, 30–31.

2. See, for example, Bushnell, "Some Social Aspects of the Chicago Stock Yards, Chapter One, Industry at the Chicago Stockyards"; Breckinridge and Abbott, "Housing Conditions in Chicago"; Talbert, *Chicago's Stockyards Community*; Montgomery, *American Girl*; Kennedy, *Wages*; Miller, "Rents and Housing Conditions in the Stock Yards District of Chicago" (M.A. thesis); and Abbott, *Tenements*. Other reports and surveys can be found in the University of Chicago Settlement House Papers and the Mary McDowell Papers at the Chicago Historical Society. See later notes for specific citations. For a cogent discussion of this scholarly tradition at the University of Chicago, see Stow Person, *Ethnic Studies at Chicago, 1905–45* (Urbana: University of Illinois Press, 1987).

3. Slayton, *Back of the Yards*.

4. Somer, *Personal Space*, 4.

5. In using the terms "Americanization," "acculturation," and "assimilation" I have intentionally taken—to borrow Philip Gleason's phrase—"a more relaxed position" toward these concepts. The Back of the Yards between the wars was moving toward greater sociocultural heterogeneity while at the same time it retained meaningful ties to the first generation and the Old Country. By 1941 structural assimilation was under way, though hardly complete and irreversible. Individual rates of acculturation varied, of course, but overall the neighborhood moved steadily toward inclusiveness and further away from divisiveness based on ethnic origins. Gleason, "American Identity and Americanization," 39. See also Harold J. Abramson, "Assimilation and Pluralism," in *Harvard Encyclopedia of American Ethnic Groups*, ed. Stephan Thernstrom (Cambridge: Harvard University Press, 1980).

6. My notions of community and its composition in nineteenth- and twentieth-century urban America have been greatly influenced by Thomas Bender's essays in *Community and Social Change in America*.

7. Somer, *Personal Space*, 10.

8. Tuan, *Topophilia*, 214. Among works that are especially suggestive for historians are Peirce Lewis's and D. W. Meinig's articles in Meinig, *Interpretation of Ordinary Landscapes;* David Ward's essays in *Cities and Immigrants;* and Michael Conzen, ed., *The Making of the American Landscape* (New York: Unwin Hyman, 1990).

9. Asa Briggs, "The Sense of Place," in Briggs, *Collected Essays*, 1:87–88; Conzen, "Community Studies, Urban History, and American Local History," 289–90.

10. Aaron, "Treachery of Recollection," 7, 10; Grele, "On Using Oral History Collections," 572; Sternsher, *Hitting Home*, 3–4; Bodnar, *Workers' World*, 2–5; Bodnar, Simon, and Weber, *Lives of Their Own*, 269–70; Banks, *First Person America*, xii–xxv. For a general introduction to the use of oral history, see Herbert T. Hoover, "Oral History in the United States," in *The Past before Us*, ed. Michael Kammen (Ithaca: Cornell University Press, 1980), 391–407. For a warning on inappropriate uses of oral history, see Michael H. Frisch, "The Memory of History," *Radical History Review* 25 (October 1981): 9–23. On the shortcomings of recollections gathered long after the events as opposed to contemporary observations, see McElvaine, *Down and Out*, 4, 367 n. 4. For an introduction to life histories as used in ethnographic research, see L. L. Langness and Gelya Frank, *Lives: An Anthropological Approach to Biography* (Novato, Calif.: Chandler and Sharp, 1981).

11. Aguilar, "Insider Research," 15.

Chapter 1: The Setting

1. Wade, *Chicago's Pride*, 11–15, 25–33, 47–48; Walsh, *Meat Packing*, 11, 12, 20–21, 24, 46, 50, 51, 57, 59, 60, 63; Yeager, *Competition and Regulation*, 11–13; Commission on Chicago Historical and Architectural Landmarks, *Union Stock Yard Gate*, 6–8; Grand, *Stockyards*, 8–9; Fowler, *Men, Meat and Miracles*, 17–18, 39; Solzman, *Waterway Industrial Sites*, 24; Herbst, *Negro*, 5.

2. Wade, *Chicago's Pride*, 48–50; Yeager, *Competition and Regulation*, 14, 30; Pierce, *Chicago*, 2:93; Commission, *Gate*, 8; Grand, *Stockyards*, 9; Fowler, *Men, Meat and Miracles*, 40; Abbott, *Tenements*, 133.

3. Wade, *Chicago's Pride*, 48–57, 82; Walsh, *Meat Packing*, 73–74, 75, 79, 85, 104; Grand, *Stockyards*, 9–10; Pierce, *Chicago*, 2:94; *Week in Chicago*, 35; Barrett, *Work and Community*, 19; Rosen, *Limits of Power*, 92, 152–60; Fowler, *Men, Meat and Miracles*, 41, 44–46.

4. Wade, *Chicago's Pride*, 53, 180; Walsh, *Meat Packing*, 80; Grand, *Stockyards*, 24, 30–32, 90–91; Commission, *Gate*, 11; photographs of the National Live Stock Bank, Chicago Historical Society; Herr, *Seventy Years*, 22, 160; Pierce, *Chicago*, 3:192n, 204; German Press Club of Chicago, *Prominent Citizens and Industries of Chicago*, 87.

5. Wade, *Chicago's Pride*, 53, 56; Dainty, *Darling-Delaware Centenary*, 127; Grand, *Stockyards*, 219–20; Fowler, *Men, Meat and Miracles*, 41–43.

6. Wade, *Chicago's Pride*, 56, 181; Joseph Hamzik, "Saga of Dexter Park Ave., Remnant of a Bygone Era," *Back of the Yards Journal*, 20 May 1970, Brighton Park Branch, Chicago Public Library; Grand, *Stockyards*, 11, 15; *Chicago Tribune* clipping, 11 June 1947, Box 1, Chicago Stockyards Collection, University of Illinois at Chicago Library; Pierce, *Chicago*, 3:140; Fowler, *Men, Meat and Miracles*, 4.

7. Commission, *Gate*, 2–4.

8. Commission, *Gate*, 8, 11; Grand, *Stockyards*, 15; *Week in Chicago*, 35; Wade, *Chicago's Pride*, 48, 99; Pierce, *Chicago*, 3:141.

9. Wade, *Chicago's Pride*, 65, 99–100; Fowler, *Men, Meat and Miracles*, 31–32, 34–35; Commission, *Gate*, 8–11; Pierce, *Chicago*, 3:108–9, 114–15, 119–20; Yeager,

Competition and Regulation, 16–17, 49–67; Slayton, *Back of the Yards,* 17; Barrett, *Work and Community,* 18–19; Herr, *Seventy Years,* 163–65, 192; German Press Club of Chicago, *Prominent Citizens,* 87–88.

10. Robert Mitchell, "The North American Past: Retrospect and Prospect," in Mitchell, ed., *North America,* 19. The discussion that follows draws upon dozens of photographs housed at the Chicago Historical Society. A major premise of this work, as noted in the Introduction, is that the cultural landscape (the entire local landscape including industrial, residential, and ethnic elements) greatly influenced the nature of everyday life in the Back of the Yards and ultimately helped to create a "sense of place" among residents. In turn, this territorial association significantly contributed to a growing sense of community during the 1930s. I acknowledge a debt to James Borchert and his creative use of photographs to personalize his moving study *Alley Life in Washington.* Especially important is his essay in appendix B, "Photographs and the Study of the Past." Most of the Chicago Historical Society photographs of the Back of the Yards can be found under the following headings: "Communities: Back of the Yards," "Stockyards," "Halsted" (Street), and "Ashland" (Avenue). Contemporary scholarly pieces that also include poignant photographs are Bushnell, "Some Social Aspects of the Chicago Stock Yards, Chapter One, Industry at the Chicago Stock Yards," and by the same author, "Some Social Aspects of the Chicago Stock Yards, Chapter Two, The Stock Yards Community at Chicago"; see also Breckinridge and Abbott, "Housing Conditions in Chicago." In addition, I have conducted field observations in the Back of the Yards and photographed the industrial and residential areas of the community in the company of individuals who lived there during the time under study.

11. Wilson, *McDowell,* 26; Simons, *Packingtown,* 10; Sanborn Map Company of New York, "Chicago: Packing Houses and Union Stockyards," 1901, Chicago Historical Society; Pierce, *Chicago,* 3:123–24; interviews with R. Johnston and S. M.; Commission, *Gate,* 10.

12. Simons, *Packingtown,* 9; Fowler, *Men, Meat and Miracles,* 44; interviews with A. Kloris, P. Jasaitas, S. M., E. Baranowsky, J. and C. Dahm, J. Fabian, J. and R. Gallik, Mrs. E. H., M. Jensen, M. Matusek, V. Mikolaitas, M. Shalack, S. Vasilenko, and F. and G. Young; Sinclair, *The Jungle,* 28; Slayton, *Back of the Yards,* 15.

13. Interviews with R. Johnston, S. M., and R. Jablonsky; Chicago Historical Society photographs; Leslie F. Orear and Stephen H. Diamond, *Out of the Jungle* (Chicago: Hyde Park Press, 1968); Grand, *Stockyards,* 15.

14. Chicago Historical Society photographs; Breckinridge, "Housing," passim; Bushnell, "Some Social Aspects," passim; Sinclair, *The Jungle,* 28; interview with F. and G. Young.

15. Lynch, *Image of the City,* 62–66; Miles Richardson, "Introduction," in Richardson, *Place: Experience and Symbol,* 1.

16. German Press Club of Chicago, *Prominent Citizens,* 80; Joseph Hamzik, "Early Railroads Caused Great Distress in Back of the Yards," *Back of the Yards Journal,* 30 December 1970, Brighton Park Branch, Chicago Public Library; *Chronological History of St. Augustine's Church,* 53; interviews with M. Dluhy, S. and S. Wozniak, and F. and G. Young. For a discussion of earlier efforts to establish safer railroad rights-of-way through residential areas of the city, see Rosen, *Limits of Power,* 135–39.

17. Hamzik, "Early Railroads."

18. These conclusions are based on daily behavioral patterns detailed in the oral histories as people spoke of living near these tracks. Particular mention should be made of the interviews with J. and R. Paluck and A. Suvada.

19. Wade, *Chicago's Pride*, chaps. 1 and 2.

20. Joseph Hamzik, "Portion of Pershing Road Was Once a Union Stock Yards Canal Slip," *Back of the Yards Journal*, 4 October 1972, Brighton Park Branch, Chicago Public Library; Pacyga, "Packinghouses," 79; Fowler, *Men, Meat and Miracles*, 35; interviews with A. Falat, E. Fredericks, J. Gelatka, Mrs. E. H., M. M., and J. Weber; Solzman, *Waterway*, 23–24.

21. Wilson, *McDowell*, 157–64; Central Manufacturing District, *Speaking of Ourselves*, 6–21, Stockyards Collection, Box 2, University of Illinois at Chicago Library; Joseph Hamzik, "General John J. Pershing Visits Back of the Yards," *Back of the Yards Journal*, 27 September 1972, Brighton Park Branch, Chicago Public Library; idem, "'Mr. Klu' Called All-America Congressman," *Brighton Park Life*, 14 December 1967, ibid.; idem, "Perishing Road Once Proposed as Highway," *Brighton Park Life*, 28 September 1972, ibid.

22. Bushnell, "Some Social Aspects," 302–3; Breckinridge, "Housing," 464–67; Chicago Historical Society photographs; interview with S. and S. Wozniak.

23. Wilson, *McDowell*, 144–45; Joseph Hamzik, "A Back of the Yards Alderman Once Defeated the World's Richest Woman," *Back of the Yards Journal*, 10 June 1970, Brighton Park Branch, Chicago Public Library.

24. Wilson, *McDowell*, 145–57; Simons, *Packingtown*, 11.

25. Carl Sandburg, "Chicago," in *Poems of the Midwest*, selected by Elizabeth McCausland (Cleveland: World, 1946), 27.

Chapter 2: The Context

1. Wade, *Chicago's Pride*, 69; James J. O'Toole, "The Story of 'Back of the Yards,'" in "'Back o' the Yards' 1870 to 1890," Chicago Historical Society; "The Back-of-the-Yards Area," 2–3, University of Chicago Settlement House Papers, Box 1, ibid.; Donnellan, "Back of the Yards Neighborhood Council" (M.A. thesis), 6–7; Slayton, *Back of the Yards*, 20–21.

2. Grand, *Stockyards*, 12; Wade, *Chicago's Pride*, 70–74; *Journal Town of Lake*, 16 September 1937; "Map of Chicago Showing Growth of the City by Annexations and Accretions," Chicago Historical Society.

3. O'Toole, "Story"; Wade, *Chicago's Pride*, 154, 157; Philpott, *Slum*, 14; Rosen, *Limits of Power*, 94.

4. *Illinois Staats-Zeitung*, 4 August 1879, Chicago Foreign Language Press Survey (hereafter cited as FLPS); Wade, *Chicago's Pride*, 157–58, 276; Pierce, *Chicago*, 3:333; Joseph Hamzik, "How 'Back of the Yards' Triumphed over Earlier Names," *Back of the Yards Journal*, 23 December 1970, Brighton Park Branch, Chicago Public Library; "Back-of-the-Yards Area," 4; Pacyga, "Packinghouses," 72–73; Miller, "Rents and Housing Conditions in the Stock Yards District of Chicago, 1923" (M.A. thesis), photograph of Laflin Street between pp. 6 and 7; Burgess, *Census Data, 1920*, 441–58.

5. "'Back o' the Yards' 1870 to 1890," Chicago Historical Society; Koenig, *Archdiocese*, 853–57; Zunz, *Changing Face of Inequality*, 67; "Back-of-the-Yards Area," 4; Herbst, *Negro*, 14, 19; interviews with R. R. Ehrlicher and M. Pratl; Fowler, *Men, Meat and Miracles*, 79; Burgess, *Census Data, 1920*, 451–52.

6. *St. Augustine's*, 19; Wade, *Chicago's Pride*, 158–59; Koenig, *Archdiocese*, 91, 93; Pacyga, "Packinghouses," 10; Bullard, "Distribution of Chicago's Germans, 1850–1914," 11, 26, Chicago Historical Society; Townsend, "Germans of Chicago" (Ph.D. diss.), 10; Burgess, *Census Data, 1920*, 457.

7. Herbst, *Negro*, 21; Donnellan, "Council," 15; Pacyga, "Packinghouses," 10; *St.*

Augustine's, 51; *Journal Town of Lake,* 14 September 1939; *Abendpost,* 5 August 1911, FLPS; Bodnar, *Transplanted,* 173; interview with J. and V. Lebensorger.

8. O'Toole, "Story"; *Journal Town of Lake,* 16 September 1937; Bushnell, "Some Social Aspects," 290; *St. Augustine's,* 21, 91, 208, 264; *Journal Town of Lake,* 16 September 1936; *Journal Town of Lake* clipping, 9 July 1939, Joseph Meegan Collection, Back of the Yards Branch, Chicago Public Library; interview with J. Weber.

9. Prohibition Survey of the Stock Yards Community, 1926, Mary McDowell Papers, Box 2, CHS; Kennedy, *Wages,* 62; Zygmuntowicz, "Back of the Yards Neighborhood Council and Its Health and Welfare Services" (M.S.W. thesis), 11.

10. Golab, *Destinations,* 142; Galush, "Both Polish and Catholic," 411; Greene, *Slavic Community,* 33, 47; Lopata, *Polish Americans,* 48–49; Somer, *Personal Space,* 15. Because the Mexican migration into the Back of the Yards came after 1920, I will not discuss it here; it will be treated at length in chapter 4.

11. Both quotations are from Galush, "Both Polish and Catholic," 407, 411, 423; Golab, *Destinations,* 143; Greene, *Slavic Community,* 47; Koenig, *Archdiocese,* 219, 363, 496, 519, 647, 870–73. For an introduction to the architecture of Chicago Catholic churches and to the connection between these centers of worship and the ethnicity of those who used them, see Edward R. Kantowicz, "To Build the Catholic City," *Chicago History* 14 (Fall 1985): 4–27.

12. Zygmuntowicz, "Back of the Yards," 5; Slayton, *Back of the Yards,* 21; Wade, *Chicago's Pride,* 157; Koenig, *Archdiocese,* 515.

13. Pacyga, "Crisis and Community," 168; *Journal Town of Lake,* 14 September 1939; Pacyga, "Packinghouses," 171, 196; Kantowicz, *Polish-American Politics in Chicago,* 149; Koenig, *Archdiocese,* 515–17; Greene, *For God,* chap. 6; Greene, *American Immigrant Leaders,* 114; Lopata, *Polish Americans,* 49–50; Bodnar, *Transplanted,* 156–57; interviews with G. Kober, M. Pratl, and J. Shimanis.

14. Wade, *Chicago's Pride,* 157; Herbst, *Negro,* 16; Burgess, *Census Data, 1920,* 443, 446, 451–52; Pacyga, "Packinghouses," 27, 182–83; Lopata, *Polish Americans,* 121; Koenig, *Archdiocese,* 496; *Journal Town of Lake,* 14 September 1939.

15. *Journal Town of Lake,* 14 September 1939; Rudolf Bubenicek, "History of Czechs in Chicago," mimeographed pages, Czechoslovak Museum, Library, and Archives; Janus Horak, "Assimilation of Czechs in Chicago" (Ph.D. diss.), 29, 42, 52, 75–76; Kennedy, *Wages,* 5–6; Cada, *Panorama,* 30–34.

16. Stolarik, *Growing up on the South Side,* 21, 66–67; *Journal Town of Lake,* 14 September 1939; Zahrobsky, "Slovaks in Chicago" (M.A. thesis), 18–22, 26, 33–40.

17. Koenig, *Archdiocese,* 645–47; Palickar, "Slovaks of Chicago," 187, 193; Abbott, *Tenements,* 134–35; Marriage and Baptism Records, Saint Michael the Archangel Parish.

18. Quotation from Fainhauz, *Lithuanians in Multi-ethnic Chicago until World War II,* 11–12, 35–36, 38–39, 96–97, 105, 114–15, 117, 139–140; Koenig, *Archdiocese,* 363–65; Greene, *For God,* 145, 149; Herbst, *Negro,* 23, 30n; Kucas, *Lithuanians in America,* 250.

19. Burgess, *Census Data, 1920,* 441, 443–46, 448, 451–52; *St. Augustine's,* 304–5; interviews with S. Maack and P. Mrowca.

20. Chicago Transit Authority, *Historical Information,* 4, 6, 12, 17, 34, 38, Chicago Historical Society; Lind, *Chicago Surface Lines,* 221, 228, 254, 309, 315, 320; "Report on the Chicago Elevated Road," Chicago Stockyards Collection, Box 1, University of Illinois at Chicago Library; *Chicago Tribune* clipping, 11 June 1947, ibid.

21. Breckinridge, "Housing Conditions," 433–36, 442–43.

22. Shaw, *Jack-Roller*, 34; Wilson, *McDowell*, 26–27; Abbott, *Tenements*, 138, 174.

23. Porteous, *Environment and Behavior*, 177–78; Breckinridge, "Housing Conditions," 449–52; Abbott, *Tenements*, 261.

24. Grand, *Stockyards*, 226–27; Breckinridge, "Housing Conditions," 464; Duis, *Saloon*, 102; interview with J. and C. Dahm.

25. Wright, *Building the Dream*, 128; Bushnell, "Some Social Aspects," 303–5; Philpott, *Slum*, 286.

26. Wilson, *McDowell*, 31–36; Slayton, *Back of the Yards*, 173.

27. Wilson, *McDowell*, 26–27; Bushnell, "Some Social Aspects," 300; Philpott, *Slum*, 78.

28. Wilson, *McDowell*, 52–63; Slayton, *Back of the Yards*, 175–77.

29. Breckinridge, "Housing Conditions," 434; Miller, "Rents," 15; Abbott, *Tenements*, 133; Slayton, *Back of the Yards*, 20. For more on the health risks involved in employment in the packinghouses, see Barnard, "Study of the Industrial Diseases of the Stockyards" (M.A. thesis); also Barrett, *Work and Community*, 69–71.

30. Greene, *Slavic Community*, 43; interviews with A. Kloris and P. Jasaitas.

Chapter 3: At Home

1. Barrett, *Work and the Community*, 189, 198–99; Fowler, *Men, Meat and Miracles*, 94, 100.

2. Fowler, *Men, Meat and Miracles*, 101–3, 141; Barrett, *Work and Community*, chap. 7; Pacyga, "Crisis and Community," 167–76; interviews with A. and S. Kobylar, M. M., and A. Prusak.

3. Prohibition Survey of the Stock Yards Community, 5–6, 8, 12–13, 16–18, 30, Mary McDowell Papers, Box 2, CHS; Lopata, *Polish Americans*, 36; Hicks, *Republican Ascendancy*, 131–32; Leuchtenberg, *Perils of Prosperity*, 207–8; Burgess, *Census Data, 1920*, 441–58; Burgess, *Census Data, 1930*, table 1.

4. Miller, "Rents and Housing Conditions" (M.A. thesis), 15; Lensing, "Unemployment Study in the Stockyards District" (M.A. thesis), 33–37; Slayton, *Back of the Yards*, 20, 87–95; Barrett, *Work and Community*, 64; Burgess, *Census Data, 1930*, table 8; maps of Central Manufacturing District, Chicago Stockyards Collection, Box 1, University of Illinois at Chicago Library; interviews with R. Aulinskis, E. Cieplak, A. Falat, Mrs. E. H., L. Jackson, L. and N. Klink, Mrs. X., Mrs. Y., Mrs. Z., S. Maack, M. M., R. and R. Matha, M. Matusek, B. and S. Nowicki, E. Odell, and A. Suvada.

5. Herbst, *Negro*, 10; Miller, "Rents," 6, 8–11, 14; Abbott, *Tenements*, 131–33, 139; Fowler, *Men, Meat and Miracles*, 216; interviews with R. Aulinskis, J. and R. Gallik, M. Kaleta, L. and N. Klink, A. and S. Kobylar, S. Maack, R. and R. Matha, M. Mega, V. Mikolaitas, E. Odell, J. and R. Paluck, J. Shimanis, J. Siska, A. Suvada, S. Vasilenko, and J. Weber.

6. Miller, "Rents," passim; Abbott, *Tenements*, 132, 136, 139, 227, 232, 241, 249, 258–59, 266; Back-of-the-Yards Area, 8–10, 18–20, 26–58, Settlement House Papers, Box 1, CHS; "Prohibition Survey," 23, 28–29, ibid.

7. Abbott, *Tenements*, 139, 344, 359, 361; Miller, "Rents," 19–20, 21, 24; WPA, *Housing*, community area 61, p. 33; Barrett, *Work and Community*, 101; Bodnar, *Transplanted*, 82–83; Gabaccia, *From Sicily*, 80; Cohen, "Embellishing a Life of Love," 269–70; Handlin, *American Home*, 375; interviews with J. Fabian, S. Fetta, R. Jablonsky, M. Mega, S. Nemec, J. Sukie, A. Suvada, C. Roszak, V. Koenigshofer, J. Drzazga, S. Vasilenko, and S. and S. Wozniak.

8. Breckinridge and Abbott, "Housing Conditions in Chicago," 442, 444, 449–52;

Burgess, *Census Data, 1920,* 441–58; Burgess, *Census Data, 1930,* table 1; overcrowding, Mary McDowell Papers, Box 2, CHS: WPA, *Housing,* 32.

9. WPA, *Housing,* 27, 28; Burgess, *Census Data, 1930,* table 10; data on dwellings, McDowell Papers, Box 2, CHS; Cohen, "Embellishing," 268; Greene, *For God and Country,* 51–58; Greene, *Slavic Community,* 56; Bodnar, *Transplanted,* 180–81; Barton, *Peasants and Strangers,* 101; Gabaccia, *From Sicily,* 74; Lensing, "Unemployment Study," 73; interviews with R. Aulinskis, A. Chaloupka, M. Ostrowski, R. Cwik, A. Jablonsky, A. Kloris, P. Jasaitas, S. Nemec, C. Nicholson, E. Odell, J. and R. Paluck, and M. Pratl.

10. Golab, *Destinations,* 153–54; Barton, *Peasants,* 102; Bodnar, *Transplanted,* 134, 180–82; Mormino, *Immigrants,* 114; Burgess, *Census Data, 1930,* table 10; Back-of-the-Yards Area, 17, Settlement House Papers; Belknap, "Summer Activities," 7; Barrett, *Work and Community,* 104–7; Palickar, "Slovaks of Chicago," 188, 194; interviews with R. Aulinskis, R. Cwik, M. Davis, L. and N. Klink, M. Mega, E. Niez, and B. and S. Nowicki.

11. Morawska, *For Bread,* 159, 187; Barrett, *Work and Community,* 90–107; Miller, "Rents," 20; Burgess, *Census Data, 1920,* 602–3; McElvaine, *Depression,* 181; Lensing, "Unemployment Study," 38; Bodnar, *Transplanted,* 78–80; Tentler, *Wage-Earning,* chap. 6; Wandersee, *Women's Work,* chap. 4; Kessler-Harris, *Work,* 218–19, 229; Maurine Weiner Greenwald, *Women, War, and Work* (Westport, Conn.: Greenwood Press, 1980), 4–7; Blackwelder, *Women,* 32–33, 66, 169–70; interviews with R. Aulinskis, E. Baranowsky, A. Chaloupka, M. Ostrowski, R. Cwik, E. Cieplak, J. and C. Dahm, R. Ehrlicher, A. Zeilner, S. Fetta, A. and C. Harkabus, A. and A. Havelka, Mrs. E. H., R. Jablonsky, M. Jensen, M. Kaleta, L. and N. Klink, G. Kober, A. Korcheck, Mrs. X., Mrs. Y., Mrs. Z., S. Maack, M. M., M. Mega, S. Nemec, B. and S. Nowicki, J. and R. Paluck, M. Pratl, J. Siska, S. Vasilenko, and F. and G. Young.

12. Talbert, *School and Industry,* 10, 41–42; Montgomery, *American Girl,* 2–8; Belknap, "Summer Activities," 11; Tentler, *Wage-Earning,* chap. 4; Bodnar, *Transplanted,* 182, 190–91; Barton, *Peasants,* 161–62, 172; Wandersee, *Women's Work,* 13, 60–66; Banks, *America,* 56; McElvaine, *Depression,* 181, 185; interviews with R. Cwik, E. Cieplak, A. Falat, S. Fetta, A. and C. Harkabus, J. Gelatka, A. and A. Havelka, R. Jablonsky, L. and N. Klink, G. Kober, A. and S. Kobylar, S. Lachowicz, S. Maack, M. M., R. and R. Matha, P. Mrowca, C. Nicholson, E. Odell, J. and R. Paluck, C. Roszak, V. Koenigshofer, J. Drzazga, J. Shimanis, J. Siska, A. Suvada, S. Vasilenko, and F. Young.

13. Interviews with R. Johnson, A. Kobylar, and Mr. K.

14. Study of the Educational and Industrial Life of Girls in Settlement Groups Ages 14–18, Mary McDowell Papers, Box 2, CHS; interviews with R. Aulinskis, R. Johnston, A. Kloris, P. Jasaitas, Mr. K., Mrs. K., M. Kapral, J. Shimanis, J. Sukie, Mrs. X., Mrs. Y., and Mrs. Z.

15. *Denni Hlasatel,* 13 October 1922, FLPS; Hayner, "The Effect of Prohibition in Packingtown" (M.A. thesis), 52–53; Prohibition Survey, 16, 29, McDowell Papers, Box 2, CHS; Bernstein, *Society,* 276; McElvaine, *Depression,* 7; Anderson, *This Was Harlem,* 235; Heleniak, "New Orleans," 289–90; Wandersee, *Women's Work,* 28; Biles, *Memphis in the Great Depression,* 51; Keyssar, *Work,* 289.

16. James, *Banks,* 2:1221, 1376; *Osadne Hlasy,* 3 April 1931, FLPS.

17. Teaford, *American City,* 77; James, *Banks,* 2:1221, 1345–46, 1370; *Journal Town of Lake,* 10 February 1938, 10 November 1938, 3 August 1939, 2 November 1939; Slayton, *Back of the Yards,* 190; Trout, *Boston,* 77; interviews with R. Ehrlicher, A.

Zeilner, R. R. Ehrlicher, A. Falat, A. and C. Harkabus, J. and R. Gallik, A. and A. Havelka, R. Jablonsky, A. Korcheck, J. and V. Lebensorger, M. M., M. Matusek, V. Mikolaitas, C. Nicholson, E. Niez, J. and R. Paluck, C. Roszak, V. Koenigshofer, J. Drzazga, M. Shalack, H. Tobias, S. Vasilenko, and S. and S. Wozniak. For repayments by Sherman State Bank, see *Journal Town of Lake*, 8 April 1937, 17 February 1938, 25 May 1939, 17 August 1939. For a revealing account of the consequences of the closing of community banks, see Shannon, *Depression*, 75–82.

18. Brandenburg, "Relief Statistics, 1928–31," 7, 18, 24; Biles, *Big City Boss in Depression and War*, 22–23; Bernstein, *Society*, 17–18, 276–77; Teaford, *American City*, 75–77; Mayer and Wade, *Chicago*, 358–60; Leuchtenburg, *Franklin D. Roosevelt and the New Deal*, 19–21; Bodnar, *Lives*, 186; Trout, *Boston*, 81; Morawska, *For Bread*, 159; Keyssar, *Work*, 289–90; Heleniak, "New Orleans," 301; Lyle W. Dorsett, "Kansas City and the New Deal" in Braeman, Bremner, and Brody, *New Deal*, 2:408; David J. Maurer, "Relief Problems and Politics in Ohio," in ibid., 2:78; Bowly, *Poorhouse*, 8; Lensing, "Unemployment Study," 87.

19. Burchard, *Fact Book*, districts 58–61, 63, 67, 68; Wirth and Bernert, *Local Community Fact Book of Chicago*, area 61, table E; Lensing, "Unemployment Study," 11; Van Sickle, "Lake Forest," 116–22.

20. Survey of Twelve Typical Chicago Commission Firms' Cattle Receipts 1932 Compared with 1938, Chicago Stockyards Collection, Supplement, Box 1, University of Illinois at Chicago Library; Bird, *Scar*, 246; Wilson, "Hull-House," 318; Keyssar, *Work*, 290; Van Sickle, "Lake Forest," 121; Lensing, "Unemployment Study," 8, 29, 31, 75; interviews with R. Aulinskis, R. Cwik, E. Cieplak, J. and C. Dahm, M. Davis, R. Ehrlicher, A. Zeilner, R. R. Ehrlicher, J. Fabian, A. Falat, S. Fetta, J. Gelatka, A. and C. Harkabus, A. Jablonsky, R. Jablonsky, L. Jackson, E. Niez, and J. Shimanis.

21. Illinois Emergency Relief Commission, *Monthly Bulletin on Relief Statistics*, January 1934, passim, February 1934, 1–4, March 1934 to January 1935, p. 4 in each issue, January 1936, 10; Burchard, *Fact Book*, area 61; Back-of-the-Yards Area, 14, Settlement House Papers, Box 1, CHS; Trout, *Boston*, 86. See also the community-based maps on p. 12 of the March 1935 issue of the *Monthly Bulletin on Relief Statistics* and the chart on relief districts in the January 1937 issue (also p. 12).

22. Bushnell, "Some Social Aspects of the Chicago Stock Yards, Chapter Two"; Bosch, "Public Outdoor Poor Relief in Chicago" (M.A. thesis), 1, 52–56, 113; Brown, *Public Relief*, 222–23.

23. Social Service Department Reports, March 1936, August 1936, September 1936, July 1937, August 1937, October 1937, March 1938, May 1938, June 1938, University of Chicago Settlement House Papers, Box 20, CHS; Lensing, "Unemployment Study," 13–14, 18–20, 27–28, 71, 91, 103; Terkel, *Hard Times*, 116, 136, 487; Bird, *Scar*, 35, 141–42; Shannon, *Depression*, 48–49, 50–51; Wilson, "Hull-House," 318; Bonnie Fox Schwartz, "Unemployment Relief in Philadelphia, 1930–1932: A Study of the Depression's Impact on Voluntarism," in Sternsher, *Hitting Home*, 65; McElvaine, *Depression*, 176; Bodnar, *Lives*, 217–18; Wandersee, *Women's Work*, 30–31; Blackwelder, *Women*, 8, 10; Kessler-Harris, *Work*, 252; Mormino, *Immigrants*, 214; Morawska, *For Bread*, 216–18; interviews with E. Baranowsky, A. Chaloupka, M. Ostrowski, E. Cieplak, J. and C. Dahm, M. Dluhy, R. Ehrlicher, A. Zeilner, R. R. Ehrlicher, E. Fredericks, A. and C. Harkabus, J. and R. Gallik, Mrs. E. H., L. Jackson, A. Kloris, P. Jasaitas, A. Korcheck, V. Mikolaitas, P. Mrowca, S. Nemec, C. Nicholson, E. Niez, B. and S. Nowicki, A. Prusak, C. Roszak, V. Koenigshofer, J. Drzazga, M. Shalack, A. Suvada, S. Vasilenko, J. Weber, and S. and S. Wozniak.

24. Social Service Department Reports, November 1938, January 1939, February 1939, Settlement House Papers, Boxes 19 and 20, CHS; Lensing, "Unemployment Study," 24, 44, 55; Brown, *Public Relief*, 277–78; Terkel, *Hard Times*, 444, 481–82; Bird, *Scar*, 30–32; Shannon, *Depression*, 140; Federal Writers Project, "The Depression in Harlem," in Sternsher, *Hitting Home*, 106–7, 110; Blumberg, *New Deal and the Unemployed*, 27; McElvaine, *Depression*, 176–77; interviews with J. Fabian, S. Fetta, A. Jablonsky, R. Jablonsky, L. Jackson, M. Kaleta, M. M., M. Matusek, V. Mikolaitas, E. Odell, C. Roszak, V. Koenigshofer, J. Drzazga, M. Shalack, and H. Tobias.

25. University of Chicago Settlement Report for Joint Emergency Relief Fund of Cook County, Mary McDowell Papers, Box 3, CHS; Neighborhood House and Minor Agencies Giving Family Relief, ibid.; Social Service Department Reports, June 1938, November 1938, Settlement House Papers, Boxes 19 and 20, CHS; Lensing, "Unemployment Study," 59–60, 65, 76, 81, 85; Brown, *Public Relief*, 224, 242–43, 254–56; Wilson, "Hull-House," 317–18, Terkel, *Hard Times*, 111, 496; Shannon, *Depression*, 140, 142; McElvaine, *Depression*, 178; Morawska, *For Bread*, 219; Patterson, *Poverty*, 57; interviews with E. Baranowsky, A. Chaloupka, M. Ostrowski, M. Davis, A. Falat, S. Fetta, E. Fredericks, A. Jablonsky, R. Jablonsky, L. Jackson, A. Kloris, P. Jasaitas, A. Korcheck, Mr. K., Mrs. K., M. Kapral, R. and R. Matha, V. Mikolaitas, P. Mrowca, C. Roszak, V. Koenigshofer, J. Drzazga, M. Shalack, H. Tobias, and F. and G. Young.

26. Social Service Department Reports, November 1936, January 1938, July 1939, November 1940, Settlement House Papers, Boxes 19 and 20, CHS; Lensing, "Unemployment Study," 63, 65, 69, 74, 83, 85–86; Brown, *Public Relief*, 248; Wilson, "Hull-House," 317; interviews with E. Baranowsky, M. Dluhy, J. Fabian, A. Falat, S. Fetta, E. Fredericks, A. and A. Havelka, A. Korcheck, R. and R. Matha, V. Mikolaitas, P. Mrowca, C. Roszak, V. Koenigshofer, J. Drzazga, and M. Shalack.

27. Lensing, "Unemployment Study," 7, 41–42, 56; Brandenburg, "Relief Statistics," 8; Terkel, *Hard Times*, 164; McElvaine, *Depression*, 172–73; Trout, *Boston*, 87; interviews with E. Cieplak, J. Fabian, A. Falat, S. Fetta, A. and C. Harkabus, A. and A. Havelka, A. Jablonsky, R. Jablonsky, L. and N. Klink, A. Kloris, P. Jasaitas, A. and S. Kobylar, Mr. K., Mrs. K., M. Kapral, M. Matusek, V. Mikolaitas, M. Pratl, and M. Shalack.

28. Porteous, "Home," 383; Porteous, *Environment*, 62, 270; WPA, *Housing*, 27, tables D and E, 29, table F, 30, table G; Aaron, *Strenuous Decade*, 60; Handlin, *Home*, 370; Cohen, "Embellishing," 273; interviews with R. Aulinskis, E. Cieplak, J. and C. Dahm, M. Dluhy, R. Ehrlicher, A. Zeilner, S. Fetta, A. and A. Havelka, A. Jablonsky, M. Jensen, J. and V. Lebensorger, S. Maack, M. M., C. Nicholson, E. Odell, C. Roszak, V. Koenigshofer, J. Drzazga, J. Shimanis, and J. Siska.

29. WPA, *Housing*, 30, table I; *Sixteenth Census*, table 6; Lensing, "Unemployment Study," 51; interviews with R. Aulinskis, A. Chaloupka, M. Ostrowski, R. Cwik, E. Cieplak, J. Fabian, S. Fetta, J. and R. Gallik, A. and A. Havelka, Mrs. E. H., M. Jensen, L. and N. Klink, Mr. K., Mrs. K., M. Kapral, S. Maack, M. M., R. and R. Matha, M. Mega, V. Mikolaitas, P. Mrowca, S. Nemec, E. Niez, E. Odell, J. and R. Paluck, C. Roszak, V. Koenigshofer, J. Drzazga, J. Sukie, A. Suvada, H. Tobias, S. Vasilenko, and F. and G. Young.

30. WPA, *Housing*, 30, table J; Lensing, "Unemployment Study," 9, 77, 85; interviews with R. Aulinskis, A. Chaloupka, M. Ostrowski, R. Cwik, E. Cieplak, J. and C. Dahm, M. Davis, A. Falat, S. Fetta, A. and C. Harkabus, J. and R. Gallik, A. and A. Havelka, R. Jablonsky, M. Jensen, L. and N. Klink, A. Kloris, P. Jasaitas, Mr. K., Mrs. K., M. Kapral, S. Lachowicz, M. M., R. and R. Matha, M. Mega, S. Nemec, C.

Nicholson, E. Odell, J. and R. Paluck, C. Roszak, V. Koenigshofer, J. Drzazga, J. Shimanis, J. Siska, and J. Sukie.

31. Cohen, "Embellishing," 269–70; Wright, *Building the Dream*, 124, 169; Lensing, "Unemployment Study," 72; interviews with R. Aulinskis, E. Baranowsky, A. Chaloupka, M. Ostrowski, R. Cwik, E. Cieplak, J. and C. Dahm, M. Dluhy, R. Ehrlicher, A. Zeilner, R. R. Ehrlicher, J. Fabian, A. Falat, S. Fetta, A. and C. Harkabus, A. and A. Havelka, A. Jablonsky, R. Jablonsky, M. Jensen, M. Kaleta, Mr. K., Mrs. K., M. Kapral, A. Kloris, P. Jasaitas, A. and S. Kobylar, S. Lachowicz, J. and V. Lebensorger, S. Maack, M. M., R. and R. Matha, M. Mega, V. Mikolaitas, S. Nemec, E. Niez, G. Niez, C. Nicholson, E. Odell, J. and R. Paluck, J. Shimanis, J. Siska, A. Suvada, S. Vasilenko, J. Weber, and S. and S. Wozniak.

32. Burgess, *Census Data, 1930*, table 11; *Sixteenth Census*, table 6.

33. Belknap, "Summer Activities," 18, 46–47; Cohen, "Embellishing," 263, 274; interviews with E. Cieplak; Mr. K., Mrs. K., M. Kapral, S. Maack, H. Tobias, S. Vasilenko, J. Weber, and F. and G. Young.

34. Interviews with J. and C. Dahm, R. Ehrlicher, A. Zeilner, A. Falat, S. Fetta, A. Jablonsky, A. Kloris, P. Jasaitas, S. Lachowicz, M. M., R. and R. Matha, M. Mega, V. Mikolaitas, G. Niez, J. and R. Paluck, M. Pratl, A. Prusak, C. Roszak, V. Koenigshofer, J. Drzazga, and J. Shimanis.

35. This paragraph and the one that follows were derived from interviews with R. Aulinskis, E. Baranowsky, A. Chaloupka, M. Ostrowski, R. Cwik, J. and C. Dahm, M. Davis, R. Ehrlicher, A. Zeilner, R. R. Erlicher, J. Fabian, A. Falat, S. Fetta, E. Fredericks, A. and A. Havelka, A. Jablonsky, R. Jablonsky, M. Jensen, M. Kaleta, L. and N. Klink, A. Kloris, P. Jasaitas, G. Kober, A. and S. Kobylar, A. Korcheck, Mr. K., Mrs. K., M. Kapral, S. Lachowicz, Mrs. X., Mrs. Y., Mrs. Z., J. and V. Lebensorger, S. Maack, M. M., R. and R. Matha, M. Matusek, M. Mega, V. Mikolaitas, S. Nemec, C. Nicholson, E. Niez, G. Niez, B. and S. Nowicki, E. Odell, J. and R. Paluck, J. Shimanis, J. Siska, A. Suvada, H. Tobias, S. Vasilenko, J. Weber, S. and S. Wozniak, and F. and G. Young; Lensing, "Unemployment Study," 50, 53, 77.

36. Interviews with R. Aulinskis, R. Cwik, J. Fabian, A. Falat, M. Kaleta, A. Kloris, P. Jasaitas, A. Korcheck, Mr. K., Mrs. K., M. Kapral, S. Lachowicz, S. Maack, M. M., R. and R. Matha, C. Nicholson, E. Odell, J. and R. Paluck, A. Suvada, H. Tobias, S. Vasilenko, J. Weber, and, F. and G. Young.

37. Wilson, "Hull-House," 317–18; Terkel, *Hard Times*, 76, 111, 116, 493; Aaron, *Strenuous Decade*, 58–61; Schwartz, "Philadelphia," 65; Federal Writers Project, "Harlem," 106–7; Bird, *Scar*, 37–39, 43, 275; Morawska, *For Bread*, 218–21; Blackwelder, *Women*, 8, 10, 169; Trout, *Boston*, 14–15, 178; Gabaccia, *From Sicily*, 92–93, 96; Mormino, *Immigrants*, 215; Maurer, "Ohio," 97; Patterson, *Poverty*, 42.

38. Cavan and Ranck, *Family and the Depression*, viii, 3, 4, 56, 73, 85, 93, 103, 150–51, 153, 171.

39. Morawska, *For Bread*, 216, 299; Banks, *America*, 53; interviews with A. Chaloupka, M. Ostrowski, J. and C. Dahm, R. Ehrlicher, A. Zeilner, A. Falat, A. and S. Kobylar, A. Korcheck, S. Lachowicz, Mrs. X., Mrs. Y., Mrs. Z., J. and V. Lebensorger, M. M., M. Matusek, G. Niez, C. Roszak, V. Koenigshofer, J. Drzazga, and H. Tobias.

Chapter 4: On the Block

1. Jakle, Brunn, and Roseman, *Human Spatial Behavior*, 92–93; Porteous, "Home," 385–86, 390; Porteous, *Environment*, 61, 78, 93.

2. Handlin, *American Home*, 170, 175; Borchert, *Alley Life*, 96; Gabaccia, *From*

Sicily, 93; interviews with A. and A. Havelka, M. Jensen, A. and S. Kobylar, S. Lachowicz, G. Niez, E. Odell, H. Tobias, and F. and G. Young.

3. Cohen, "Embellishing," 269; Belknap, "Summer Activities," 14; interviews with J. Fabian, S. Fetta, A. and A. Havelka, A. Jablonsky, A. Korcheck, S. Lachowicz, Mrs. X., Mrs. Y., Mrs. Z., S. Maack, R. and R. Matha, M. Mega, V. Mikolaitas, P. Mrowca, S. Nemec, C. Nicholson, J. and R. Paluck, C. Roszak, V. Koenigshofer, J. Drzazga, J. Sukie, A. Suvada, H. Tobias, and F. and G. Young.

4. Data calculated from a list of stores and businesses, district 61, Mary McDowell Papers, Box 2, CHS; Gabaccia, *From Sicily,* 72.

5. Interviews with J. and R. Gallik, R. Jablonsky, G. Niez, and E. Odell; Kraut, "Butcher, the Baker, the Pushcart Peddler," 81; Golab, *Destinations,* 144; Greene, *Slavic Community,* 48; Barton, *Peasants,* 72.

6. This paragraph and the preceding one draw from interviews with J. and R. Gallik, R. Jablonsky, A. Kloris, P. Jasaitas, S. Lachowicz, G. Niez, and F. and G. Young; Lensing, "Unemployment Study," 18, 49, 63–64, 77, 94; Mormino, *Immigrants,* 215.

7. Tuan, *Topophilia,* 215; Briggs, *Collected Essays,* 1:95–96; Jakle, *American Small Town,* 5, 9–10; Golab, *Destinations,* 116, 119, 154; Porteous, *Environment,* 62, 278; Seamon, "Heidegger's Notion," 49; Gabaccia, *From Sicily,* 105; Bodnar, *Transplanted,* 178–79; interviews with A. Chaloupka, M. Ostrowski, J. and R. Gallik, R. Jablonsky, A. Kloris, P. Jasaitas, S. Lachowicz, M. Mega, V. Mikolaitas, S. Nemec, and J. Sukie.

8. Interviews with E. Baranowsky, E. Cieplak, R. Ehrlicher, A. Zeilner, J. and R. Gallik, M. Jensen, A. and S. Kobylar, G. Niez, E. Odell, M. Pratl, A. Prusak, and J. Siska; Lensing, "Unemployment Study," 69.

9. Interviews with R. Cwik, E. Cieplak, R. Ehrlicher, A. Zeilner, J. Fabian, A. Falat, E. Fredericks, Mrs. E. H., A. Jablonsky, M. Jensen, G. Kober, S. Maack, M. Mega, V. Mikolaitas, S. Nemec, G. Niez, E. Odell, A. Prusak, J. Shimanis, J. Siska, A. Suvada, and J. Weber; Handlin, *Home,* 211; Abbott, *Tenements,* 137; Melosi, *Garbage in the Cities,* 23, 161; Borchert, *Alley Life,* 97; Gabaccia, *From Sicily,* 93.

10. Interviews with E. Baranowsky, R. Cwik, R. Ehrlicher, A. Zeilner, J. Fabian, A. Falat, S. Fetta, E. Fredericks, A. and A. Havelka, J. and R. Gallik, R. Jablonsky, A. and S. Kobylar, S. Maack, E. Niez, G. Niez, E. Odell, J. and R. Paluck, C. Roszak, V. Koenigshofer, J. Drzazga, and J. Siska; Belknap, "Summer Activities," 38, 45, 47, 52, 68, 70, 75; Terkel, *Hard Times,* 54. A similar practice of "junking" was carried on in the African-American alley communities of Washington, D.C.; Borchert, *Alley Life,* 96–97.

11. This paragraph and the preceding one draw from interviews with R. Aulinskis, A. Chaloupka, M. Ostrowski, R. Cwik, J. and C. Dahm, J. Fabian, A. Falat, S. Fetta, A. and A. Havelka, A. Jablonsky, R. Jablonsky, M. Jensen, A. Kloris, P. Jasaitas, G. Kober, A. Korcheck, Mr. K., Mrs. K., M. Kapral, S. Lachowicz, Mrs. X., Mrs. Y., Mrs. Z., S. Maack, R. and R. Matha, M. Mega, V. Mikolaitas, S. Nemec, C. Nicholson, G. Niez, J. and R. Paluck, M. Pratl, C. Roszak, V. Koenigshofer, J. Drzazga, J. Siska, A. Suvada, H. Tobias, and S. and S. Wozniak; Belknap, "Summer Activities," 44–45, 73; Gabaccia, *From Sicily,* 96–97.

12. Clark, "Stoop Is the World," 269–80; Borchert, *Alley Life,* 101–2, 108, 113; Seamon, "Heidegger's Notion," 51; Gabaccia, *From Sicily,* 105–6; Belknap, "Summer Activities," 16, 49, 104; Porteous, *Environment,* 86–87; interviews with R. Aulinskis, A. Chaloupka, M. Ostrowski, R. Cwik, E. Cieplak, J. and C. Dahm, J. Fabian, S. Fetta, M. Jensen, A. Kloris, P. Jasaitas, S. Lachowicz, R. and R. Matha, V. Mikolaitas, S. Nemec, C. Roszak, V. Koenigshofer, J. Drzazga, and J. Siska. Many of the same charac-

teristics of local street life still prevailed in the Hull House area thirty-five years later, as depicted in Suttles, *Social Order of the Slum*, 73–83.

13. Prohibition Survey of the Stockyards Community, 4, 6, 17–18, 23–24, 27, Mary McDowell Papers, Box 2, CHS; Hayner, "Prohibition," 12–13, 23, 31, 33, 39; Duis, *Saloon*, 182; Lopata, *Polish Americans*, 99; Gabaccia, *From Sicily*, 97; interviews with J. Fabian, A. and C. Harkabus, R. Jablonsky, A. and S. Kobylar, Mr. K., Mrs. K., M. Kapral, C. Nicholson, J. and R. Paluck, C. Roszak, V. Koenigshofer, and J. Drzazga.

14. Prohibition Survey, 7–17, 19–24, 26, 29, 31–32, McDowell Papers, Box 2, CHS; Hayner, "Prohibition," 16–17, 21–22, 31, 34–35, 48; Stolarik, *Growing Up*, 88, 97; interviews with A. Chaloupka, M. Ostrowski, M. Davis, J. Fabian, A. Falat, J. and R. Gallik, J. Gelatka, R. Jablonsky, M. Kaleta, A. Kloris, P. Jasaitas, A. and S. Kobylar, Mr. K., Mrs. K., M. Kapral, P. Mrowca, C. Nicholson, E. Niez, J. and R. Paluck, C. Roszak, V. Koenigshofer, J. Drzazga, J. Shimanis, and A. Suvada.

15. Interviews with E. Baranowsky, A. Chaloupka, M. Ostrowski, J. Fabian, A. Falat, A. and C. Harkabus, A. Kloris, P. Jasaitas, G. Kober, A. Korcheck, S. Lachowicz, S. Maack, R. and R. Matha, M. Mega, E. Odell, and J. and R. Paluck; McElvaine, *Depression*, 174.

16. Somer, *Personal Space*, 120; interviews with J. Fabian, Mrs. E. H., G. Kober, S. Lachowicz, and C. Nicholson.

17. *Denni Hlasatel*, 21 May 1917, Chicago Foreign Language Press Survey (hereafter cited as FLPS); *Abendpost*, 15 January 1919, FLPS; 1934 Survey of Newspaper Distribution in Area 61, Mary McDowell Papers, Box 2, CHS; Prohibition Survey, 14–15, ibid.; Hayner, "Prohibition," 24–27. See also *Denni Hlasatel*, 23 Januarzy 1920, 3 February 1920, 19 February 1920, 6 October 1922, 5 November 1922, FLPS; *Abendpost*, 18 July 1931, FLPS; *Osadne Hlasy*, 13 July 1929, FLPS.

18. *Denni Hlasatel*, 28 March 1913, 3 October 1921, FLPS; *Polonia*, 21 December 1916, FLPS.

19. *Abendpost*, 30 November 1918, 5 April 1919, FLPS; *Narod Polski*, 16 October 1918, 25 August 1920, FLPS. For an example of changing attitudes toward Polish young women attending high school rather than entering the work force after grade school, see *Dziennik Zwiazkowy*, 29 June 1917, FLPS.

20. *Dziennik Zjednoczenia*, 18 October 1921, 6 October 1927, 12 May 1928, FLPS; *Narod Polski*, 29 June 1921, FLPS; *Denni Hlasatel*, 26 January 1922, 8 September 1922, 16 September 1922, FLPS; *Osadne Hlasy*, 27 March 1931, 28 August 1931, FLPS; interview with A. and A. Havelka.

21. Interviews with E. Baranowsky, J. and C. Dahm, E. Fredericks, J. and R. Gallik, J. Gelatka, A. and A. Havelka, R. Jablonsky, A. Kloris, P. Jasaitas, A. and S. Kobylar, Mr. K., Mrs. K., M. Kapral, S. Lachowicz, J. and V. Lebensorger, R. and R. Matha, M. Matusek, M. Mega, C. Nicholson, E. Niez, J. and R. Paluck, M. Pratl, A. Prusak, J. Siska, J. Weber, and S. and S. Wozniak; Golab, *Destinations*, 130–31.

22. *Denni Hlasatel*, 19 March 1903, 7 April 1915, 29 March 1917, 29 April 1917, 28 July 1917, 20 January 1918, FLPS; *Dziennik Zjednoczenia*, 20 March 1922, FLPS; *Narod Polski*, 19 January 1921, 8 June 1921, FLPS; *Naujienos*, 3 June 1914, FLPS; *Osadne Hlasy*, 6 September 1929, 28 March 1930, 28 April 1931, 25 November 1932, 9 December 1932, 6 January 1933, 27 January 1933, 10 February 1933, 15 January 1934, FLPS; Greene, *For God*, 63; Stolarik, *Growing Up*, 66–67; Banks, *America*, 64.

23. *Narod Polski*, 28 April 1920, FLPS; *Dziennik Chicagoski*, 25 January 1922, 16 February 1922, 11 January 1928, FLPS; Palickar, "Slovaks of Chicago," 188; Trout, *Boston*, 15; Bodnar, *Transplanted*, 128–30.

24. Czecho-Slovakian School, Mary McDowell Papers, Box 2, CHS; *Journal Town of Lake*, 21 September 1938, 1; Reichman, *Czechoslovaks in Chicago*, 13; interviews with A. Chaluopka, M. Ostrowski, and M. Jensen; Record Books of the Building and Loan Associations, 1937, FLPS.

25. My opinion regarding the declining importance of nationalistic feelings among Back of the Yards residents differs from that expressed by Robert Slayton in his study of the community. He insists that strong antagonisms remained between nationalities—at both the individual and group levels—into the late 1930s. Furthermore, he contends that the Back of the Yards Neighborhood Council, created in 1939, was a timely mediator that promoted harmony among the different groups. My view is that cooperation among ethnic organizations, as evinced by their support of the Council, reflected an accommodation already well established at the grass-roots level. On the other hand, the Council did provide a community forum where the various agencies of nationalistic expression (churches, lodges, business enterprises, athletic clubs, etc.) learned to tolerate one another. My argument is that acceptance of other Euro-Americans developed from the bottom up, not from the top down. Thus the community, from the point of view of residents, was not torn apart by nationalistic segmentation as Slayton suggests. See Slayton, *Back of the Yards*, 9, 13, 129–48, 201–2, 205, 209–10, 226–27.

26. Cohen, "Embellishing," 268; Barrett, *Work and Community*, 78–81; Slayton, *Back of the Yards*, 148; Bodnar, *Transplanted*, 177; interview with R. Aulinskis.

27. Barrett, *Work and Community*, 81; Golab, *Destinations*, 112–13, 132; Gabaccia, *From Sicily*, 101–2; Greene, *Slavic Community*, 39; Stolarik, *Growing Up*, 84; Barton, *Peasants*, 161–69; Bodnar, *Lives*, 203; interviews with R. Aulinskis, E. Baranowsky, A. Chaloupka, M. Ostrowski, R. Cwik, J. and C. Dahm, M. Dluhy, R. R. Ehrlicher, J. Fabian, S. Fetta, E. Fredericks, A. and C. Harkabus, J. and R. Gallik, R. Jablonsky, L. Jackson, M. Jensen, R. Johnston, M. Kaleta, L. and N. Klink, G. Kober, A. and S. Kobylar, A. Korcheck, Mr. K., Mrs. K., M. Kapral, J. and V. Lebensorger, S. Maack, R. and R. Matha, V. Mikolaitas, P. Mrowca, S. Nemec, C. Nicholson, E. Niez, G. Niez, B. and S. Nowicki, E. Odell, J. and R. Paluck, M. Pratl, A. Prusak, C. Roszak, V. Koenigshofer, J. Drzazga, J. Shimanis, J. Siska, J. Sukie, A. Suvada, H. Tobias, S. Vasilenko, J. Weber, and S. and S. Wozniak.

28. *Juanimas*, 15 September 1936, 25 January 1937, 15 February 1937, FLPS. See also the remark of a young woman that by the 1930s there were no Lithuanian organizations for younger people in the Back of the Yards apart from church clubs; Lithuanian Organizations, Mary McDowell Papers, Box 2, CHS.

29. Spear, *Black Chicago*, 36–38; Barrett, *Work and Community*, 202–19; Tuttle, *Race Riot*, 102–3; Philpott, *Slum*, 169; interviews with R. Aulinskis, A. Chaloupka, M. Ostrowski, L. Jackson, R. Johnston, and J. Sukie.

30. Spear, *Black Chicago*, 214–16; Tuttle, *Race Riot*, 35–39, 48, 55, 57, 60–61, 199–200; Pacyga, "Packinghouses," 286–301; Philpott, *Slum*, 274; Weber, "Mexican Immigrants"; interviews with J. Gelatka, Mrs. E. H., L. and N. Klink, J. and V. Lebensorger, M. Matusek, V. Mikolaitas, and A. Prusak; Barrett, *Work and Community*, 219–22; *Narod Polski*, 6 August 1919, FLPS. For a brief but useful discussion of the spatial parameters of black Chicago before 1945, see Arnold Hirsch, *Making the Second Ghetto* (Cambridge: Cambridge University Press, 1983), 1–9.

31. Kerr, "Chicano Experience," 19, 75–80; Jones, *Mexicans*, 42–43; Frank X. Paz, Mexican-Americans in Chicago: A General Survey, 2–3, Welfare Council of Metropolitan Chicago Papers, Box 147, CHS; Minutes of the Meeting of the Committee on Minority Groups, 6–7, ibid.; Jones and Wilson, *Mexican in Chicago*, 10–12; Slayton, *Back of the*

Yards, 179; Reiser, "Chicago Area," 144–46, 149; Philpott, *Slum*, 144; Weber, "Mexican Immigrants," 135.

32. Kerr, "Chicano Experience," 22, 33, 77, 86–87, 103–4, 106; Jones, *Mexicans*, 47–49; Philpott, *Slum*, 284; Reiser, "Chicago Area," 147, 152; Weber, "Mexican Immigrants," 165, 200–204, 207–8.

33. Kerr, "Chicano Experience," 19, 28, 57, 82, 86–87, 106–7; Jones, *Mexicans*, 44–45, 50–51, 53, 91–94; Reiser, "Chicago Area," 151–52, 155; Weber, "Mexican Immigrants," 135, 150, 153–54, 156; "A Butcher Shop Their Church" clipping, Joseph Meegan Collection, Back of the Yards Branch, Chicago Public Library; Koenig, *Archdiocese*, 444–46; interviews conducted in 1924 by Robert Redfield, Robert Redfield Papers, Box 59, University of Chicago Library; *La Defensa*, 21 December 1935, FLPS; *El Mexicano*, 20 April 1934, 2 May 1934, FLPS; *El Nacional*, 10 February 1934, 4 April 1934, FLPS; *Mexico*, 29 March 1930, 17 May 1930, FLPS; interview with Joseph Meegan.

34. Sue H. Perry, Report of Study of Fifty Mexican Families of Stockyards District of Chicago, Settlement House Papers, Box 25, CHS. See also interview with Placida and Severna Gonzales, Robert Redfield Papers, Box 59, University of Chicago Library.

35. Kerr, "Chicano Experience," 22, 28–29, 33, 75, 80, 96, 105–7; Philpott, *Slum*, 284; Reiser, "Chicago Area," 150, 153, 155; Weber, "Mexican Immigrants," 135, 143, 147, 155–56, 201–2, 208–10, 258; Jones, *Mexicans*, 39, 51; Belknap, "Summer Activities," 58; Field Notes, 17–24, Robert Redfield Papers, Box 59, University of Chicago Library; *Dziennik Chicagoski*, 7 January 1928, FLPS; Fact Sheet on Mexican-Americans in Chicago, Welfare Council of Metropolitan Chicago Papers, Box 147, CHS; Minutes of Meeting of the Committee on Minority Groups, ibid; interviews with E. Baranowsky, R. Cwik, M. Dluhy, R. Jablonsky, L. Jackson, A. and S. Kobylar, M. Matusek, V. Mikolaitas, and G. Niez.

Chapter 5: Around the Corner

1. This paragraph and the next draw from interviews with R. Aulinskis, A. Chaloupka, M. Ostrowski, R. Cwik, E. Cieplak, J. and C. Dahm, R. Ehrlicher, A. Zeilner, J. Fabian, S. Fetta, Mrs. E. H., A. Kloris, P. Jasaitas, Mr. K., Mrs. K., M. Kapral, Mrs. X., Mrs. Y., Mrs. Z., J. and V. Lebensorger, M. Matusek, M. Mega, V. Mikolaitas, P. Mrowca, S. Nemec, J. and R. Paluck, A. Prusak, C. Roszak, V. Koenigshofer, J. Drzazga, J. Sukie, A. Suvada, S. Vasilenko, J. Weber, and S. and S. Wozniak; DeSaulniers, *Catholic Periodicals*, 8–13, 29; Stolarik, *Growing Up*, 76; Josef J. Barton, "Religion and Cultural Change in Czech Immigrant Communities, 1850–1920," in Miller and Marzik, *Immigrants and Religion in Urban America*, 17; Linkh, *American Catholicism*, 51.

2. *Golden Jubilee Book of Sacred Heart of Jesus Church*, 60; Annual Reports, 1904–43, Saint Basil Church; Trout, *Boston*, 88, 260.

3. Slayton, *Back of the Yards*, 131–33; Golab, *Destinations*, 113, 143; William J. Galush, "Faith and Fatherland: Dimensions of Polish-American Ethnoreligion, 1875–1975," in Miller and Marzik, *Immigrants and Religion*, 90; Bodnar, *Transplanted*, 145, 164; Greene, *For God*, 64; DeSaulniers, *Catholic Periodicals*, 23; Sanders, *Education*, 43–44; Blackwelder, *Women*, 40; interviews with A. and C. Harkabus, J. and R. Gallik, A. Kloris, P. Jasaitas, L. and N. Klink, A. and S. Kobylar, M. Mega, V. Mikolaitas, S. Nemec, and J. Siska.

4. Linkh, *American Catholicism*, 4, 7, 123, 129; Bodnar, *Transplanted*, 154, 193–95; Lopata, *Polish Americans*, 51; Barton, *Peasants*, 148, 155; Thomas and Znaniecki,

Polish Peasant in Europe and America, 252–53; Galush, "Faith," 85; Sanders, *Education*, 4, 12–13, 80–83; Hogan, *Class*, 98–99, 125–27; Belknap, "Summer Activities," 12; *Narod Polski*, 5 February 1919, FLPS; *Denni Hlasatel*, 10 August 1921, FLPS; *Osadne Hlasy*, 30 August 1929, 28 September 1929, FLPS; *Dziennik Zjednoczenia*, 19 August 1926, FLPS; interviews with R. Cwik, M. Dluhy, R. Ehrlicher, A. Zeilner, J. Fabian, S. Fetta, E. Fredericks, A. and A. Havelka, Mrs. E. H., A. Jablonsky, R. Jablonsky, A. Kloris, P. Jasaitas, A. and S. Kobylar, A. Korcheck, Mr. K., Mrs. K., M. Kapral, J. and V. Lebensorger, S. Maack, M. M., M. Mega, V. Mikolaitas, S. Nemec, G. Niez, J. and R. Paluck, A. Prusak, J. Shimanis, J. Siska, J. Sukie, A. Suvada, H. Tobias, S. Vasilenko, and J. Weber.

5. Linkh, *American Catholicism*, 11–12; Sanders, *Education*, 40–51, 60–65; Lopata, *Polish Americans*, 50–51; Barton, *Peasants*, 147–48, 151, 153; Galush, "Faith," 93–95; interviews with R. Aulinskis, A. Chaloupka, M. Ostrowski, R. Cwik, J. and C. Dahm, M. Dluhy, A. Falat, A. and C. Harkabus, A. and A. Havelka, A. Jablonsky, L. and N. Klink, A. and S. Kobylar, J. and V. Lebensorger, M. M., R. and R. Matha, V. Mikolaitas, S. Nemec, G. Niez, B. and S. Nowicki, A. Prusak, J. Shimanis, J. Sukie, and A. Suvada.

6. Linkh, *American Catholicism*, 108–10; Barton, "Religion," 3; Galush, "Faith," 96–98; Lopata, *Polish Americans*, 100, 105; Barton, *Peasants*, 151–52, 155; Sanders, *Education*, 105, 108–11, 116–17; *St. Augustine's*, 147; Record of Marriages, 1899–1943, Saint Michael the Archangel Church; interviews with E. Baranowsky, M. Davis, R. R. Ehrlicher, A. Falat, S. Fetta, A. and C. Harkabus, A. and A. Havelka, A. Jablonsky, M. Jensen, M. Kaleta, G. Kober, A. and S. Kobylar, A. Korcheck, S. Lachowicz, J. and V. Lebensorger, S. Maack, M. M., R. and R. Matha, V. Mikolaitas, S. Nemec, C. Nicholson, E. Niez, A. Prusak, C. Roszak, V. Koenigshofer, J. Drzazga, J. Shimanis, J. Siska, A. Suvada, S. Vasilenko, and J. Weber.

7. Citation from Shanabruch, *Chicago's Catholics*, 160–225; Parot, *Polish Catholics in Chicago*, 191–214; Sanders, *Education*, 51–55, 118–20, 146–51; Galush, "Faith," 91–92, 95–96; Bodnar, *Transplanted*, 145, 192–93; Linkh, *American Catholicism*, 2, 139–40; Slayton, *Back of the Yards*, 133–37, 201.

8. Life History of Rt. Rev. Ambrose L. Ondrak (autobiographical), Saul Alinsky/Industrial Areas Foundation Records, Folder 299, University of Illinois at Chicago Library; *Journal Town of Lake*, 1 December 1938; Slayton, *Back of the Yards*, 132–33; Barton, *Peasants*, 154; interviews with J. and R. Gallik, A. and S. Kobylar, M. Mega, S. Nemec, J. Siska, and H. Tobias.

9. Goodman, *Choosing Sides*, 3; Belknap, "Summer Activities," 27; Gabaccia, *From Sicily*, 102; Cranz, *Design*, 80.

10. Cranz, *Design*, 61–62, 199, 204–5; Belknap, "Summer Activities," 51–52, 54–55, 70; interviews with A. Chaloupka, M. Ostrowski, M. Dluhy, J. Gelatka, J. Meegan, R. Jablonsky, M. Kaleta, L. and N. Klink, A. and S. Kobylar, A. Korcheck, J. and V. Lebensorger, S. Maack, R. and R. Matha, and E. Niez. For the classic study of delinquent gangs in Chicago during this period, see Frederic M. Thrasher, *The Gang*.

11. *Week in Chicago*, 21; German Press Club of Chicago, *Prominent Citizens*, 124; Belknap, "Summer Activities," 22; Wilson, *McDowell*, 54–56; Cranz, *Design*, 29, 65, 81–82; Hogan, *Class*, 69–70; Rosenzweig, *Eight Hours*, 128–36; interviews with J. Meegan and L. and N. Klink.

12. This paragraph and the next are drawn from interviews with A. Chaloupka, M. Ostrowski, L. and N. Klink, J. and V. Lebensorger, M. Matusek, E. Niez, J. and R. Paluck, C. Roszak, V. Koenigshofer, J. Drzazga, J. Weber, and S. and S. Wozniak; Cranz, *Design*, 79.

13. Goodman, *Choosing Sides*, 44, 108–9; Cranz, *Design*, 87–91, 93; Wilson, *McDowell*, 26–27; Belknap, "Summer Activities," 27; Prohibition Survey of the Stockyards Community, 21, Mary McDowell Papers, Box 2, CHS.

14. Interviews with R. Cwik, S. Fetta, J. Meegan, A. and A. Havelka, R. Jablonsky, L. Jackson, L. and N. Klink, A. and S. Kobylar, A. Korcheck, Mr. K., Mrs. K., M. Kapral, J. and V. Lebensorger, R. and R. Matha, M. Matusek, M. Mega, V. Mikolaitas, E. Niez, G. Niez, J. and R. Paluck, M. Pratl, A. Prusak, C. Roszak, V. Koenigshofer, J. Drzazga, J. Sukie, H. Tobias, S. Vasilenko, and S. and S. Wozniak; Belknap, "Summer Activities," 22–23, 25, 27; "Speaking of Fun," Joseph Meegan Collection, Back of the Yards Branch, Chicago Public Library; "Davis, Sherman, Cornell Parks to Open Saturday" newspaper clipping, ibid.; *Journal Town of Lake*, 11 February 1937, 22 April 1937, 23 September 1937, 6 January 1938, 22 December 1938; Cranz, *Design*, 13, 61, 63, 65–66, 69, 70–72, 86–87, 91–96, 116.

15. Bird, *Scar*, 140; Cranz, *Design*, 77, 96; "Branch at Davis Square Aids Foreign Born" clipping, Joseph Meegan Collection, Back of the Yards Branch, Chicago Public Library; "News of Davis Square Park" clipping, ibid.; Davis Square Library, Cornell Square Library and Sherman Park Library reports, Mary McDowell Papers, Box 2, CHS; *Journal Town of Lake*, 24 August 1939; Belknap, "Summer Activities," 25; interview with L. Jackson.

16. Wilkie, "Submerged Sensuality," 653–54; Bushman and Bushman, "Early History of Cleanliness in America," 1235–38; Cranz, *Design*, 70; Banks, *America*, 60; *Journal Town of Lake*, 14 April 1938; Belknap, "Summer Activities," 16, 18, 34–35; interviews with E. Baranowsky, J. Fabian, A. Falat, S. Fetta, A. and A. Havelka, A. Korcheck, M. Pratl, J. Sukie, and J. Weber; *Sixteenth Census*, table 6; University of Chicago Settlement Handbook, Box 1, Mary McDowell Papers, CHS.

17. Cranz, *Design*, 13, 68; interviews with R. Aulinskis, A. Chaloupka, M. Ostrowski, R. Cwik, M. Dluhy, S. Fetta, A. and C. Harkabus, J. Meegan, A. and A. Havelka, R. Jablonsky, G. Kober, A. and S. Kobylar, A. Korcheck, Mr. K., Mrs. K., M. Kapral, S. Lachowicz, J. and V. Lebensorger, S. Maack, R. and R. Matha, M. Mega, V. Mikolaitas, P. Mrowca, E. Niez, G. Niez, J. and R. Paluck, A. Prusak, C. Roszak, V. Koenigshofer, J. Drzazga, H. Tobias, and S. Vasilenko.

18. Porteous, *Environment*, 26, 68; Belknap, "Summer Activities," 33, 65; Stolarik, *Growing Up*, 84; Cranz, *Design*, 199. In fact, Cary Goodman argues that the rise of organized play and the social reform movement (the playground portion, that is) destroyed the "immigrant, working-class street life" quite intentionally; see Goodman, *Choosing Sides*, xii, 15, and chap. 4.

19. Interviews with J. Meegan, R. Jablonsky, L. Jackson, M. Jensen, A. and S. Kobylar, S. Maack, V. Mikolaitas, and E. Niez; New City Schools, Mary McDowell Papers, Box 2, CHS; Attendance and Membership Report for Elementary Schools, April 1934, ibid.; Public Schools, ibid.; Seward School, 1934, ibid.; Libby School, 1934, ibid.; Belknap, "Summer Activities," 29–30; Joseph Hamzik, "Seward's Diamond Jubilee," *Back of the Yards Journal*, 17 June 1970, Brighton Park Branch, Chicago Public Library; *Journal Town of Lake*, 21 January 1937, 27 January 1938; "Truant Officer" clipping, 3 November 1940, Joseph Meegan Collection, Back of the Yards Branch, Chicago Public Library; *Official Catholic Directory*.

20. Hogan, *Class*, 44, 129–32, 169; Herrick, *Chicago Schools*, 170–73, 187–90, 201–15; Bodnar, *Transplanted*, 190–95; Belknap, "Summer Activities," 11; Tyack, Lowe, and Hansot, *Public Schools in Hard Times*, 20, 86–87, 148; Teaford, *American City*, 81; Biles, *Memphis in the Great Depression*, 65.

Chapter 6: Across the Community

1. Porteous, *Environment*, 91–93; Yi-fu Tuan, "In Place, out of Place," in Richardson, *Place: Experience and Symbol*, 3.

2. Interviews with E. Baranowsky, R. Cwik, M. Davis, M. Dluhy, R. Ehrlicher, A. Zeilner, R. R. Ehrlicher, J. Fabian, A. Falat, S. Fetta, J. and R. Gallik, J. Gelatka, A. and C. Harkabus, Mrs. E. H., A. Jablonsky, R. Jablonsky, M. Kaleta, L. and N. Klink, A. Kloris, P. Jasaitas, A. and S. Kobylar, A. Korcheck, Mr. K., Mrs. K., M. Kapral, S. Lachowicz, S. Maack, M. M., R. and R. Matha, M. Mega, P. Mrowca, S. Nemec, C. Nicholson, E. Niez, E. Odell, J. and R. Paluck, M. Pratl, A. Prusak, C. Roszak, V. Koenigshofer, J. Drzazga, A. Suvada, H. Tobias, S. Vasilenko, S. and S. Wozniak, and F. and G. Young; Social Service Department Reports, May 1936, February 1937, June 1937, October 1937, November 1937, January 1939, July 1939, January 1940, April 1940, October 1941, Settlement House Papers, Box 20, CHS; Wandersee, *Women's Work*, 30–31, 110–11.

3. Porteous, *Environment*, 78; Banks, *America*, 54, 56; Tentler, *Wage-Earning*, 86, 89, 91, 105–10; Wandersee, *Women's Work*, 116; Kessler-Harris, *Out to Work*, 255; Gabaccia, *From Sicily*, 101; interviews with R. Cwik, M. Davis, R. R. Ehrlicher, A. and S. Kobylar, Mr. K., Mrs. K., Mrs. X., Mrs. Y., Mrs. Z., J. and V. Lebensorger, M. M., R. and R. Matha, S. Nemec, M. Pratl, J. Shimanis, and A. Suvada. Spatial independence, it should be noted, seldom triggered a family crisis. Unmarried young adults who were working generally lived at home and were still bound by family rules. They also, whether fourteen or twenty-four, ordinarily turned over their entire paychecks to their mothers or fathers. In return the child—who was considered a child until she or he married—received the fourteen cents a day needed for streetcar fare and a little spending money for the week, normally between fifty cents and three dollars. One informant recalled with a chuckle that on the day before his wedding he cautiously asked his mother if he could keep his last week's paycheck. For women the strings were even shorter and weekly allowances smaller. They seldom earned enough to afford their own apartments and thus had to follow family traditions carefully. Nonetheless, employment patterns of the 1930s created in many of these women a growing sense of freedom that, during wartime, would get even stronger. Rosie the Riveter may have served her apprenticeship during the depression. Interviews with R. Aulinskis, R. Cwik, M. Davis, R. R. Ehrlicher, E. Fredericks, A. and S. Kobylar, M. M., R. and R. Matha, S. Nemec, E. Niez, J. Shimanis, and A. Suvada.

4. See *1925 Chicago* (New York: Sanborn Map Company, 1925, corrected to 1949), 49; *Journal Town of Lake*, 23 February 1939, 23 March 1939, 30 March 1939, 13 April 1939, 27 April 1939, 25 May 1939; Joseph Hamzik, "The Schoenstadts bring Nickelodeons to the Yards Area," *Back of the Yards Journal*, 8 July 1970, Brighton Park Branch, Chicago Public Library; idem, "Crane Theatre Recalls Memories of Yesterday," *Back of the Yards Journal*, 19 November 1970, ibid.; Brief Report of a Study Made of the Organization, Program and Services of the University of Chicago Settlement, 1927–1928, 5, Settlement House Papers, Box 19, CHS; Belknap, "Summer Activities," 75; McElvaine, *Depression*, 298; interviews with R. Aulinskis, E. Baranowsky, A. Chaloupka, M. Ostrowski, J. and C. Dahm, R. Ehrlicher, A. Zeilner, J. Fabian, S. Fetta, A. and C. Harkabus, J. Gelatka, A. and A. Havelka, A. Jablonsky, R. Jablonsky, M. Jensen, M. Kaleta, A. Kloris, P. Jasaitas, A. and S. Kobylar, A. Korcheck, Mr. K., Mrs. K., M. Kapral, S. Lachowitz, J. and V. Lebensorger, S. Maack, V. Mikolaitas, P. Mrowca, C. Nicholson, E. Odell, J. and R. Paluck, A. Prusak, J. Shimanis, J. Siska, J. Sukie, A. Suvada, H. Tobias, J. Weber, and S. and S. Wozniak. For a revealing discus-

sion of moviegoing habits of working-class folk in a Massachusetts city before World War I, see Rosenzweig, *Eight Hours*, chap. 8.

5. See *1925 Chicago*, 48; *Journal Town of Lake*, 6 April 1939, 13 July 1939; Hayner, "Effect of Prohibition in Packingtown," 29; 1927–28 Report, 5, Settlement House Papers, Box 19, CHS; Rosenzweig, *Eight Hours*, 200; interviews with E. Baranowsky, J. and C. Dahm, M. Dluhy, S. Fetta, A. and C. Harkabus, R. Jablonsky, M. Jensen, M. Kaleta, L. and N. Klink, A. Kloris, P. Jasaitas, A. and S. Kobylar, S. Lachowitz, M. Matusek, C. Nicholson, E. Odell, J. and R. Paluck, A. Prusak, J. Siska, J. Sukie, J. Weber, and S. and S. Wozniak.

6. *Abendpost*, 23 October 1934, FLPS; 1927–28 Report, 6, Settlement House Papers, Box 19, CHS; Erenberg, "'Ain't We Got Fun?'" 11–18; Mayer and Wade, *Chicago*, 360–64; Biles, *Big City Boss in Depression and War*, 31–32; interviews with A. Chaloupka, M. Ostrowski, R. Cwik, R. Ehrlicher, A. Zeilner, S. Fetta, A. and C. Harkabus, J. Gelatka, A. and A. Havelka, Mrs. E. H., A. Jablonsky, R. Jablonsky, M. Jensen, L. & N. Klink, A. Kloris, P. Jasaitas, A. and S. Kobylar, S. Lachowitz, M. Matusek, C. Nicholson, B. and S. Nowicki, J. and R. Paluck, A. Prusak, J. Siska, J. Sukie, and S. and S. Wozniak.

7. Prohibition Survey of the Stockyards Community, 27, Mary McDowell Papers, Box 2, CHS; *Journal Town of Lake*, 9 February 1939, 20 September 1939; *Journal Town of Lake* clipping, Saul Alinsky/Industrial Areas Foundation Collection, Folder 571, University of Illinois at Chicago Library; 1927–28 Report, 5–6, Settlement House Papers, Box 19, CHS; Sengstock, "Chicago's Dance Bands and Orchestras," 24, 26, 30; Erenberg, "Fun," 6–7, 18; interviews with A. Chaloupka, M. Ostrowski, S. Fetta, A. and C. Harkabus, Mrs. E. H., Mr. K., Mrs. K., M. Kapral, Mrs. X., Mrs. Y., Mrs. Z., J. and V. Lebensorger, S. Maack, M. Matusek, S. Nemec, C. Nicholson, B. and S. Nowicki, E. Odell, J. and R. Paluck, M. Pratl, A. Prusak, J. Shimanis, J. Siska, and A. Suvada.

8. Interviews with R. Aulinskis, E. Baranowsky, R. Ehrlicher, A. Zeilner, A. and C. Harkabus, A. and A. Havelka, A. Jablonsky, A. Kloris, P. Jasaitas, A. Korcheck, M. M., R. and R. Matha, V. Mikolaitas, S. Nemec, C. Nicholson, and A. Prusak.

9. Interviews with A. Chaloupka, M. Ostrowski, R. Cwik, S. Fetta, J. and R. Gallik, L. Jackson, G. Kober, A. and S. Kobylar, S. Lachowitz, J. and V. Lebensorger, S. Maack, R. and R. Matha, V. Mikolaitas, S. Nemec, C. Nicholson, G. Niez, B. and S. Nowicki, E. Odell, A. Prusak, J. Shimanis, J. Siska, A. Suvada, H. Tobias, and J. Weber; Belknap, "Summer Activities," 62–63; McElvaine, *Depression*, 174; Sternsher, *Hitting Home*, 5; Bird, *Scar*, 63; Terkel, *Hard Times*, 444; Blackwelder, *Women*, 153, 160, 166; Van Sickle, "Special Place," 122; interview with Goldblatt's detective, 13 April 1934, Mary McDowell Papers, Box 2, CHS.

10. Joseph Hamzik, "Rise and Fall of Early Town of Lake Police Stations," *Back of the Yards Journal*, 18 February 1970, Brighton Park Branch, Chicago Public Library; *1925 Chicago*, 47; Bushnell, "Some Social Aspects of the Chicago Stock Yards," table XII, map 6, p. 324; Murders Committed in Chicago, 1919–21, Mary McDowell Papers, Box 2, CHS; Citizens' Police Committee, *Chicago Police Problems*, 91; *Journal Town of Lake*, 20 October 1938; *Mexico*, 23 April 1929, 1 June 1929, FLPS; interviews with A. and S. Kobylar, E. Odell, J. and R. Paluck, J. Siska, and A. Suvada.

11. Davis Square, Saul Alinsky/Industrial Areas Foundation Records, Folder 310, University of Illinois at Chicago Library; Heitzman, "Back of the Yards Neighborhood Council," 82–83; Wirth and Bernert, *Local Community Fact Book of Chicago*, data for city of Chicago and area 61; *St. Augustine's*, 212; *Journal Town of Lake*, 12 December

1937, 26 January 1939, 20 July 1939, 7 September 1939; *Back of the Yards Journal*, 16 November 1939; Bird, *Scar*, 63.

12. Shaw, *Jack-Roller*; Wilson, "Hull-House," 321; Crime in Three Chicago Districts, Mary McDowell Papers, Box 2, CHS; Thrasher, *Gang*, 16–17, 133; Belknap, "Summer Activities," 104; interviews with R. Cwik, Mrs. E. H., A. Kloris, P. Jasaitas, A. and S. Kobylar, J. and V. Lebensorger, M. Matusek, V. Mikolaitas, C. Nicholson, and J. Weber.

13. Lyle, *Dry and Lawless Years*, 19, 64–65, 68–69, 102–3, 118; interviews with R. Aulinskis, S. Fetta, E. Fredericks, J. and R. Gallik, A. and C. Harkabus, Mr. K., Mrs. K., M. Kapral, S. Maack, R. and R. Matha, J. and R. Paluck, and S. and S. Wozniak; *Chicago Tribune*, 1 June 1983, sec. 2, p. 4.

14. *Journal Town of Lake*, 1 July 1937, 21 September 1938; "Organizer Shot in Yards War" clipping, 15 July 1939, Joseph Meegan Collection, Back of the Yards Branch, Chicago Public Library; interviews with A. Chaloupka, M. Ostrowski, R. Cwik, A. Falat, S. Fetta, J. and R. Gallik, A. and A. Havelka, G. Kober, A. Korcheck, S. Lachowitz, J. and V. Lebensorger, S. Maack, R. and R. Matha, V. Mikolaitas, C. Nicholson, E. Odell, J. and R. Paluck, M. Pratl, A. Pruisak, C. Roszak, V. Koenigshofer, J. Drzazga, J. Siska, A. Suvada, and J. Weber; Monthly Report, October 1934, Settlement House Papers, Box 19, CHS; Annual Report, 1934, ibid.; 1927–28 Report, 8, ibid.

15. Davis, *Heroine*, 199–200; Davis, *Reform*, 112–21, 127; William J. Blackburn, Brief Report on the Organization, Program, and Services of the University of Chicago Settlement, Mary McDowell Papers, Box 2, CHS.

16. Philpott, *Slum*, 205–6; Davis, *Heroine*, 57; Davis, *Reform*, chap. 2 and pp. 231–32; Wright, *Building the Dream*, 128; Bremer, *Depression Winters*, 4–7, 18; The Foreign Born in Our Midst, Mary McDowell Papers, Box 2, CHS; Monthly Report, June–September 1941, Settlement House Papers, Box 19, CHS; Annual Report, 1941, ibid.; University of Chicago Settlement News, 22 March 1937, ibid., Box 6, CHS; University of Chicago Settlement Briefs, October 1938, ibid.

17. Slayton, *Back of the Yards*, 174–77; Davis, *Heroine*, 94; Davis, *Reform*, 27–29; Bremer, *Depression*, 172; letter, Head Resident to Mr. Thomas E. Wilson, 20 April 1931, Settlement House Papers, Box 25, CHS; letter, Head Resident to Stockyards Community Clearing House, 20 April 1931, ibid.; letter, Head Resident to Stockyards Community Clearing House, 25 April 1931, ibid.

18. Saint Michael the Archangel Parish Records; Saint Basil Parish Reports; Annual Report, 1918–19, Settlement House Papers, Box 19, CHS; Summary, May 1918–May 1919, ibid.

19. *Denni Hlasatel*, 8 October 1922, FLPS; Bohemian Woman's Club, Settlement House Papers, Box 20, CHS; Record of the Development of the Clubs for Unemployed Men and Women, ibid.; 1922–23 Adult Department Report, ibid.; Enrollment in English Classes . . . 1937–38, ibid., Box 25; Monthly Report, January 1934, ibid., Box 19; Monthly Report, February 1934, ibid.; Monthly Report, February 1935, ibid.; University of Chicago Settlement Activities for the Summer, 1934, ibid.; Annual Report for the Year 1939, ibid.; Annual Report, 1940, ibid.; interviews with V. Mikolaitas and H. Tobias.

20. Annual Reports, 1918–30, Settlement House Papers, Box 19, CHS; Annual Report, 1936, ibid.; Annual Report, 1940, ibid.; First Six Months of 1939, ibid.; Monthly Report, March 1938, ibid.; Monthly Report, April 1938, ibid.; Monthly Report, May 1938, ibid.; draft of Monthly Report, July 1938, ibid.; Settlement News/Briefs, 12 December 1932 to 1 December 1941, ibid., Box 6; *Our House and Neighbors* (Chicago:

University of Chicago Settlement, n.d.); Davis, *Reform*, 235–37; interviews with L. Jackson, M. Kaleta, A. and S. Kobylar, A. Korcheck, J. and V. Lebensorger, V. Mikolaitas, C. Roszak, V. Koenigshofer, J. Drzazga, J. Siska, J. Sukie, and S. Vasilenko.

21. Interviews with R. Jablonsky, M. Kaleta, Mr. K., Mrs. K., M. Kapral, J. and V. Lebensorger, and V. Mikolaitas; A Review of the Camp Farr Picture and a Proposal for Reorganization, Welfare Council of Metropolitan Chicago Papers, Box 371, CHS; Monthly Report, 1 July–1 October 1940, Settlement House Papers, Box 19, ibid.

22. Annual Report, 1928–29, Settlement House Papers, Box 19, CHS; Monthly Report, May 1935, ibid.; Monthly Report, March 1936, ibid.; Monthly Report, October 1941, ibid.; List of Mexican Activities, ibid., Box 25; Mexican Club Members, October 1936, ibid.; Translator's Note (2 June 1938) to citation from *Mexico*, 22 February 1930, FLPS; *Mexico*, 12 April 1930, ibid.; *El Nacional*, 14 April 1931; 13 May 1933; 3 June 1933, ibid.; interviews with A. and S. Kobylar, J. and V. Lebensorger, and J. Sukie; *Journal Town of Lake*, 11 March 1937.

23. Supplementary Report to the Board, 1935, Settlement House Papers, Box 19, CHS; Supplementary Report of Miss Marguerite K. Sylla, April 1937, ibid.; Monthly Report, May 1937, ibid.; Monthly Report, October 1937, ibid.; Settlement Briefs, October 1939, ibid., Box 6; Philpott, *Slum*, 286–87; Davis, *Reform*, 239–41; *Journal Town of Lake*, 13 May 1937, 11 August 1938, 19 January 1939, 1 June 1939, 19 October 1939; Junior Girls of the University of Chicago Settlement, Mary McDowell Papers, Box 2, CHS.

24. *Journal Town of Lake*, 4 March 1937, 25 March 1937, 13 April 1937, 6 May 1937, 5 August 1937.

25. *Journal Town of Lake*, 8 April 1937, 4 November 1937, 18 November 1937, 29 December 1937, 8 September 1938, 15 December 1938, 29 December 1938, 5 October 1939.

26. *Journal Town of Lake*, 30 September 1937.

27. *Journal Town of Lake*, January 1937 to December 1939; in particular, see 28 January 1937, 3 February 1937, 26 August 1937, 30 September 1937, 18 November 1937, 2 December 1937, 9 December 1937, 16 December 1937, 20 January 1938, 2 March 1938, 7 April 1938, 25 May 1938, 21 July 1938, 12 January 1939, 9 February 1939, 16 February 1939, 2 March 1939, 23 March 1939, 13 April 1939, 4 May 1939, 22 June 1939, 27 July 1939, 10 August 1939, 17 August 1939, 19 October 1939, 9 November 1939, 16 November 1939; Janowitz, *Community Press in an Urban Setting*, 10.

28. Melvin, "Changing Contexts: Neighborhood Definition and Urban Organization," 359–63; Wilson, "Hull-House," 321; Golab, *Destinations*, 123; Lopata, *Polish Americans*, 44; Conzen, "Immigrants, Immigrant Neighborhoods, and Ethnic Identity," 611–12; Tuan, *Topophilia*, 208, 210.

29. Interviews with A. and C. Harkabus, A. and A. Havelka, and M. Mega; Back o' the Yards Old Timers' Scrapbook, Back of the Yards Branch, Chicago Public Library; *Journal Town of Lake*, 30 September 1937, 21 September 1938, 8 June 1939; "Back o' Yards Club Catches a Bygone Flavor" clipping, June 1939, Joseph Meegan Collection, Back of the Yards Branch, Chicago Public Library; "Back o' Yards Old Timers to Swap Stories" clipping, 23 June 1940, ibid.; "Back o' the Yards Old Timers Club, Second Meeting" program, 9 June 1939, ibid.

Chapter 7: The Neighborhood Council

1. Connolly, "Study of Change," 20–35; interview with J. Meegan; Slayton, *Back of the Yards*, 193, 196–97.

2. Packingtown Youth Conference flier, Joseph Meegan Collection, Back of the Yards Branch, Chicago Public Library; *Journal Town of Lake*, 15 December 1938, 4 May 1939, 19 October 1939; Slayton, *Back of the Yards*, 195–96; Brody, *Butcher Workmen*, 167–68.

3. Slayton, *Back of the Yards*, 194–200; interview with J. Meegan; Connolly, "Study of Change," 34–36; Brody, *Butcher Workmen*, 177. The involvement of the PWOC in the first two years of the Council's operation (the years under consideration here) is open to some debate. Scholars who center their research on the unions generally emphasize labor's role in the establishment of the Back of the Yards Neighborhood Council. Robert Slayton, on the other hand, who received special access to the Council records and to Joseph Meegan himself, downplays the importance of the PWOC leaders in the management of the early Council (Slayton, *Back of the Yards*, chaps. 9 and 10). The Council's nonunion leadership and the local labor organizers clearly developed a warm relationship that manifested itself in the former's energetic support of the union in a 1946 strike. However, it is questionable whether the labor organizers could have been as dominant during 1939–41 as they later claimed. Unions did not seem entirely trustworthy to either the residents or the clergy, especially with an acknowledged Communist such as Herb March at the forefront of the PWOC. Even though the *Journal* was upbeat in its portrayal of union activity and Bishop Sheil openly worked with the labor organizers, the PWOC's role within the Council had to be understated during these first few years. Open, unabashed use of the Council by the union organizers for their own ends would have destroyed the community organization and discredited the union movement locally. That did not happen. The two organizations learned to cooperate and to depend on each other for guidance and support. The Council, of course, outlasted the local packing industry by many years. For a pro-labor account of the union's role in the creation of the Council, see Hoehler, "Community Action by the United Packinghouse Workers of America." As examples of the *Journal*'s positive approach to union activity, see *Journal Town of Lake*, 25 May 1939; *Back of the Yards Journal*, 16 November 1939; *Back of the Yards Journal* clipping, 25 April 1940, Saul Alinsky/Industrial Areas Foundation Records, Box 572, University of Illinois at Chicago Library.

4. Slayton, *Back of the Yards*, 201–2; *Journal Town of Lake*, 9 March 1939, 4 May 1939, 29 June 1939, 6 July 1939, 13 July 1939, 20 July 1939; "Back of the Yards Seeks a Cure for Own Ills" clipping, Joseph Meegan Collection, Back of the Yards Branch, Chicago Public Library.

5. Miles Richardson, "Place and Culture: A Final Note," in Richardson, *Place*, 65; *The Call to a Community Conference*, Joseph Meegan Collection, Back of the Yards Branch, Chicago Public Library; Back of the Yards Neighborhood Council Mass Meeting Agenda, ibid.; open letter headed "Dear Friends," ibid.; Porteous, *Environment*, 84–86; *Back of the Yards Journal*, 16 November 1939.

6. Saul D. Alinsky, "A Departure in Community Organization," reprint, Joseph Meegan Collection, Back of the Yards Branch, Chicago Public Library; *New World* clipping, 4 October 1940, ibid.; "Council Gives Name of Its Applicant" clipping, ibid.; *Back of the Yards Journal* clipping, 30 April 1941, ibid.; Kahn, "Catholic Church."

7. Porteous, *Environment*, 80–81; "Back o' the Yards" song sheet, Joseph Meegan Collection, Back of the Yards Branch, Chicago Public Library; 1927–28 Report, 10, Settlement House Papers, Box 19, CHS; Richardson, "Introduction," in *Place*, 1; inter-

views with A. Chaloupka, M. Ostrowski, M. Dluhy, R. Ehrlicher, A. Zeilner, J. Fabian, A. and C. Harkabus, J. Gelatka, A. and A. Havelka, S. Lachowitz, J. and V. Lebensorger, M. Matusek, J. Meegan, V. Mikolaitas, J. and R. Paluck, C. Roszak, V. Koenigshofer, J. Drzazga, J. Sukie, and H. Tobias.

8. Back of the Yards Neighborhood Council statement, Joseph Meegan Collection, Back of the Yards Branch, Chicago Public Library; "Begin Work on 47th St. Playground" clipping, ibid.; "New Playground to Be Ready for Use in Spring" clipping, ibid.; "Playlots to Be done for Summer Use" clipping, ibid.; "Donkeys Are Coming Here Tuesday" clipping, ibid.; *Chicago Sunday Tribune* clipping, 15 September 1940, ibid.; *Back of the Yards Journal* clipping, n.d., ibid.; "Here and There about the Fair" clipping, ibid.; *Back of the Yards Journal* clipping, 26 September 1940, ibid.; "Forecast: Ten Fair Nights Coming Soon" clipping, ibid,; "Davis Square to Open Infant Care Station" clipping, ibid.; *Back of the Yards Journal*, 30 November 1939.

9. The Joseph Meegan Collection at the Back of the Yards Branch of the Chicago Public Library contains many newspaper clippings from both Chicago and out of town publications commenting on the early achievements of the Council. The collection also contains complete copies of longer pieces on the early Council, including *Miller's Chicago Letter*, 20 September 1939; Edward Skillin, Jr., "Back of the Stockyards," *Commonweal*, 29 November 1940; and Robert A. Senser, "Jungle Drama," *St. Anthony Messenger*, June 1941. Others can be found in the Back o' the Yards Old Timers' Scrapbook, which is also at the Back of the Yards Branch. See also Kathryn Close, "Back of the Yards," *Survey Graphic*, December 1940. The best scholarly account of the early years of the Council can be found in Robert Slayton's *Back of the Yards*.

10. "Plans to Spur Spirit of Play by Hot Lunches" clipping, Joseph Meegan Collection, Back of the Yards Branch, Chicago Public Library; "1,000 Children Hosts to Bishop at Park—and Lunch Is Free" clipping, ibid.; "Ready for School Lunch" clipping, ibid.; "Davis Free Lunch Kitchen Is Becoming Streamlined" clipping, ibid.; letter to "Reverend and Dear Father" from Joseph B. Meegan, n.d., ibid.; "76,000 School Children Get Milk for One Cent" clipping, ibid.; *Back of the Yards Journal* clipping, n.d., ibid.; "State, National Leaders Praise Free Lunches" clipping, ibid.; "Kids Drink Milk with Vitamins, Government O.K." clipping, ibid.; "Youth Forum Brings 200 to 1st Meet" clipping, ibid.; *Back of the Yards Journal* clipping, 23 October 1941, ibid.; "Stores Agree to Hire Our Local People" clipping, ibid.; "Buy Now in Your Own Back Yard" clipping, ibid.; "Star's Clothing Employs Only Local People" clipping, ibid.; "Typical Scene at Infant Welfare Station" clipping, ibid.; "Business Men Play Santa" clipping, ibid.; "Church, Labor, Business Work Hand in Hand" clipping, ibid.; "Church, Labor Heads Praise Business Men" clipping, ibid.; Don't Tell a Soul—It's a Secret" clipping, ibid.; "Filled Hall Greets C. of C. Banquet" clipping, ibid.; "C. of C. Big Jamboree Sale of Year" clipping, ibid.; *Back of the Yards Journal*, 21 September 1939, 7 December 1939, 14 December 1939; Slayton, *Back of the Yards*, 212-14; Kahn, "Catholic Church," passim.

11. *Back of the Yards Journal*, 16 November 1939, 7 December 1939; "In Our Churches" clipping, Joseph Meegan Collection, Back of the Yards Branch, Chicago Public Library; "Guardian Angel Home Is True Haven of Mercy" clipping, ibid.; "BYNC Members Speak at City Rotary Meeting" clipping, ibid.; "Out of the Great Melting Pot That Constitutes Back of the Yards" clipping, ibid.; "Back of the Yards Is Talking" clipping, ibid.; "1940—A Year of Progress Back o' Yards" clipping, ibid.

12. *Back of the Yards Journal*, 16 November 1939; "Journal to Give Week's Proceeds to B.Y.N.C." clipping, Joseph Meegan Collection, Back of the Yards Branch, Chicago Public Library; "At the Jamboree Dance" clipping, ibid.; Settlement Data Sheet, Sep-

tember 1939, Mary McDowell Papers, Box 1, CHS; untitled history of settlement, ca. 1960, Settlement House Papers, Box 1, CHS; interview with J. Meegan.

13. Election Records, Municipal Research Library, Chicago City Hall; *Journal Town of Lake*, 2 March 1939; Biles, *Boss*, 11–13, 21, 39, 60; Allswang, *Peoples*, 55; Gottfried, *Cermak*, 308; Gosnell, *Machine Politics*, 96, 121; McElvaine, *Depression*, 185; Patterson, *Poverty*, 52; Terkel, *Hard Times*, 506; *Statistical History of the United States* (New York: Basic Books, 1976), 1077; Bayor, *Neighbors in Conflict*, 147; interviews with R. Aulinskis, A. Chaloupka, M. Ostrowski, E. Cieplak, J. and C. Dahm, M. Davis, R. Ehrlicher, A. Zeilner, R. R. Ehrlicher, A. Falat, S. Fetta, A. and C. Harkabus, Mrs. E. H., A. Jablonsky, R. Jablonsky, L. Jackson, M. Jensen, M. Kaleta, L. and N. Klink, A. Kloris, P. Jasaitas, Mr. K., Mrs. K., M. Kapral, Mrs. X., Mrs. Y., Mrs. Z., J. and V. Lebensorger, M. M., R. and R. Matha, M. Matusek, M. Mega, V. Mikolaitas, E. Niez, G. Niez, M. Pratl, A. Prusak, C. Roszak, V. Koenigshofer, J. Drzazga, J. Siska, J. Sukie, H. Tobias, and J. Weber.

14. Allswang, *Bosses, Machines and Urban Voters*, 105–16; Gottfried, *Cermak*, 30–47, 92–93, 235–36, 241–43, 308, 328 ff.; Allswang, *Peoples*, 21, 136–37; Sternsher, *Hitting Home*, 9, 33; Keyssar, *Work*, 297; Gosnell, *Machine Politics*, chaps. 2 and 3; Lyle W. Dorsett, "Kansas City and the New Deal," in Braeman, Bremner, and Brody, *New Deal*, 2:410; Stave, *New Deal and the Last Hurrah*, 112, 162–64; interviews with E. Baranowsky, A. Chaloupka, M. Ostrowski, R. Cwik, E. Cieplak, J. and C. Dahm, M. Davis, M. Dluhy, R. R. Ehrlicher, J. Fabian, A. Falat, S. Fetta, E. Fredericks, A. and C. Harkabus, A. and A. Havelka, Mrs. E. H., R. Jablonsky, L. and N. Klink, A. Kloris, P. Jasaitas, A. and S. Kobylar, A. Korcheck, Mr. K., Mrs. K., M. Kapral, S. Lachowitz, Mrs. X., Mrs. Y., Mrs. Z., J. and V. Lebensorger, S. Maack, M. M., R. and R. Matha, M. Matusek, M. Mega, V. Mikolaitas, S. Nemec, C. Nicholson, E. Niez, G. Niez, J. and R. Paluck, A. Prusak, C. Roszak, V. Koenigshofer, J. Drzazga, J. Shimanis, J. Sukie, A. Suvada, H. Tobias, S. Vasilenko, J. Weber, and F. and G. Young; *Journal Town of Lake*, 27 May 1937, 24 June 1937, 23 September 1937, 21 October 1937, 2 December 1937, 20 January 1938, 24 March 1938, 30 June 1938, 1 September 1938, 15 December 1938, 9 February 1939, 20 September 1939; "Ward Superintendent Promises Weekly Service in 14th" clipping, Joseph Meegan Collection, Back of the Yards Branch, Chicago Public Library. For a thorough and revealing review of the literature concerning whom Americans blamed for the depression, see Sternsher, "Victims of the Great Depression," 135–77.

15. *Journal Town of Lake*, 2 February 1939, 23 February 1939; *Back of the Yards Journal* clipping, 25 April 1940, Saul Alinsky/Industrial Areas Foundation Records, Box 572, University of Illinois at Chicago Library; interviews with A. and A. Havelka, Mr. K., Mrs. K., M. Kapral, and J. Sukie; *Denni Hlasatel*, 1 June 1922, 24 October 1922, 6 November 1922, 1 April 1923, FLPS; *Abendpost*, 3 November 1929, 3 November 1934, FLPS; *Osadne Hlasy*, 28 October 1932, 15 May 1935, FLPS; Lithuanian political situation, Mary McDowell Papers, Box 2, CHS; Settlement News, 13 April 1936, Settlement House Papers, Box 6, CHS; Allswang, *Peoples*, 42, 55, 57–59, 78; White, "Lithuanians and the Democratic Party," 3, 11–12, 25, 32, 40–41, 46–48, 50–56.

16. "Large Group Attends Green Inaugural" clipping, Joseph Meegan Collection, Back of the Yards Branch, Chicago Public Library; *Journal Town of Lake*, 7 April 1938, 28 April 1938, 3 November 1938, 16 February 1939, 7 September 1939; Election Records, Municipal Reference Library, Chicago City Hall; interviews with R. Aulinskis, M. Davis, R. Ehrlicher, A. Zeilner, L. Jackson, M. Jensen, Mr. K., Mrs. K., M. Kapral, R. and R. Matha, S. Nemec, E. Niez, and B. and S. Nowicki.

17. *Journal Town of Lake*, 21, January 1937, 28 October 1937, 23 November 1937, 6 January 1938, 10 March 1938, 28 April 1938, 16 June 1938, 21 September 1938, 27 October 1938, 31 August 1939, 2 November 1939; "BYNC Will Help Enroll Men for CCC Projects" clipping, Joseph Meegan Collection, Back of the Yards Branch, Chicago Public Library; "Paulina Street Paving Soon to Be Completed" clipping, ibid.; *Chicago Tribune*, 9 July 1984, sec. 2, p. 1; Adult Education Program, Tilden-Englewood District, 7 January 1938, Settlement House Papers, Box 25, CHS; letter, C. Myers Bardine to Miss Sylla, 14 January 1936, ibid., Box 18; Report of the University of Chicago Settlement, Program Year 1935–36, ibid., Box 19; letter, M. H. Bickham to Miss Sylla, 20 May 1936, ibid., Box 18; letter, Charles H. Good to Miss Sylla, 22 April 1938, ibid.; Work Assignment—Transfer—Reinstatement Forms, National Youth Administration of Illinois, ibid.; Report for April 1939, ibid., Box 19; Memorandum, Works Progress Administration, 25 October 1939, ibid., Box 18; letter, Marguerite K. Sylla to Miss Emma Schoembe, 29 March 1940, ibid.; Certification of Sponsors' Contribution, Works Progress Administration, ibid.; Bernstein, *Society*, 151, 156–59; Biles, *Boss*, chap. 4; Terkel, *Hard Times*, 76–77; McElvaine, *Depression*, 178; Bird, *Scar*, 207; Dorsett, *Franklin D. Roosevelt and the City Bosses*, 88; Blumberg, *New Deal and the Unemployed*, 46–47; Trout, *Boston*, 182–83; Blackwelder, *Women*, 117; interviews with E. Baranowsky, A. Chaloupka, M. Ostrowski, E. Cieplak, R. Ehrlicher, A. Zeilner, A. Falat, A. Jablonsky, R. Jablonsky, L. and N. Klink, A. Kloris, P. Jasaitas, S. Lachowitz, Mrs. X., Mrs. Y., Mrs. Z., M. M., M. Matusek, M. Mega, V. Mikolaitas, J. and R. Paluck, C. Roszak, V. Koenigshofer, J. Drzazga, J. Sukie, H. Tobias, S. Vasilenko, S. and S. Wozniak, and F. and G. Young.

18. *Journal Town of Lake*, 21 January 1937, 10 March 1938; *Back of the Yards Journal*, 30 November 1939; "875 Boys and Girls of District Get NYA Jobs" clipping, Joseph Meegan Collection, Back of the Yards Branch, Chicago Public Library; "N.Y.A. Places 120 Local Young People" clipping, ibid.; "NYA Is Dutch Uncle to 92 on S.W. Side" clipping, ibid.; Bernstein, *Society*, 161–63; Bird, *Scar*, 133; interviews with Mr. K., Mrs. K., M. Kapral, and J. Meegan.

19. *Monthly Bulletin on Relief Statistics*, December 1936, CHS; Monthly Reports, April 1937, October 1939, January 1940, October 1940, December 1940, Settlement House Papers, Box 19, CHS; Brief Notes of Our House and Neighbors, 31 October 1941, ibid., Box 6; *Journal Town of Lake*, 27 January 1938, 6 October 1938, 8 June 1939, 25 May 1939; Banks, *America*, 51.

Chapter 8: Postscript

1. Parish Reports, Saint Basil Church; parish records, Saint Michael the Archangel Church.

2. "Back of the Yards Neighborhood Council," series of articles printed in the *Washington Post*, 4–9 June 1945, reprint, Saul Alinsky/Industrial Areas Foundation Records, Folder 6, University of Illinois at Chicago Library; John Bartlow Martin, "Certain Wise Men," *McCall's*, March 1949; "The Voice from Back of the Yards," *Central Manufacturing District Magazine*, April 1954, 26–31; Millspaugh and Breckenfeld, *Human Side of Urban Renewal*, 178–219; Henry, "Study of the Leadership of a 'People's Organization'"; Fisher, *Let the People Decide*, 46–59; Slayton, *Back of the Yards*, chap. 10; Jablonsky, "Back of the Yards Neighborhood Council"; Slayton, "New City," 156.

3. Alinsky, *Reveille for Radicals*, x–xii, 47–49, 167; *Back of the Yards Journal* clipping, 25 April 1940, Joseph Meegan Collection, Back of the Yards Branch, Chicago Public Library.

4. Slayton, "New City," 157–59; Zunz, *Changing Face of Inequality*, 78.

References

Manuscript Collections

Saul Alinsky/Industrial Areas Foundation Records, University of Illinois at Chicago Library

Annual Parish Reports, 1913–43, Saint Basil Church, Chicago, Illinois

Back o' the Yards Old Timers' Scrapbook, Back of the Yards Branch, Chicago Public Library

Chicago Foreign Language Press Survey, University of Chicago Library (cited as FLPS)

Chicago Stockyards Collection, University of Illinois at Chicago Library

Joseph Hamzik Collection, Brighton Park Branch, Chicago Public Library

Illinois Emergency Relief Commission Monthly Bulletin, 1934–37, Chicago Historical Society

Journal Town of Lake, 1937–39, Back of the Yards Branch, Chicago Public Library

Mary McDowell Papers, Chicago Historical Society

Joseph Meegan Collection, Back of the Yards Branch, Chicago Public library

Miscellaneous pamphlets, clippings, and booklets, Balzekas Lithuanian Museum and Library, Chicago, Illinois

Miscellaneous pamphlets, clippings, and booklets, Czechoslovak Museum, Library and Archives, Berwyn, Illinois

Parish Baptismal, Marriage, and Death Records, 1899–1943, Saint Michael the Archangel Church, Chicago, Illinois

Photographic Archives, Chicago Historical Society

Robert Redfield Papers, University of Chicago Library

Sanborn Fire Insurance Maps, Chicago Historical Society

University of Chicago Settlement House Papers, Chicago Historical Society

Welfare Council of Metropolitan Chicago Papers, Chicago Historical Society

Oral History Informants

R. Aulinskis, E. Baranowsky, A. Chaloupka, E. Cieplak, R. Cwik, C. Dahm, J. Dahm, M. Davis, M. Dluhy, J. Drzazga, R. Ehrlicher, R. R. Ehrlicher, J. Fabian, A. Falat, S. Fetta, E. Fredericks, J. Gallik, R. Gallik, J. Gelatka, Mrs. E. H., A. Harkabus, C. Harkabus, A. Havelka, A. Havelka, A. Jablonsky, R. Jablonsky, P. Jasaitas, M. Jensen, R. Johnston, M. Kaleta, M. Kapral, L. Klink, N. Klink,

A. Kloris, G. Kober, A. Kobylar, S. Kobylar, V. Koenigshofer, A. Korcheck, Mr. K.,
Mrs. K., S. Lachowicz, J. Lebensorger, V. Lebensorger, M. M., S. M., S. Maack,
R. Matha, R. Matha, M. Matusek, J. Meegan, M. Mega, V. Mikolaitas, P. Mrowca,
S. Nemec, C. Nicholson, E. Niez, G. Niez, B. Nowicki, S. Nowicki, E. Odell,
H. Ostrowski, M. Ostrowski, J. Paluck, R. Paluck, M. Pratl, A. Prusak, C. Roszak,
M. Shalack, J. Shimanis, J. Siska, J. Sukie, A. Suvada, H. Tobias, S. Vasilenko,
J. Weber, S. Wozniak, S. Wozniak, Mrs. X., Mrs. Y., F. Young, G. Young, Mrs. Z.,
A. Zeilner

Secondary Sources

Aaron, Daniel. "The Treachery of Recollection: The Inner and the Outer History." In *Essays on History and Literature*, ed. Robert H. Bremner. Columbus: Ohio State University Press, 1966.

Aaron, Daniel, and Robert Bendiner, eds. *The Strenuous Decade*. Garden City, N.Y.: Doubleday, 1970.

Abbot, Edith. *The Tenements of Chicago*. Chicago: University of Chicago Press, 1936.

Aguilar, John L. "Insider Research: An Ethnography of a Debate." In *Anthropologists at Home*, ed. Donald A. Messerschmidt. Cambridge: Cambridge University Press, 1981.

Alilunas, Leo J., ed. *Lithuanians in the United States: Selected Studies*. San Francisco: R. and E. Research Associates, 1978.

Alinsky, Saul. *Reveille for Radicals*. New York: Vintage Books, 1969.

Allswang, John M. *Bosses, Machines and Urban Voters*. Rev. ed. Baltimore: Johns Hopkins University Press, 1986.

———. *A House for all Peoples: Ethnic Politics in Chicago, 1890–1936*. Lexington: University Press of Kentucky, 1971.

Anderson, Jervis. *This Was Harlem: A Cultural Portrait, 1900–1950*. New York: Farrar, Straus and Giroux, 1982.

Banks, Ann. *First Person America*. New York: Knopf, 1980.

Barrett, James R. *Work and Community in the Jungle: Chicago's Packinghouse Workers, 1894–1922*. Urbana: University of Illinois Press, 1987.

Barton, Josef. *Peasants and Strangers: Italians, Rumanians, and Slovaks in an American City, 1890–1950*. Cambridge: Harvard University Press, 1975.

Bayor, Ronald H. *Neighbors in Conflict*. Baltimore: Johns Hopkins University Press, 1978.

Bender, Thomas. *Community and Social Change in America*. Baltimore: Johns Hopkins University Press, 1978.

Bernstein, Irving. *A Caring Society: The New Deal, the Worker, and the Great Depression*. Boston: Houghton Mifflin, 1985.

Biles, Roger. *Big City Boss in Depression and War: Mayor Edward J. Kelly of Chicago*. DeKalb: Northern Illinois University Press, 1984.

———. *Memphis in the Great Depression*. Nashville: University of Tennessee Press, 1986.

Bird, Caroline. *The Invisible Scar*. New York: David McKay, 1966.

Blackwelder, Julia Kirk. *Women of the Depression: Caste and Culture in San Antonio, 1929–1939*. College Station: Texas A&M University Press, 1984.

Blumberg, Barbara. *The New Deal and the Unemployed: The View from New York City*. Lewisburg, Pa.: Bucknell University Press, 1979.

Bodnar, John. *The Transplanted: A History of Immigrants in Urban America*. Bloomington: Indiana University Press, 1985.

———. *Workers' World: Kinship, Community, and Protest in an Industrial Society, 1900–1940*. Baltimore: Johns Hopkins University Press, 1982.

Bodnar, John, Roger Simon, and Michael P. Weber. *Lives of Their Own: Blacks, Italians, and Poles in Pittsburgh, 1900–1960*. Urbana: University of Illinois Press, 1982.

Borchert, James. *Alley Life in Washington: Family, Community, Religion, and Folklife in the City, 1850–1970*. Urbana: University of Illinois Press, 1980.

Bowly, Devereux, Jr. *The Poorhouse: Subsidized Housing in Chicago, 1895–1976*. Carbondale: Southern Illinois University Press, 1978.

Braeman, John, Robert H. Bremner, and David Brody, eds. *The New Deal: The State and Local Levels*. Columbus: Ohio State University Press, 1975.

Breckinridge, Sophonisba P., and Edith Abbott. "Housing Conditions in Chicago, III: Back of the Yards." *American Journal of Sociology* 16 (January 1911): 433–68.

Bremer, William. *Depression Winters: New York Social Workers and the New Deal*. Philadelphia: Temple University Press, 1984.

Briggs, Asa. *The Collected Essays of Asa Briggs*. Urbana: University of Illinois Press, 1985.

Brody, David. *The Butcher Workmen*. Cambridge: Harvard University Press, 1964.

Brown, Josephine Chapin. *Public Relief*. New York: Henry Holt, 1940.

Budreckis, Algirdas. *Lithuanians in America*. Dobbs Ferry, N.Y.: Oceana, 1976.

Burchard, Edward L. *District Fact Book*. Chicago: Chicago Board of Education, 1935.

Burgess, Ernest, and Charles Newcomb. *Census Data of the City of Chicago, 1920*. Chicago: University of Chicago Press, 1931.

———. *Census Data of the City of Chicago, 1930*. Chicago: University of Chicago Press, 1933.

Bushman, Richard L., and Claudia L. Bushman. "The Early History of Cleanliness in America." *Journal of American History* 74 (March 1988): 1213–1238.

Bushnell, Charles J. "Some Social Aspects of the Chicago Stock Yards. Chapter One. Industry at the Chicago Stock Yards." *American Journal of Sociology* 7 (September 1901): 145–70.

———. "Some Social Aspects of the Chicago Stock Yards. Chapter Two. The Stock Yards Community at Chicago." *American Journal of Sociology* 7 (November 1901): 289–330.

———. "Some Aspects of the Chicago Stock Yards. Chapter Three. The Relation of the Chicago Stock Yards to the Local Community." *American Journal of Sociology* 7 (January 1902): 433–74.

Cada, Joseph. *Czech-American Catholics*. Chicago: Benedictine Abbey Press, 1964.

———. *Panorama*. Cicero, Ill.: Czechoslovakian National Council of America, 1970.

Cavan, Ruth Shonle, and Katherine Howland Ranck. *The Family and the Depression*. Chicago: University of Chicago Press, 1938; reprint ed., New York: Arno Press and New York Times, 1971.

Chicago Fact Book Consortium. *Local Community Fact Book*. Chicago: University of Illinois, Chicago Circle, 1984.

Chronological History of St. Augustine's Church. Chicago, 1936.

Citizens' Police Committee. *Chicago Police Problems*. Chicago: University of Chicago Press, 1931.

Clark, John G. "The Stoop Is the World." In *Growing up in America*, ed. N. Ray Hiner and

Joseph M. Hawes. Urbana: University of Illinois Press, 1985.

Cohen, Lizabeth A. "Embellishing a Life of Labor: An Interpretation of the Material Culture of American Working-Class Homes, 1885–1915." In *Common Places: Reading in American Vernacular Architecture*, ed. Dell Upton and John Michael Vlach. Athens: University of Georgia, 1986.

Commission on Chicago Historical and Architectural Landmarks. *Union Stock Yard Gate*. Chicago: Commission on Chicago Historical and Architectural Landmarks, 1976.

Conzen, Kathleen Neils. "Community Studies, Urban History, and American Local History." In *The Past before Us*, ed. Michael Kammen. Ithaca: Cornell University Press, 1980.

———. "Immigrants, Immigrant Neighborhoods, and Ethnic Identity: Historical Issues." *Journal of American History* 66 (December 1979): 603–15.

Cranz, Galen. *The Politics of Park Design: A History of Urban Parks in America*. Cambridge: MIT Press, 1982.

Dainty, Ralph B. *Darling-Delaware Centenary*. Chicago: Darling-Delaware, 1981.

Davis, Allen F. *American Heroine: The Life and Legend of Jane Addams*. New York: Oxford University Press, 1978.

———. *Spearheads for Reform: The Social Settlements and the Progressive Movement, 1890–1914*. New Brunswick: Rutgers University Press, 1984.

DeSaulniers, Lawrence B. *The Response in American Catholic Periodicals to the Crises of the Great Depression, 1930–1935*. New York: University Press of America, 1984.

Dorsett, Lyle W. *Franklin D. Roosevelt and the City Bosses*. Port Washington, N.Y.: Kennikat Press, 1977.

Droba, Daniel. *Czech and Slovak Leaders in Metropolitan Chicago*. Chicago: Slavonic Club of the University of Chicago, 1934.

Duis, Perry R. *The Saloon*. Urbana: University of Illinois Press, 1983.

Elder, Glen. *Children of the Depression*. Chicago: University of Chicago Press, 1974.

Erenberg, Lewis A. "'Ain't We Got Fun?'" *Chicago History* 14 (Winter 1985–86): 4–21.

Fainhauz, David. *Lithuanians in Multi-ethnic Chicago until World War II*. Chicago: Lithuanian Library Press and Loyola University Press, 1977.

Fisher, Robert. *Let the People Decide: Neighborhood Organizing in America*. Boston: Twayne, 1984.

Fowler, Bertram B. *Men, Meat and Miracles*. New York: Julian Messner, 1952.

Gabaccia, Donna R. *From Sicily to Elizabeth Street: Housing and Social Change among Italian Immigrants, 1880–1930*. Albany: State University of New York Press, 1984.

Galush, William. "Both Polish and Catholic: Immigrant Clergy in the American Church." *Catholic Historical Review* 70 (July 1984): 407–27.

German Press Club of Chicago. *Prominent Citizens and Industries of Chicago*. Chicago: W. P. Dunn, 1901.

Gleason, Philip. "American Identity and Americanization." In *Harvard Encyclopedia of American Ethnic Groups*, ed. Stephan Thernstrom. Cambridge: Harvard University Press, 1980.

Golab, Caroline. *Immigrant Destinations*. Philadelphia: Temple University Press, 1977.

Golden Jubilee Book of Sacred Heart of Jesus Church. Chicago, 1960.

Goodman, Cary. *Choosing Sides: Playground and Street Life on the Lower East Side*. New York: Schocken Books, 1979.

Gosnell, Harold F. *Machine Politics, Chicago Model*. New York: Greenwood Press, 1937.

Gottfried, Alex. *Boss Cermak of Chicago: A Study of Political Leadership*. Seattle: University of Washington Press, 1962.

Grand, W. Joseph. *Illustrated History of the Union Stockyards*. Chicago: Thomas Knapp, 1896.

Greene, Victor R. *American Immigrant Leaders, 1800–1910: Marginality and Identity*. Baltimore: Johns Hopkins University Press, 1987.

———. *For God and Country*. Madison: State Historical Society of Wisconsin, 1975.

———. *The Slavic Community on Strike: Immigrant Labor in Pennsylvania Anthracite*. Notre Dame: University of Notre Dame Press, 1968.

Grele, Ronald J. "On Using Oral History Collections: An Introduction." *Journal of American History* 74 (September 1987): 570–78.

Handlin, David P. *The American Home: Architecture and Society, 1815–1915*. Boston: Little, Brown, 1979.

Heleniak, Roman. "Local Reaction to the Great Depression in New Orleans, 1929–1933." *Louisiana History* 10 (Fall 1969): 289–306.

Herbst, Alma. *The Negro in the Slaughtering and Meat-Packing Industry in Chicago*. Boston: Houghton Mifflin, 1932; reprint ed., New York: Arno Press and New York Times, 1971.

Herr, Alexander. *Seventy Years in the Chicago Stockyards*. New York: Vantage Press, 1968.

Herrick, Mary J. *The Chicago Schools: A Social and Political History*. Beverly Hills, Calif.: Sage, 1971.

Hicks, John D. *Republican Ascendency*. New York: Harper and Row, 1960.

Hogan, David. *Class and Reform: School and Society in Chicago, 1880–1930*. Philadelphia: University of Pennsylvania Press, 1985.

Jablonsky, Thomas J. "Back of the Yards Neighborhood Council." In *American Community Organizations*, ed. Patricia Mooney Melvin. New York: Greenwood Press, 1986.

Jakle, John. *The American Small Town: Twentieth Century Place Images*. Hamden: Archon Press, 1982.

Jakle, John, Stanley Brunn, and Curtis C. Roseman. *Human Spatial Behavior*. North Scituate, Mass.: Duxbury Press, 1976.

James, F. Cyril. *The Growth of Chicago Banks*. 2 vols. Chicago: J. and J. Harper, 1938; reprint ed., New York: Harper and Row, 1969.

Janowitz, Morris. *The Community Press in an Urban Setting*. Chicago: University of Chicago Press, 1967.

Jones, Anita. *Conditions Surrounding Mexicans in Chicago*. Chicago: University of Chicago Press, 1928; reprint ed., San Francisco: R. and E. Research Associates, 1971.

Jones, Robert C., and Louis R. Wilson. *The Mexican in Chicago*. Chicago: Comity Commission of the Chicago Church Federation, 1931.

Kantowicz, Edward. *Polish-American Politics in Chicago, 1888–1940*. Chicago: University of Chicago Press, 1975.

Kennedy, J. C. *Wages and Budgets in the Chicago Stock Yards District*. Chicago: University of Chicago Press, 1914.

Kessler-Harris, Alice. *Out to Work: A History of Wage-Earning Women in the United States*. New York: Oxford University Press, 1982.

Keyssar, Alexander. *Out of Work: The First Century of Unemployment in Massachusetts*. Cambridge: Cambridge University Press, 1986.

Koenig, Harry C., ed. *A History of the Parishes of the Archdiocese of Chicago*. Chicago: New World, 1980.

Kraut, Alan M. "The Butcher, the Baker, the Pushcart Peddler: Jewish Foodways and Entrepreneurial Opportunities in the East European Immigrant Community, 1880–1940." *Journal of Popular Culture* 6 (Winter 1983): 71–83.

Kucas, Antanas. *Lithuanians in America*. Trans. Joseph Boley. Boston: Encyclopedia Lithuanica, 1975.

Leuchtenberg, William E. *The Perils of Prosperity*. Chicago: University of Chicago Press, 1958.

———. *Franklin D. Roosevelt and the New Deal, 1932–1940*. New York: Harper and Row, 1963.

Lind, Alan R. *Chicago Surface Lines*. Park Forest, Ill.: Transport History Press, 1979.

Linkh, Richard M. *American Catholicism and European Immigrants*. Staten Island, N.Y.: Center for Migration Studies, 1975.

Lopata, Helena Znaniecki. *Polish Americans: Status Competition in an Ethnic Community*. Englewood Cliffs, N.J.: Prentice-Hall, 1976.

Lyle, John H. *The Dry and Lawless Years*. Englewood Cliffs, N.J.: Prentice-Hall, 1960.

Lynch, Kevin. *Image of the City*. Cambridge: MIT Press, 1960.

McElvaine, Robert. *Down and Out in the Great Depression: Letters from the Forgotten Man*. Chapel Hill: University of North Carolina Press, 1983.

———. *The Great Depression: America, 1929–1941*. New York: Times Books, 1984.

Mayer, Harold, and Richard C. Wade. *Chicago: Growth of a Metropolis*. Chicago: University of Chicago Press, 1969.

Meinig, D. W., ed. *The Interpretation of Ordinary Landscapes: Geographical Essays*. New York: Oxford University Press, 1979.

Melosi, Martin V. *Garbage in the Cities*. Chicago: Dorsey Press, 1981.

Melvin, Patricia Mooney. "Changing Contexts: Neighborhood Definition and Urban Organization." *American Quarterly* 37 (1985): 357–67.

Miller, Randall M., and Thomas D. Marzik. *Immigrants and Religion in Urban America*. Philadelphia: Temple University Press, 1977.

Millspaugh, Martin, and Gurney Breckenfeld. *The Human Side of Urban Renewal*. New York: Ives Washburn, 1958.

Mitchell, Robert, ed. *North America: The Historical Geography of a Changing Continent*. Totowa, N.J.: Rowman and Littlefield, 1987.

Montgomery, Louise. *The American Girl in the Stockyards District*. Chicago: University of Chicago Press, 1913.

Morwaska, Ewa. *For Bread with Butter: The Life-Worlds of East Central Europeans in Johnstown, Pennsylvania, 1890–1940*. Cambridge: Cambridge University Press, 1986.

Mormino, Gary Ross. *Immigrants on the Hill: Italian-Americans in St. Louis, 1882–1982*. Urbana: University of Illinois Press, 1986.

Official Catholic Directory. New York: P. J. Kenedy, 1934.

Pacyga, Dominic A. "Crisis and Community." *Chicago History* 6 (Fall 1977): 167–76.

Palickar, Stephen J. "The Slovaks of Chicago." *Illinois Catholic Historical Review* 4 (October 1921): 180–96.

Parot, Joseph John. *Polish Catholics in Chicago 1850–1920*. DeKalb: Northern Illinois University Press, 1981.

Patterson, James T. *America's Struggle against Poverty: 1900–1980*. Cambridge: Harvard University Press, 1981.

Philpott, Thomas. *The Slum and the Ghetto: Neighborhood Deterioration and Middle-Class Reform, Chicago, 1880–1930*. New York: Oxford University Press, 1978.

Pierce, Bessie Louise. *A History of Chicago*. 3 vols. New York: Knopf, 1937–57.

Porteous, J. Douglas. *Environment and Behavior: Planning and Everyday Life*. Reading, Mass.: Addison-Wesley, 1977.

————. "Home: The Territorial Core." *Geographical Review* 66 (October 1976): 383–90.

Reichman, John J. *Czechoslovaks in Chicago*. Chicago: Czechoslovak History Society of Illinois, 1937.

Reiser, Mark. "The Mexican Immigrant in the Chicago Area during the 1920s." *Journal of the Illinois State Historical Society* 66 (Summer 1973): 144–58.

Richardson, Miles, ed. *Place: Experience and Symbol*. Baton Rouge: Geoscience Publications, 1984.

Rosen, Christine Meisner. *The Limits of Power: Great Fires and the Process of City Growth in America*. Cambridge: Cambridge University Press, 1986.

Rosenzweig, Roy. *Eight Hours for What We Will: Workers and Leisure in an Industrial City, 1870–1920*. Cambridge: Cambridge University Press, 1983.

Sanders, James W. *The Education of an Urban Minority: Catholics in Chicago, 1833–1965*. New York: Oxford University Press, 1977.

Sanders, M. K. *The Professional Radical*. New York: Harper and Row, 1970.

Seamon, David. "Heidegger's Notion of Dwelling and One Concrete Interpretation as Indicated by Hassan Fathy's *Architecture For the Poor*." In *Place: Experience and Symbol*, ed. Miles Richardson. Baton Rouge: Geoscience Publications, 1984.

Sengstock, Charles A., Jr. "Chicago's Dance Bands and Orchestras." *Chicago History* 16 (Spring 1987): 22–37.

Shanabruch, Charles. *Chicago's Catholics: The Evolution of an American Identity*. Notre Dame: University of Notre Dame Press, 1981.

Shannon, David, ed. *The Great Depression*. Englewood Cliffs, N.J.: Prentice-Hall, 1960.

Shaw, C. R. *The Jack-Roller*. Chicago: University of Chicago Press, 1930.

Simons, A. J. *Packingtown*. Chicago: Charles H. Kerr, n.d.

Sinclair, Upton. *The Jungle*. New York: Grosset and Dunlap, 1906.

Sixteenth Census of the United States: Population and Housing, Chicago. Washington, D.C.: Department of Commerce, 1943.

Slayton, Robert A. *Back of the Yards: The Making of a Local Democracy*. Chicago: University of Chicago Press, 1986.

————. "New City." In *Local Community Fact Book*, ed. Chicago Fact Book Consortium. Chicago: University of Illinois, Chicago Circle, 1984.

Solzman, David M. *Waterway Industrial Sites: Chicago Case Study*. Department of Geography Research Paper no. 107. Chicago: University of Chicago, 1966.

Somer, Robert. *Personal Space: The Behavioral Basis of Design*. Englewood Cliffs, N.J.: Prentice-Hall, 1969.

Spear, Alan H. *Black Chicago: The Making of a Negro Ghetto*. Chicago: University of Chicago Press, 1967.

Stave, Bruce M. *The New Deal and the Last Hurrah: Pittsburgh Machine Politics*. Pittsburgh: University of Pittsburgh Press, 1970.

Sternsher, Bernard, ed. *Hitting Home*. Chicago: Quadrangle Books, 1970.

————. "Victims of the Great Depression: Self-Blame/Non-Self-Blame, Radicalism, and Pre-1929 Experiences." *Social Science History* 1 (Winter 1977): 136–77.

Stolarik, M. Mark. *Growing up on the South Side: Three Generations of Slovaks in Bethlehem, Pennsylvania, 1880–1976*. Lewisburg, Pa.: Bucknell University Press, 1985.

Suttles, Gerald D. *The Social Order of the Slum: Ethnicity and Territory in the Inner City.* Chicago: University of Chicago Press, 1968.

Talbert, Ernest L. *A Study of Chicago's Stockyards Community.* Chicago: University of Chicago Press, 1912.

Teaford, Jon C. *The Twentieth-Century American City: Problem, Promise, and Reality.* Baltimore: Johns Hopkins University Press, 1986.

Tentler, Leslie Woodcock. *Wage-Earning Women: Industrial Work and Family in the United States, 1900–1930.* New York: Oxford University Press, 1982.

Terkel, Studs. *Hard Times.* New York: Pantheon, 1970.

Thomas, William I., and Florian Znaniecki. *The Polish Peasant in Europe and America.* Ed. Eli Zaretsky. Urbana: University of Illinois Press, 1984.

Thrasher, Frederic. *The Gang.* Chicago: University of Chicago Press, 1963.

Trout, Charles H. *Boston, the Great Depression, and the New Deal.* New York: Oxford University Press, 1977.

Tuan, Yi-fu. *Topophilia: A Study of Environmental Perception, Attitudes, and Values.* Englewood Cliffs, N.J.: Prentice-Hall, 1974.

Tuttle, William J., Jr. *Race Riot: Chicago in the Red Summer of 1919.* New York: Atheneum, 1972.

Tyack, David, Robert Lowe, and Elisabeth Hansot. *Public Schools in Hard Times: The Great Depression and Recent Years.* Cambridge: Harvard University Press, 1984.

Van Sickle, Frederick Mercer. "A Special Place: Lake Forest and the Great Depression, 1929–1940." *Illinois Historical Journal* 79 (Summer 1986): 113–26.

Wade, Louise Carroll. *Chicago's Pride: The Stockyards, Packingtown, and Environs in the Nineteenth Century.* Urbana: University of Illinois Press, 1987.

Walsh, Margaret. *The Rise of the Midwestern Meat Packing Industry.* Lexington: University Press of Kentucky, 1982.

Wandersee, Winifred D. *Women's Work and Family Values: 1920–1940.* Cambridge: Harvard University Press, 1981.

Ward, David. *Cities and Immigrants: A Geography of Change in Nineteenth Century America.* New York: Oxford University Press, 1971.

Weber, Harry P. *An Outline History of Chicago Traction.* Chicago, 1936.

A Week in Chicago. Chicago: Rand McNally, 1887.

Wilkie, Jacqueline S. "Submerged Sensuality: Technology and Perceptions of Bathing." *Journal of Social History* 19 (Summer 1986): 649–64.

Wilson, Edmund. "Hull-House in 1932: III." *New Republic,* 1 February 1933, 317–322.

Wilson, Howard E. *Mary McDowell.* Chicago: University of Chicago Press, 1928.

Wirth, Louis, and Bernert, Eleanor H., eds. *Local Community Fact Book of Chicago.* Chicago: University of Chicago Press, 1949.

Works Progress Administration. *Housing in Chicago Communities.* Chicago: Chicago Planning Commission, 1940.

Wright, Gwendolyn. *Building the Dream: A Social History of Housing in America.* Cambridge: MIT Press, 1981.

Yeager, Mary. *Competition and Regulation: The Development of Oligopoly in the Meat Packing Industry.* Greenwich, Conn.: JAI Press, 1981.

Zunz, Olivier. *The Changing Face of Inequality: Urbanization, Industrial Development, and Immigrants in Detroit, 1880–1920.* Chicago: University of Chicago Press, 1982.

Unpublished Secondary Sources

Barnard, Floyd. "A Study of the Industrial Diseases of the Stockyards." M.A. thesis, University of Chicago, 1910.

Belknap, E. Clinton. "Summer Activities of Boys Back of the Yards in Chicago." M.A. thesis, University of Chicago, 1937.

Bosch, Allan Whitworth. "Public Outdoor Poor Relief in Chicago, 1907–1914." M.A. thesis, University of Chicago, 1950.

Brandenburg, Clorinne McCulloch. "Chicago Relief and Service Statistics, 1928–31." M.A. thesis, University of Chicago, 1932.

Connolly, Michael Patrick. "An Historical Study of Change in Saul D. Alinsky's Community Organization Practice and Theory, 1939–1972." Ph.D. diss., University of Minnesota, 1976.

Donnellan, Elizabeth Anne. "The Back of the Yards Neighborhood Council." M.A. thesis, Loyola University, 1940.

Hayner, Norman Sylvester. "The Effect of Prohibition in Packingtown." M.A. thesis, University of Chicago, 1921.

Heitzman, W. A. "Back of the Yards Neighborhood Council: A Study of the Community Organization Approach to Juvenile Delinquency." M.A. thesis, University of Chicago, 1946.

Henry, Patrick J. "A Study of the Leadership of a 'People's Organization': The Back of the Yards Neighborhood Council." M.A. thesis, Loyola University, 1959.

Hoehler, Fred K., Jr. "Community Action by the United Packinghouse Workers of America—CIO in the Back-of-the-Yards Neighborhood of Chicago." M.A. thesis, University of Chicago, 1947.

Horak, Janus. "Assimilation of Czechs in Chicago." Ph.D. diss., University of Chicago, 1920.

Kahn, Bernard. "The Catholic Church and Its Relationship to the Back-of-the-Yards Neighborhood Council: A Study in Community Political Behavior." M.A. thesis, University of Chicago, 1949.

Kerr, Louise Año Nuevo. "The Chicano Experience in Chicago." Ph.D. diss., University of Illinois at Chicago Circle, 1976.

Lensing, Genevieve Ann. "An Unemployment Study in the Stockyards District." M.A. thesis, University of Chicago, 1932.

Miller, Alice Mae. "Rents and Housing Conditions in the Stock Yards District of Chicago." M.A. thesis, University of Chicago, 1923.

Pacyga, Dominic A. "Villages of Packinghouses and Steel Mills: The Polish Workers on Chicago's South Side." Ph.D. diss., University of Illinois at Chicago, 1981.

Townsend, Andrew Jacke. "The Germans of Chicago." Ph.D. diss., University of Chicago, 1927.

Weber, David Stafford. "Anglo Views of Mexican Immigrants: Popular Perceptions and Neighborhood Realities in Chicago, 1900–1940." Ph.D. diss., Ohio State University, 1982.

White, John P. "Lithuanians and the Democratic Party." Ph.D. diss., University of Chicago, 1953.

Zahrobsky, Mary Lydia. "The Slovaks in Chicago." M.A. thesis, University of Chicago, 1924.

Zygmuntowicz, Evelyn. "The Back of the Yards Neighborhood Council and Its Health and Welfare Services." M.S.W. thesis, Loyola University, 1950.

Index

Books in the Series

*The American Backwoods Frontier: An Ethnic and
Ecological Interpretation*
Terry G. Jordan and Matti Kaups

The City Beautiful Movement
William H. Wilson

*The Rough Road to Renaissance: Urban Revitalization
in America, 1940–1985*
Jon C. Teaford

Greenways for America
Charles E. Little

Bravo 20: The Bombing of the American West
Richard Misrach, with Myriam Weisang Misrach

*The Spanish-American Homeland: Four Centuries in
New Mexico's Río Arriba*
Alvar W. Carlson

Nuclear Landscapes
Peter Goin

The Last Great Necessity: Cemeteries in American History
David Charles Sloane

*Measure of Emptiness: Grain Elevators in the
American Landscape*
Frank Gohlke, with a concluding essay by John C. Hudson

To Build in a New Land: Ethnic Landscapes in North America
edited by Allen G. Noble

Jens Jensen: Maker of Natural Parks and Gardens
Robert E. Grese

*The Pennsylvania Barn: Its Origin, Evolution, and Distribution
in North America*
Robert F. Ensminger

*Pride in the Jungle: Community and Everyday Life in
Back of the Yards Chicago*
Thomas J. Jablonsky

*The Four-Cornered Falcon: Essays on American Space
and the Natural Scene*
Reg Saner

Thomas J. Jablonsky, born in the Back of the Yards neighborhood of Chicago, now lives in Los Angeles, where he is associate professor of geography and director of the Program on the Environment and the City at the University of Southern California. He received his B.A. and M.A. in history from California State University, Los Angeles, and his Ph.D. in history from the University of Southern California. His teaching and research interests are in historical urban geography. He is the author of *The Home, Heaven, and Mother Party: Female Anti-Suffragists in America, 1870–1920*.

Pride in the Jungle:
Community and Everyday Life in Back of the Yards Chicago
Designed by Ann Walston
Composed by The Composing Room of Michigan, Inc.,
in Bodoni Book with Poster Bodoni Compressed display
Printed by The Maple Press Company
on 60-lb. Glatfelter Offset